FEATS AND WISDOM OF THE ANCIENTS

FEATS AND WISDOM
OF THE ANCIENTS

BY THE EDITORS OF TIME-LIFE BOOKS

CONTENTS

SAGES

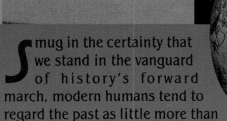

S mug in the certainty that we stand in the vanguard of history's forward march, modern humans tend to regard the past as little more than a backdrop for current achievements. Progress, we think, has been a steady, linear advance, leading inexorably from superstition to enlightenment, from primitivism to sophistication, from ignorance to knowledge.

This comfortable assumption is being challenged, however, as archaeologists, historians, and other scholars point out evidence hinting that humankind's progress has been less a lockstep march than a lurching dance, with steps forward and steps back, with bursts of genius ahead of its time and lost knowledge that even now rests unretrieved—or is gone forever. The destruction of the Alexandria Library, the greatest repository of learning in the ancient world, resulted in the permanent loss of untold numbers of monumental works of literature and science.

Fortunately, other advances of the ancients have been recorded on substances hardier than papyrus, giving us a glimmer of the level of sophistication of so-called primitive humans. So small a thing as the clay pot shown above, for instance, suggests to some scholars that ancient Andean Indians, long thought to have lacked a written language, may have had one after all *(page 13)*. We now know that the roots of democracy may have been planted in Sumer as early as 3000 BC. And there is evidence that the first notation by humans—perhaps even an attempt at astronomy or arithmetic—may date back to 35,000 BC.

How much more did our ancestors know? In our own ignorance, we are just beginning to learn the answer.

The Tragedy of Alexandria

It was the sum and apex of ancient knowledge, a matchless monument to the human intellect—and, ultimately, the victim of human bigotry and ignorance. The Alexandria Library held uncounted masterpieces of science and literature, the sole copies of works now vanished from the earth.

The institution was founded near the end of the fourth century BC by Ptolemy I, a Macedonian Greek general under Alexander the Great, and, rumor had it, Alexander's illegitimate half brother. Following Alexander's death in the year 323 BC, it fell to Ptolemy to rule Egypt, including the cosmopolitan port city to which Alexander had given his name.

A shrewd and farsighted king whose dynasty would hold sway in Egypt for almost 300 years, Ptolemy in his youth had probably studied with Alexander under the great philosopher

Aristotle, and he had an appreciation of learning that he would pass down to most of his successors. He wanted to crown his kingdom with a center of knowledge and research, attracting the civilized world's finest philosophers, scientists, poets, and scholars and freeing them from financial worries so that they could devote their complete attention to research, writing, and lecturing.

The library itself was the jewel of Ptolemy's grand scheme, though not the whole of the plan. It was attached to a university and a research institute—called the Museum, after the Muses, the nine Greek goddesses of the arts and sciences. An estimated 14,000 students at the Museum studied physics, engineering, astronomy, medicine, mathematics, geography, biology,

philosophy, and literature under the world's best teachers. Everything that these revered pedagogues required was provided for them: comfortable apartments, a dining hall, a chemical laboratory, an observatory, an anatomical theater for observing operations and dissections, and a zoological and botanical garden.

Details of the library's physical layout are uncertain, but scholars do know that it was divided into two parts. The main facility, known as the Royal Library, was evidently a building next to the Museum. Some distance away in the city's old Egyptian quarter was a second library, housed in the Serapeum, the pagan Temple of Serapis. Both buildings were repositories for books handwritten on papyrus scrolls.

To assemble a book collection superior to all others, the Ptolemys and their librarians spared no effort. Legions of learned men, assistants, and highly trained slaves ceaselessly organized, classified, and copied huge stacks of rolls that seemed always to be increasing. At times the library's methods of obtaining the best versions of coveted works were not overscrupulous. While many rolls were purchased fairly by the Ptolemys' minions, ships docking at Alexandria had to surrender any works on board to the library—after which cheap copies would be

returned to their hapless owners.

Obviously, since copyists sometimes made mistakes, originals or authenticated versions of valued works were considered far more desirable. Ptolemy III is supposed to have "borrowed" from the city of Athens the official rolls containing the works of the foremost Greek tragedians, Aeschylus, Sophocles, and Euripides. He left a large deposit as security. But instead of returning the scrolls, the king simply forfeited the deposit, and he sent back copies to the furious Athenians.

Such zeal paid off. By the time that Julius Caesar conquered Egypt in the middle of the first century BC, the collection of volumes at the Royal Library numbered between 300,000 and 500,000, with perhaps 50,000 more in the Serapeum. Even though it sometimes took many scrolls to make up a complete book, the number of works at the Alexandria Library would compare respectably to that of a good college library today. But modern books are printed in thousands of copies and cataloged by machines. In an era when books were written, copied, and cataloged by hand, half a million volumes was a truly stupendous number. In fact, in 1450, before the invention of movable type, all of Europe possessed only a tenth as many books as had been housed in the Alexandria Library.

No one is sure precisely what was there. The Ptolemys' mission—never wholly fulfilled—was to acquire an edition of every work by every Greek author. In addition, library translators rendered into Greek important works from India, Persia, and Africa, and the Hebrew

scriptures. The literary wealth alone must have been staggering, and the scientific and philosophical holdings equally vast. The shelves of dramatic poets, for example, probably contained not just the 44 greatest Greek plays extant today but all 123 tragedies of Sophocles, along with most or all of the 90 tragedies of Aeschylus, the 92 of Euripides, and the 54 comedies of Aristophanes. Furthermore, thanks to the Ptolemys' support, Alexandria fostered much of the intellectual inquiry of its day, and it generated an enormous amount of scientific research and writing. Even after Egypt became part of the Roman Empire in 30 BC, the library continued as the scientific capital of the world.

But if the library's growth is one of the most inspiring stories in humankind's intellectual journey, its ending was that trek's most tragic event.

Little more is known about the library's destruction beyond the basic facts. Its first brush with disaster came in 48 BC during Julius Caesar's conquest of Egypt. Several thousand volumes were accidentally consumed in a fire started by Caesar's troops at the harbor. Luckily for Alexandria, the famous general Mark Antony later made up at least part of the loss by requisitioning 200,000 volumes of the Pergamon Library in Asia Minor. The love-besotted Roman soldier presented them as a gift to Egypt's brilliant queen Cleopatra.

Unfortunately, there was no Mark Antony to save the library from the savage attack that all but destroyed it. In AD 391, the Christian emperor Theodosius I, at the urging of Alexandria's fanatical bishop Theophilos, ordered the Temple ↻

The Alexandria Library was founded by Ptolemy I *(far left)* and was the repository of works by ancient Greece's greatest intellectuals, among them, from left to right, tragedians Sophocles, Aeschylus, and Euripides, and philosopher Aristotle.

of Serapis to be destroyed. A mob attacked the Serapeum and burned most of its priceless contents. It appears likely that Christians also pillaged the larger Royal Library, although it is not known exactly how much of that repository perished at their hands.

In any case, whatever was left of the Alexandria Library was finished off after about AD 640 when Arab legions swept through Egypt on their mission to conquer the world for Islam. It is reported that the Arab military governor, baffled by the dusty scrolls in the library, asked Mecca what to do with them. Burn them, he was told, for "either the manuscripts contain what is in the Koran, in which case we do not have to read them, or they contain what is contrary to the Koran, in which case we must not read them." The books were used as fuel for Alexandria's 4,000 public baths. There were evidently enough left to heat bath water for several months. The last of the treasures of antiquity blazed brightly one last time and were gone. Enlightened Arab scholars later recovered from other sources some important works of Greek science and philosophy, such as the writings of Aristotle and Archimedes. But it would be centuries before humankind could begin to reconstruct the knowledge that was lost at Alexandria. □

Alexandrian Scholars

Here are only a handful of the great thinkers who were associated with the Alexandria Library during its 600-year history:

- Euclid (fourth century BC) was a Greek mathematician whose *Elements of Geometry*, used as a textbook for more than 2,000 years, is one of the most important books in Western thought and education.

- Apollonius of Perga (third century BC) was a mathematician who first demonstrated elliptic, parabolic, and hyperbolic curves. The great sixteenth-century German astronomer Johannes Kepler, who first described the elliptical orbits of planets, owed his discovery to Apollonius.

- Archimedes of Syracuse (third century BC) was a mathematician, physicist, engineer, and inventor. A Renaissance-style genius, he is credited with having invented the Archimedes screw, a kind of pump, and other mechanical devices. He is perhaps most famous for discovering his First Principle—that a solid body immersed in liquid is buoyed up by a force equal to the weight of the liquid displaced—while taking a bath.

- Aristarchus of Samos (third century BC) was an astronomer who, 1,700 years before Copernicus, discovered that the earth moves around the sun. Aristarchus also argued that day and night are the result of the earth turning on its axis.

- Herophilus of Thrace (around 300 BC) is remembered as "the father of scientific anatomy." He was the first scientist to prove that the brain, not the heart, was the organ of thought.

- Eratosthenes (third century BC) was an all-around genius. A director of the library, a mathematician, astronomer, geographer, and philosopher, he also wrote poetry and was a literary and theater critic. Using only reasoning and his powers of observation, he accurately calculated the sizes of the earth, sun, and moon.

- Hipparchus of Nicea (second century BC) was an astronomer who made the first known Western chart of the constellations and estimated the brightness of stars.

- Hero, or Heron, of Alexandria (first century AD) was a mathematician and inventor. One of his writings described a steam engine. Probably because unlimited slave power made it unnecessary, this invention was not developed. Hero is also said to have written the first book on robots. □

Strings That Bound an Empire

When Spanish conquistadores chanced upon the vast Incan empire in the 1500s, they found people who were, in many respects, at least as advanced as themselves—with the notable difference that the Inca had no conventional form of writing. What the emperor and his subjects used instead was the *quipu,* a bundle of elaborately knotted strings with which they recorded virtually every important aspect of their civilization. The system worked "with such accuracy that not so much as a pair of sandals would be missing" from the empire's gross store of goods, marveled Spaniard Pedro de Cieza de León in an account he wrote of his 1549 travels in the New World.

A quipu—the Quechuan word for "knot"—typically consisted of a main cord from which were hung about a hundred strings of various colors and lengths. Often more strings were hung from the primary strings, making for a bundle of as many as several thousand strings.

The position and number of knots on a string had precise meaning. A single knot at the top signified 1,000, a knot at the next level was 100, and a knot at the end of the string was the number 1. A cluster of four knots, depending on their location, represented 4,000, 400, 40, or 4. Read from right to left, the strings provided a formidable database. Colors may have added further meaning—white for peace, yellow for

gold or corn, red for blood or war.

The quipu was integral to Incan life. While the emperor referred to it for strategic matters, such as the size of his army, an Incan family used its quipu to keep a precise accounting of property such as gold, silver, clothing, corn, or llamas. Upper-class males were expected to learn how to read a quipu, and each district of the empire employed a few expert *quipucamayocs,* or knot keepers, to keep quipus on matters such as tax revenues and census data.

But while quipus functioned primarily as tallies, they also had verbal components. Cieza de León and others reported that they were used as aids in tracking and recounting the oral history of the Inca. Although the chroniclers were vague as to exactly how the system worked, they indicated that the quipus were used to call to mind songs, legends, laws, and traditions. And it was

by quipu that the Incan king received the fatal news that the Spanish had landed on his shores.

Although they extended and perfected the art, the Inca were not the first to use knotted strings for recordkeeping. There is evidence that an earlier Andean people may have used quipus for tallying around the year 700. Moreover, the *I Ching*—an ancient Chinese book of philosophy and divination—indicates that, probably in the first millennium BC, the Chinese "were governed by means of the system of knotted strings." Even today, laborers in the Ryukyu Islands between Japan and Taiwan knot ropes to record workdays, and Bolivian and Peruvian Indians—descendants of the Inca—use a device they call a *chimpu* to keep track of livestock. □

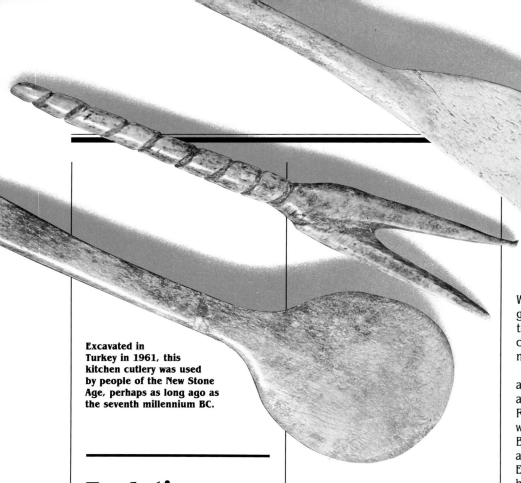

Excavated in Turkey in 1961, this kitchen cutlery was used by people of the New Stone Age, perhaps as long ago as the seventh millennium BC.

Spoons for Escargots

While Europeans ate with their fingers and their knives until the sixteenth century, a number of ancient civilizations had table manners that were more refined.

The Greeks and Romans, for example, crafted spoons from bronze and sometimes from silver; the Romans had forks as well. But it was the Egyptians, as early as 3000 BC, who fashioned the most ornate and intricate cutlery. Some of the Egyptian spoons even had spiked handles—used for extracting snails from their shells. □

Evolutionary Thinking

In the nineteenth century, Charles Darwin stunned the world with his theory of evolution—the idea that all forms of life evolved through a natural selection process that favored the survival of the fittest. The range and depth of evidence Darwin used to support his theory were unprecedented, but the basic idea was not, in fact, altogether new. Some 1,800 years earlier, the Roman philosopher-poet Lucretius seemed to anticipate Darwin in arguing that the earth had once produced numerous species of creatures that were unable to secure food, protect themselves, or reproduce properly. Because they lacked these essential survival skills, the philosopher opined, the creatures became extinct. □

Calendar of Stone

Ancient Mayan astronomers put the exact length of the year at 365.2420 days. The modern Gregorian calendar puts it at 365.2425 days. Since the actual duration of a year is precisely 365.2422 days, the old Mexican Indian calendar was more accurate than the one commonly used today.

The complex Mayan calendar was not, however, a very portable one. A stela *(left)* from the Mayan ruins at Copan in Honduras displays calendric symbols adding up to one day—July 26, 736, by Gregorian reckoning. □

A Lima Bean Language?

Workers excavating a Mochica Indian grave site in Peru during the mid-1930s may have been disappointed at one of their finds: A small llama-hide pouch turned out to contain nothing more valuable than dried lima beans. But for a Peruvian archaeologist by the name of Rafael Larco Hoyle, the discovery helped confirm a long-held theory: The Mochica—Andean Indians who flourished from about AD 100 to 800 and were eventually absorbed by the Incan empire—communicated through marks on *pallares,* a kind of lima bean.

Decorated with lines, dots, and colors, lima beans appear frequently in Mochica art. So, too, do runners—many pieces of Mochica pottery often depict men dashing across a desert carrying pouches similar to the one found in the grave. Often the two themes are combined; much of the pottery shows lima beans with men's faces, arms, and legs.

While it was widely assumed that the Mochica had no form of writing, Larco Hoyle maintained the lima bean designs were actually crude hieroglyphics, and he found similarities between some of the painted beans and the figures drawn by the Maya, who had a script. Larco Hoyle argued that the system of runners, used by the Inca to carry *quipus* from town to town *(below),* was really a Mochica idea. Not all scholars are convinced that the painted lima beans were communication tools. Some think that they may have been recordkeeping devices, like the quipus *(page 11).* Others believe that they were used in divination or gambling, and that the runners carrying bags of beans were merely playing a game. □

Atomic theory began not with Albert Einstein but with the Greek philosopher Democritus, who speculated in the fifth century BC that all matter is composed of irreducible particles "infinite in number and imperceptible because of the minuteness of their size."

Graven in Clay

Perhaps as long as 5,000 years before true writing arose in Sumer, Mesopotamian merchants and overseers may have come up with a useful precursor to it.

According to Middle Eastern scholar Denise Schmandt-Besserat, by the ninth millennium BC people were using small clay tokens in geometric forms in order to represent the commodities that they were buying, selling, or storing. Based on inscriptions on later tablets, Schmandt-Besserat determined that each shape and design had a specific meaning: A round disk with a cross indicated a sheep, a rectangle represented a granary, and a triangle etched with several lines meant metal. Spheres in a variety of sizes stood for different numbers.

Toward the end of the fourth millennium BC, people began placing the tokens in round clay envelopes about the size of tennis balls. While the clay was still soft, it was marked to show precisely what was inside and then sealed. The system was tamperproof, but it was also unwieldy, and over time it gave way to written tablets.

Not every scholar agrees with the idea that the markings on the envelopes led to writing. Some believe that the earliest instance of writing has been lost and that it actually developed simultaneously with—and independently of—the clay spheres. □

BC High

Five thousand years ago, Sumer had high schools not unlike our modern ones, except that they catered almost exclusively to the elite members of society.

The schools were originally founded for the purpose of teaching script to the children of the wealthy, preparing them for careers as governmental or religious scribes. But curricula eventually expanded, and students could learn botany, zoology, mineralogy, geography, mathematics, theology, grammar, linguistics, and even creative writing.

Archaeologists have found Sumerian workbooks, or practice tablets, dating back to 2500 BC. □

MCCLVI + DXLVIII = ?

Hampered by their own unwieldy numerals, the Romans devised a pocket-size calculator to handle simple problems. A crude form of the bead abacus still widely used in the Far East, the Romans' counting board (below) was a small metal tablet. It had several long grooves toward the bottom—each reflecting a higher power of ten—and a matching number of short grooves above. Little spheres in the grooves could be moved up or down to add or subtract. Some of the devices had a few grooves to the right for fractions. □

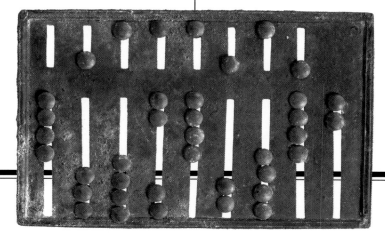

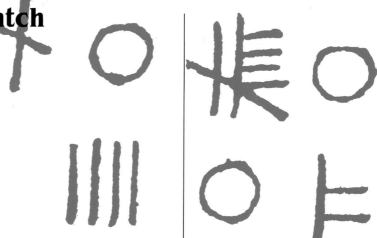

Starting from Scratch

The concept of zero is crucial to technology, computation, and advanced mathematics. But who pioneered this vital nothing? Several ancient peoples independently evolved the notion of nullity, among them the Babylonians, Chinese, Maya, and Indians.

The zero's story begins with a blank: The Babylonians, perhaps as early as the first millennium BC, and the Chinese, around the fourth century BC, left an empty space to denote the absence of a number. Around 300 BC, the Babylonians filled in the blank with a symbol that suggests a pair of wedges, one atop the other, but that appeared only in astronomical texts, never at the end of a number, and was not used in computation.

The Chinese were evidently able to make sophisticated calculations using only a blank. Their first recorded use of an "oh" shape to indicate zero may have been as late as AD 1247. An excerpt from a 1247 manuscript *(upper right)* shows a Chinese numerical sequence that includes zero in its current form. However, some Indochinese inscriptions from the seventh century bear the modern 0.

More than 1,500 years before the Spanish conquest, the Maya were designing a zero that would ultimately assume a host of shapes and meanings. At times a simple shell, the zero was drawn differently to denote the first day of each month. It was also personified as the god of death, a figure whose hand gripped his lower jaw as if to tear it off—a technique used in human sacrifice. Pictured thus, zero stood for completion. But like the Babylonians, the Maya used zero chiefly to monitor the heavens, not for earthly applications.

In India, the zero first appeared around 200 BC in a Hindu manuscript as a cluster of dots called a *sunya,* or "blank." Over centuries, Hindu mathematicians developed zero's properties, finally giving the symbol its modern form. In the ninth century, the Arabs discovered the Hindu number system and translated *sunya* to *sifr,* which, as the system spread across Europe, was Latinized to *cifra,* or "cipher," and *zepharum,* or "zero." □

An Ancient Bestseller

The *T'ung Shu*—or *Book of Myriad Things*—is almost certainly the world's oldest continuously published book.

Now called an almanac, it started as China's imperial astronomical calendar more than 4,000 years ago, reputedly under the aegis of the emperor Yao—who, according to tradition, reigned from 2357 to 2255 BC. By the time it was available in printed form in the ninth century AD, the calendar had taken on the characteristics of agricultural aid and farmer's almanac.

Over the years, the almanac's contributors have included wise men of the Buddhist, Muslim, Taoist, and Christian faiths. And the book has grown from specialized beginnings to encompass fortune-telling, divination, earth magic, herbal medicine, palmistry, charms, moral codes, dictionaries, predictions, legends, lucky and unlucky days, numerology, and even telegram and telex charts.

Still influential, the almanac continues to sell more than one million copies every year. □

Mathematics' Long March

From decimal fractions to higher numerical equations, the ancient Chinese made significant contributions to the advancement of mathematics.

The development of the decimal system has been traced back to the China of 1300 BC. (The Babylonians may have had a similar system even earlier, but their method used a base of sixty rather than ten.) Both the Chinese and the Babylonians also used negative numbers. Curiously, the Chinese wrote positive numbers in red, negative numbers in black—the reverse of today's Western accounting conventions.

By the third century AD, Chinese mathematicians could compute the approximate value of pi, and by the fifth century, they calculated pi to ten decimal places—a feat unmatched in the West until the sixteenth century. □

"You can have a lord, you can have a king, / But the man to fear is the tax collector!" This Sumerian proverb, from a tablet inscribed around 1800 BC and first translated in 1934, seems remarkably timely.

Gilgamesh Lobbies Congress

Greece may not have been the cradle of democracy after all. Government by the people seems to have blossomed first in ancient Sumer, the desert land lying between the Tigris and the Euphrates rivers in what is now southern Iraq.

What may have been the world's first bicameral congress convened around 3000 BC, almost 2,500 years before the golden age of Athens. According to the great Sumerian epic poem *The Tale of Gilgamesh* (a portion of the saga is on the tablet shown below), the rising and powerful Sumerian city-state Erech was being threatened by a neighbor, Kish, which feared Erech's growing might and was poised to attack its rival. The warrior-king Gilgamesh, Erech's bold ruler, met with what the poem calls "the convened assembly of the elders of his city" to ask them to support resistance against Kish. To his frustration, this upper house voted instead to buy peace by submitting. Undeterred, the king demanded a vote from a lower house made up of men who could bear arms. The hawks won the day.

Nothing more is known about this congress. There are no records from the age of Gilgamesh—writing had barely been invented then —and the tablets that provide this tantalizing glimpse of representative democracy in the ancient Near East were probably written more than a thousand years later. □

Mysterious Marks

When Harvard archaeologist Alexander Marshack slipped the 32,000-year-old fragment of carved reindeer bone *(above)* under his microscope one day in 1965, he felt he had caught a glimpse into the mind of Cro-Magnon man. Under the lens, a serpentine series of incised markings—long regarded merely as random or decorative doodlings of the sort sometimes found on other Ice Age artifacts—suddenly seemed to Marshack to have been made deliberately, repetitively, and with a variety of tools. The scientist concluded that the bone, a tool fragment excavat-ed in the Dordogne region of France in 1911, contained the earliest known human notation. It appears that human beings—cave dwellers—had achieved a form of written communication thousands of years before history's first true writing appeared.

Theorizing even more broadly, Marshack proposed that the artifact's topic was astronomy: Some Cro-Magnon sky gazer had marked the passage of the seasons by chronicling the phases of the moon in a bone "notebook." Marshack has since detected what he views as lunar calendars on some fifteen other Ice Age objects; still other notations, he believes, may be hunters' tallies of animal kills.

Marshack's calendar theory is not universally accepted; some scientists see no particular meaning to the bone markings, while others suggest interpretations that differ from Marshack's. In the latter category is Jean de Heinzelin, a geologist-archaeologist whose explanation of the artifact is no less startling than Marshack's: De Heinzelin suggests that the object's cryptic dashes and dots may constitute the earliest known arithmetic. The people of the last Ice Age, he proposes, had a number system based on ten and were familiar with prime numbers. □

No Stones in the Sky

In the fifth century BC, the Greek philosopher Diogenes of Apollonia, merely by using his powers of observation and reasoning, concluded that "meteors move in space and frequently fall to earth."

More than two millennia later, this perfectly correct notion was dismissed as nothing more than nonsense by the French chemist Antoine Lavoisier, one of the most noted scientists of the Enlightenment. Stones could not fall to earth, Lavoisier asserted, because there are no stones in the sky. □

No Omens in the Sky

While medieval Europeans regarded a comet's appearance with terror and superstitious awe, Greek philosophers in the fifth century BC knew comets for the phenomena they really are—natural objects that reappear regularly in the heavens. Some experts believe that even before the Greeks, ancient Babylonian astronomers understood the true nature of comets. By the first century AD, the Roman historian Seneca was stating—correctly—that comets have orbits, just as the planets themselves do. □

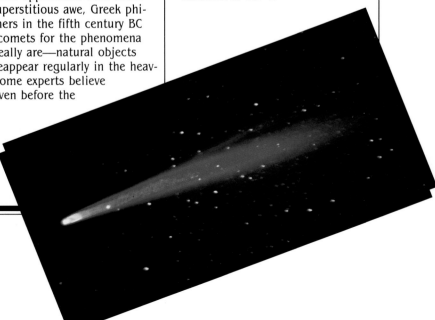

The Transylvanian Tablets

Archaeologists digging into a prehistoric mound in the Transylvanian town of Tartaria in 1961 were only hoping to shed new light on a previously excavated Rumanian site nearby. What they found was dazzling: three small clay tablets *(pictured here)* with signs that looked like writing. Carbon-14 dating suggested that the tablets might date from around 4000 BC, and thus the find hinted at a startling conclusion: Writing might not have originated in the Mesopotamian civilization of Sumer, as had long been thought, but in the barbarian wilderness of eastern Europe.

The three tablets, found in the mound's lowest stratum, were preserved along with some human bones in what had apparently been a sacrificial pit. They bore pictorial symbols resembling inscriptions on tablets both from Sumer and from the highly advanced Minoan civilization of Crete. But if the carbon dating was correct, the Tartaria tablets, made by a primitive Stone Age farming tribe called the Vinca, predated Sumerian writing by one millennium and Minoan writing by two. This idea seemed far-fetched, and indeed there were major problems with it. If writing began in Stone Age Europe rather than in Bronze Age Sumer, it seemed illogical that it leaped to far-off Sumer a thousand years before it reached the much closer island of Crete. Furthermore, prehistorians had already traced the evolution of writing in Mesopotamia, from its pictographic beginnings to a sophisticated system of cursive script. No such evolution had ever been suggested in eastern Europe.

Some experts propose that the carbon dating for the Tartaria tablets was wrong. Others suggest that the tablets were somehow displaced in the mound and that they might have reflected a later period of Vinca culture, one that followed Sumerian writing by a good many years. There is also a theory that the Tartaria inscriptions are not writing at all but a primitive people's uncomprehending copy of "magical" symbols brought to them on the pots and jars of merchants from the more advanced civilization of the Near East. By the time the Transylvanian farmers were copying these pictographs, this theory holds, the Sumerians had long since abandoned such crude script and gone on to more complex forms of writing. □

Credit for discovering how to measure right triangles usually goes to sixth-century BC philosopher Pythagoras. But the Babylonians came up with the Pythagorean theorem more than a millennium earlier, in about 1800 BC.

INVENTORS

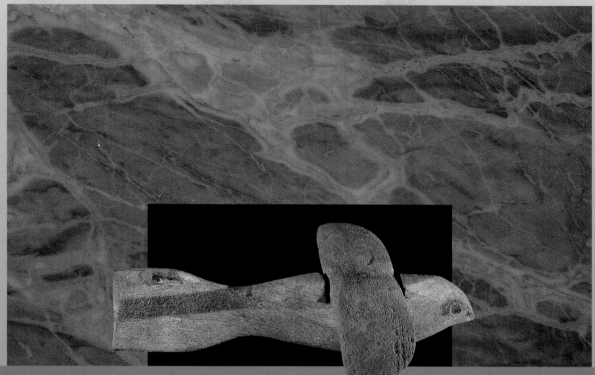

Curiosity and ingenuity may not be unique to the human species, but they are certainly among humanity's hallmarks. The youngest child, like the earliest human being, might observe a pebble rolling down a hill, wonder at its movement, pick it up and examine it, toss it, tinker with it—rolling it down a steeper incline or nudging it across a level plane. From such idle tinkering, some vanished person, nameless now for untold millennia, invented the wheel.

For all of the rich fertility of the human intellect, the progress of invention has followed a ragged course, reaching almost explosive levels during certain eras—as when civilization itself dawned in Sumer around 3000 BC—then abating for thousands of years at a time. Moreover, many an innovation has been swept into oblivion by the turbulent currents of history. It is known now, for instance, that the first steam engine was invented not by Scottish engineer and inventor James Watt in the eighteenth century but by an Alexandrian scholar by the name of Hero in the first century AD. Similarly, although Wilbur and Orville Wright pioneered aviation, the brothers may not have been the first people to understand the basics of aerodynamics. The little working model of a glider that is shown above is not a twentieth-century toy but a 2,100-year-old artifact from an Egyptian tomb *(page 28)*. This artifact has suggested to some people that not only did our ancient ancestors understand flight, but they may even have achieved it.

"The best of the new," in the thought-provoking words of an old Russian proverb, "is often the long forgotten past."

Ancient Electricity?

While excavating ruins of a 2,000-year-old village near Baghdad, Iraq, in 1936, workers discovered a mystifying artifact. It was a small earthenware vase in which was set a soldered sheet-copper tube about one inch wide and four inches long. The bottom of the tube was sealed with a crimped copper disk; an iron rod, seemingly corroded by acid, projected through an asphalt plug at the top.

German archaeologist Wilhelm König, then living in Iraq, examined the object and reached a startling conclusion: If the tube had been filled with an acidic solution, it would have served as a rudimentary electric battery. Such batteries, he speculated, may have been used by ancient artisans to electroplate metals. He pointed out that similar objects had been found at other sites in the region, along with thin copper and iron rods that might have been used to link an array of such batteries.

In 1940, Willard F. M. Gray, an engineer at the General Electric High Voltage Laboratory in Pittsfield, Massachusetts, read of König's theory in an article by German rocket scientist Willy Ley. Using drawings and details supplied by Ley, Gray made a replica of the so-called Baghdad battery. When he filled it with a copper sulfate solution, it generated about half a volt of electricity. In the 1970s, West German Egyptologist Arne Eggebrecht took Gray's experiment further. He built a Baghdad battery and charged it with freshly pressed grape juice, as he theorized the ancients might have done. Then he used current from the battery to electroplate a

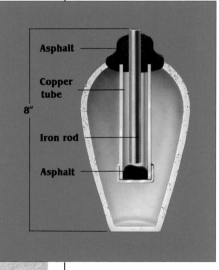

Asphalt

Copper tube

8"

Iron rod

Asphalt

A cross-section view of a Baghdad battery replica shows an iron rod, insulated with asphalt, protruding from a sealed copper tube. When the copper tube is filled with an electrolyte, the device produces an electric current.

silver statuette with gold *(left)*.

Eggebrecht was all but certain he had confirmed the development and use of electric batteries some 1,800 years before their modern invention by Alessandro Volta in 1799. Moreover, he held that many supposedly gold artifacts from ancient times are really silver, plated with gold in the same manner as his experimental statuette.

Others are not so sure; doubters have observed that the alleged battery might have held only a scroll or a cosmetic. The fact that a modern replica can be made to generate electricity is interesting, they say, but not conclusive proof that this was the object's purpose. □

Topography on Papyrus

Topographical maps—which graphically show natural and artificial features of a given terrain—came into use in the eighteenth century. But there is one such map that is older by almost 3,000 years.

Known as the Turin Papyrus because it is housed in the Egyptian Museum in Turin, Italy, this chart was drawn up around the year 1150 BC. Without question, it is the oldest geological map in the world, and its concern for topographical detail marks the origin of geological thought. Sixteen inches high and six feet across, the Turin map details a ten-mile stretch of land known as Wadi Hammamat and displays roads, quarries, gold mines, and a few buildings that once stood on the site. One of the roads shown, connecting the Nile

Pink shading on the Turin Papyrus map *(top)* corresponds to the actual tint of mountain rocks *(right)* depicted in the photograph; brown streaks on the mountain at the map's top center represent veins of gold. Arrows point to an ancient road still used today.

and the Red Sea, is still in use.

Unlike modern geological maps, which use sophisticated drafting tools and aerial surveys, the Turin scroll is a freehand drawing. It uses color—pink, brown, black, and white—to distinguish topographical features. The shades correspond to the true hues of the landscape: Pink and brown that tint a mountain on the map closely approximate pinkish granitic

rock at the site, while purplish and dark gray indicate similar shades of earth in a nearby quarry.

This pioneering map is attributed to the ancient draftsman Amennakht, chief scribe during the reign of Egypt's Ramses IV. Amennakht is also said to have mapped the burial site of his pharaoh, tinting the sarcophagus reddish brown to match the color of the stone used to fashion the coffin. □

Ancient Secrets of Precious Metal

Fashioned from alloys of precious metals, these masks from Peru *(above)* and Ecuador *(below)* display the skills of pre-Columbian metalworkers.

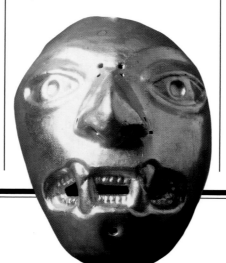

For more than three millennia, a burial pit in the southern highlands of Peru hid a golden secret. Clutched in a skeleton's fingers was the earliest evidence of metalworking ever to be unearthed in the New World.

The bones were discovered in 1971 by archaeologists who were excavating an Andean grave site some 3,500 years old. Together with several lapis lazuli beads, the fleshless hand held nine small flakes of finely hammered gold foil. At this same burial site were stone implements—two bowls, three hammers, and a small an-vil—that seemed to make up a gold-working kit. The find meant that the tradition of metalworking in the Americas was 700 years older than previously supposed.

By the time of the Spanish conquest in the sixteenth century, generations of South American Indian metalsmiths had produced an astonishing trove of gold and silver artifacts—or so the conquistadors thought. But when they melted down the looted treasures, the Spanish were often disappointed. It turned out that Andean artisans, possibly to conserve their supplies of noble metals, had learned the techniques of alloying them with copper and treating the finished works so that their surfaces shone with pure gold. Some of the native metallurgists devised a method of depletion gilding, treating their creations with a corrosive chemical that removed only the copper from the surface, leaving behind a film of pure gold. Other artisans plated the copper objects with a thin coating of precious metal.

Metalsmiths of the Moche culture, who inhabited valleys on the northern coast of Peru from about 100 BC to AD 800, were masters of these two techniques. A cache of Moche treasures recently uncovered near the Ecuadorian border included copper alloys that had been plated with gold or silver. Laboratory examination revealed that the plating was remarkably thin and even, measuring less than two microns in certain places.

Perhaps the most startling achievement of the ancient metalsmiths was their manipulation of platinum, one of the rarest and most precious of ornamental metals. From the first through the third centuries AD, Indians of the Choco region of present-day Colombia mined platinum to make jewelry. They discovered that they could work platinum by grinding it into a powder and mixing it with gold dust. Using charcoal fires intensified with forced air drafts from blowpipes, the artisans melted the gold and used it to coat the platinum particles. While the mixture was still hot, they hammered it out and then repeated the process, eventually producing a malleable form of platinum. This technique, called sintering, would not be mastered by Europeans until the nineteenth century. □

The Durable Pillar of Delhi

In the courtyard of the Ktub Minar Mosque in Delhi, India, stands a six-ton iron pillar more than twenty-three feet high. Raised in the fourth century AD, the smooth, blue-black column has long puzzled those who marvel at its size and wonder why this particular pillar—unlike other, similar iron shafts in the region—remains in almost perfect condition, exhibiting only a faint dusting of rust after standing exposed to the elements for 1,600 years.

Until a few decades ago, many experts held that such a huge piece of metal could not have been formed even in the most advanced European foundries before the nineteenth century. Now, however, most agree that the Delhi pillar was not forged in one piece but fashioned from a number of smaller pieces of hot wrought iron that were hammered together using a now-vanished technique known as forge welding.

According to some metallurgists, this method of manufacture may account for the pillar's resistance to corrosion. Repeated hammering and heating, they say, would have permitted a layer of oxide and slag to come to the surface and form a protective coating. Others, though, contend that the basic composition of the pillar—

which is higher in phosphorus and lower in manganese than is modern iron—accounts for its durability. Still others believe that although the pillar's composition and its means of fabrication may have helped, its rustless condition owes a great deal more to the relatively dry, pollution-free atmosphere of Delhi. □

A pottery bottle with a screw-top cap was discovered in 1985 in a Mayan tomb. Prior to that time, the threaded screw was believed to be solely an Old World innovation.

The Steel of Islam

When Christians set out to wrest the Holy Land from the Muslims in the Middle Ages, they met with steely resistance—Saracen swords so strong and sharp that they could fell a Crusader or bisect a feather floating in midair with almost equal ease. The blades were made of Damascus steel, a high-carbon metal whose unusual properties cannot be duplicated even today; modern metallurgists have attempted in vain to penetrate the lost secrets of its manufacture.

Damascus steel got its name because Europeans first encountered it—much to their sorrow—in Syria, whose premier city was Damascus. In fact, this extraordinary steel was made in India, where it was called *wootz*. Traders sold it in India, Persia, Turkey, and Russia, where it was forged into weaponry and other items. The best blades—including the ones that were used against the Crusaders—are thought to have been produced in Persia. However, the origins of the steel may have predated the Crusades by about 1,300 years. Alexander the Great is believed to have encountered Damascus steel during his conquests sometime in the fourth century BC.

The art of making Damascus steel was lost in the middle of the nineteenth century when firearms became humankind's weapon of choice. Contemporary scientists can only guess at the precise techniques of heating, cooling, and forging that must have gone into

A Fatal Offering

Legend has it that in the first century AD, an obscure craftsman brought a gift to the august Roman emperor Tiberius. The offering was a drinking cup, not noteworthy for its beauty, but extraordinary indeed in its properties. It looked like silver but was much lighter, and when its maker hurled it against a stone floor, it did not break, as silver might have done. Instead, it dented in the manner of bronze. The metalsmith promptly repaired the damage with a small hammer. The emperor was amazed.

The story of the metalworker's gift was recorded some years after Tiberius's death in AD 37 in the writings of the court wit Petronius and the natural historian Pliny. Petronius recounted that it was made of "a kind of glass which could not be broken," and Pliny said it was "a vitreous combination which was flexible and ductile."

What was the strange cup made of? Petronius and Pliny seemed themselves doubtful of claims made for the vessel. Based on their descriptions of it, however, modern experts have speculated that it might have been fashioned from aluminum. Like aluminum, the metal resembled silver but was lighter in weight. It could be worked and shaped. And, when questioned by Tiberius, the craftsman revealed that it was extracted from clay—just as aluminum is.

If the metal truly were aluminum, the ancient metalsmith was centuries ahead of his time. Although its compounds are common, metallic aluminum does not occur in nature and is not known to have been isolated until 1825. Today, aluminum can be obtained only through sophisticated chemical and electrical processes. If Tiberius's supplicant produced the metal 2,000 years ago, he must have used a different method.

Regrettably, the emperor saw to it that the world would never unravel the mystery. The gift-bearer boasted that the secret of the metal was known only to him and the gods; Tiberius, fearing the new metal would render silver and gold valueless, decided to narrow the field. He had the metalworker beheaded, leaving the answer to the cup's riddle to the gods alone. □

its manufacture. The only certainty is that ancient smiths found the secret of infusing steel with a high-carbon content while avoiding the brittleness that usually earmarks high-carbon steel. Their much-prized blades possessed not only strength but a distinctive beauty. During the manufacture of wootz, carbon precipitated out of

the steel in a way that ultimately gave the finished blades intricate surface markings that resembled the patterns of damask textiles.

Hoary records indicate that the most exotic part of the procedure had to do with various methods of quenching the forged blades. An ancient text from Asia Minor, for instance, tells how the blade should be quenched by plunging it into the body of a muscular slave, thereby transferring his strength to the cherished blade. □

A network of wavy lines typical of true Damascus steel can be seen *(closeup, above)* on the blade of this eighteenth-century scimitar from Persia.

Remains of an Ancient Miner

Long before the first Europeans arrived in Chile, South American Indians mined copper in the bleak Atacama Desert—sometimes with fatal results. In 1899, miners working the still-rich lodes there unearthed the body of an ancient colleague who apparently had died in a cave-in centuries earlier. The corpse had been almost completely mummified by the region's intense, dry heat. Its hands seemed still to grope forward, as if to dig. Even more macabre, over time the body had become impregnated with copper, which had turned it an eerie greenish black. □

Iron Sentinel of Kottenforst

Like the pillar of Delhi *(page 23)*, the so-called Iron Man of Kottenforst is notable for its lack of rust. The Iron Man, which stands on an old imperial hunting ground near Bonn, West Germany, is a squared, solid pillar seven feet long, with about half its length protruding above ground.

Its age and origins are not absolutely certain, but it is probably a boundary marker planted in the early seventeenth century and overlooked by scavengers who later uprooted similar posts to sell as scrap metal. The Iron Man may owe its relatively rust-free state to the hundreds of tourists who touch it every year, perhaps to test the local legend that young women who touch and kiss the pillar will soon find a suitable husband. □

A Riddle Cast in Aluminum

The ancient metalsmith who made the strange cup for Tiberius *(page 24)* may have erred in thinking that his metallurgical secret was exclusive to him and the gods. In 1956, archaeologists excavating a third-century-AD grave site in the Chinese province of Jiangsu unearthed about twenty belt ornaments. Some were found to be composed of 85 percent aluminum, alloyed with manganese and copper. The alloy was unusually pure, similar to the type used in modern aircraft.

Some metallurgists have dismissed this oddity as merely the result of a freak accident at an ancient smelter. Others, though, have speculated that the Chinese devised an aluminum refining process, now lost, that did not require the massive energy used in today's refineries. □

The Lights That Fail

Nectar of the Nile

Long before Egypt had its pyramids, it had beer.

In 1989, archaeologists excavating the ancient city of Hierakonpolis on the banks of the Nile River in southern Egypt uncovered a 5,400-year-old brewery where beer apparently was concocted from a mixture of river water, half-baked bread, wheat malt, and date juice. The brewery is the oldest ever to be found. □

An Egyptian brewery worker forces fermented grain through a sieve in this statuette from the twenty-sixth century BC.

Enthusiasts thirsting for anomalies sometimes build a precarious structure of speculation from evidence that is readily explained in other ways. Consider, for example, the curious notion that the ancient Egyptians used electric light.

This fancy centers on wall carvings such as the one that is shown above. The art comes from a subterranean room in the temple of Dendera on the east bank of the Nile north of Luxor. Built in the last century BC and the first century AD, the temple is sacred to the sky goddess Hathor. Beneath it are nine underground chambers, their limestone walls covered with hieroglyphics and reliefs. Archaeologists have yet to fully interpret the walls' messages. No serious schol-

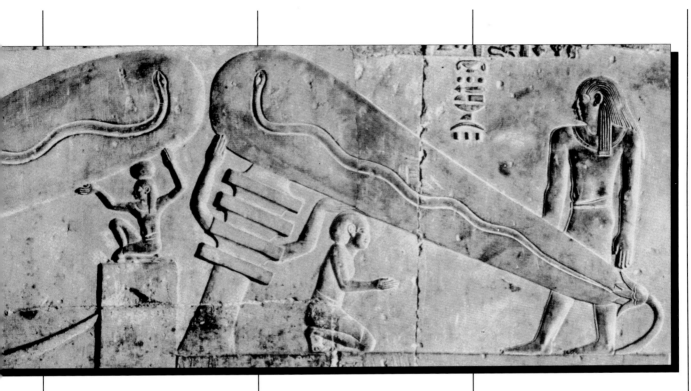

ar, however, subscribes to the anomalists' conclusion: that the large, clublike objects that dominate this scene and several others are light bulbs.

Highlights of this light bulb theory run as follows: The wavy lines inside the "bulbs" are filaments (or, failing that, electric eels that some ancient artist depicted to get across the point that the clubs generated energy). The lines extending from the lotus-shaped bases of the clubs are electrical wires or cables that connect to a rectangular box—a high-voltage generator.

More orthodox interpretations of Dendera's walls require no such wild surmise. The "light bulbs," say most archaeologists, represent the emergence of a serpent form of the god Harsomthus, a son of Hathor, from a lotus. The "electrical wires" are merely the stems of the blossoms. The rectangular "generator" is a pedestal for a minor diety whose upraised arms help support the unwieldy club above it.

Nevertheless, the anomalists contend, there is the matter of the absence of soot: Surely the ancient artist used electric light in creating his subterranean works. If he used torches or oil lamps, there would be soot on the walls.

Again, the more likely explanation is a prosaic one. The artist, not relishing the notion of dirt on his creations, merely wiped the temple walls clean.

In dismissing the light bulb the-ory, the experts add a final point: At the time that the temple was built, Egypt was a province of Rome. It seems highly improbable that the ingenious and acquisitive Romans would have overlooked such a startling phenomenon as electricity, leaving it utterly unrecorded in the annals they bequeathed from their time. □

In AD 577, while enemy armies advanced across the north China plain, the beleaguered women of the Northern Qi kingdom made matches to start the cooking fires. This simple invention did not appear in Europe until 1530.

Soaring through Ancient Skies

As he sorted through dusty, discarded exhibits in the basement of the Cairo Museum of Antiquities one day in 1969, Egyptologist Khalil Messiha noticed something decidedly odd. In a box marked "bird objects," Messiha found a peculiar artifact marked "Special Register No. 6347." The other items in the box were clearly figurines of ordinary birds, but item 6347 looked distinctly nonavian. It had straight wings, a sleek, tapered body, and a vertical tail fin.

Checking museum records, Messiha found that the object, dating from around 200 BC, had been discovered in a tomb near Saqqara, Egypt, in 1898. The antiquarian realized with a shock that he was the first person to see the artifact in more than seven decades. To his twentieth-century eyes, 6347 appeared to be not a bird but an airplane—a 2,100-year-old scale model of a working glider.

Messiha's conclusion provoked an immediate controversy that was only heightened by the findings of a committee of scientists appointed by Egypt's Ministry of Culture to investigate the matter. The committee concluded that the seven-inch-long model, built of light sycamore wood and weighing only 1.11 ounces, seemed to incorporate principles of aircraft design that had taken modern engineers decades of experimentation to discover and perfect. Moreover, they found, the glider worked. More than two millennia after its construction, it still sailed easily through the air at only the slightest flick of the hand.

Yet, the plane may not have been a glider at all. A jagged spot on the lower tail suggests that a component broke off over the years, leading some investigators of oddities and anomalies to speculate that the model may once have included a propulsion mechanism of some kind.

Theirs is not the majority view. Other researchers suggest the model was intended as a toy or a weathervane and its apparent aerodynamic sophistication is a mere coincidence.

Still, the theorists favoring the possibility of ancient flight point out that the early Egyptians frequently made scale models of things they built—including temples, chariots, and ships—and they maintain that the glider is in fact a miniature of a full-size ancient aircraft.

The Egyptians were not alone, however, in leaving behind tantalizing hints of ancient flight. "To operate a flying machine is a great privilege," a Babylonian text called the *Halkatha* records. "Knowledge of flying is most ancient, a gift of the gods of old for saving lives."

Another Babylonian work, the *Sifr'ala of Chaldea*, contains a detailed—if fragmentary—account of how to construct and fly an airplane. Although the text dates back more than 5,000 years, it contains specific comments on copper and graphite airplane parts and describes the effects of wind resistance on stability.

In 468 BC, the Greek mathematician Archytas took a step beyond theory and modeled a wooden pigeon that actually flew. Hailed as a wonder of the ancient world, the pigeon was powered by an internal mechanism of balanced weights and a mysterious, unknown propulsive agent. Some modern scholars theorize that Archytas used a variation of the jet principles demonstrated centuries later by the Greek scientist Hero. Hero designed a rotating boiler that showed the propulsive effect of a jet of steam. Suspended above a fire, his device spun about as steam shot from its four nozzles.

The early Chinese also had a lively interest in the possibilities of flight. Records inscribed on bamboo tablets some 2,000 years old tell of how the emperor Shun, who reigned between 2258 and 2208 BC, built a flying craft to escape his parents' plot to kill him. Not only did the emperor effect a successful flight, the story goes, but he also tested a primitive parachute, landing unharmed after making his getaway.

Four and a half centuries later, Emperor Cheng Tang is said to have ordered his engineer, Ki-Kung-Shi, to design a "flying chariot," the term still used by the Chinese to describe an airplane. According to legend, the emperor ordered the machine destroyed after a successful flight so that its secrets would not fall into the wrong hands.

In the fourth century AD, the scribe Ko-Hung wrote of a "flying car," fashioned from the wood of a jujube tree, that used "ox leather straps fastened to rotating blades to set the machine in motion." The craft may have been imaginary, but Ko-Hung's description calls to mind a helicopter.

The writings of ancient India are perhaps the richest in tales of aviation. The *Mahabharata,* a work that was probably begun in the fourth century BC, tells of an "aerial chariot, with the sides of iron and clad with wings."

The Hindu *Samara Sutradhara,* an eleventh-century-AD collection of texts dating back to antiquity, holds a wealth of information on flight, treating many aspects of aircraft design and even advising on the proper clothing and diet for pilots. "The aircraft which can go by its own force like a bird is called a Vimana," runs one passage. "The body must be strong and durable and built of light wood, shaped like a bird in flight with wings outstretched. Within it must be placed the mercury engine, with its heating apparatus made of iron underneath."

The text goes on to describe "the energy latent in mercury" at some length; unfortunately, though, it offers little information on how that energy was utilized. Caution, the ancient scholars explained, made them discreet, for "any person not initiated in the art of building machines of flight will cause mischief."

The *Ramayana,* the great Indian epic poem dating from the third century BC, describes a double-deck circular aircraft with portholes and a dome—a configuration reminiscent of twentieth-century flying saucer reports. Fueled by a strange yellowish white liquid, the craft was said to travel at the "speed of wind," attain heights that made the ocean look like "a small pool of water," and stop and hover motionless in the sky.

Although most hints of ancient aviation come from the Middle East or the Far East, the New World is not without some related mysteries. One centers on a gold trinket resting in a bank vault in Bogotá, Colombia. The little bauble is believed to have come from the Sinu culture, a pre-Incan civilization dating between the sixth and ninth centuries AD. About two inches long, the object has wings and an unusual tail arrangement. It is one of a handful of similar pre-Columbian gold trinkets, most clearly depicting birds or insects. Most antiquarians believe the pendant is itself a stylized representation of a bat or some other animal. However, other interpretations abound among theorists who think ◊

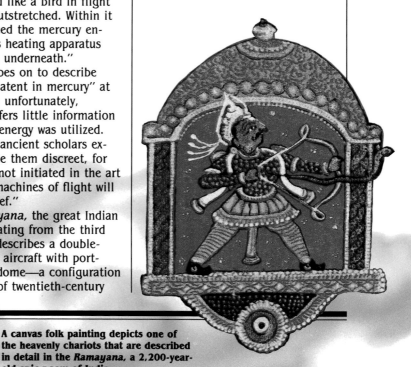

A canvas folk painting depicts one of the heavenly chariots that are described in detail in the *Ramayana,* a 2,200-year-old epic poem of India.

ancient humans mastered flight.

For example, the late biologist Ivan T. Sanderson, one-time head of a group of anomaly enthusiasts called the Society for the Investigation of the Unexplained, examined the pendant in 1969 and rejected outright the idea that it represented an animal. No known animal or insect, he claimed, has the deltoid wings and upright tail shown on the trinket. In addition, Sanderson said, although fish have upright tail fins, they usually have a counterbalancing lower one—an item missing from the pendant. "It is obviously a trinket and an artist's conception of something he had seen," he concluded. "However, it is not a representation of any kind of animal, but it looks just like a very modern, delta-winged, steep-climbing jet fighter." A few pilots and aviation engineers voiced support for Sanderson's extravagant hypothesis, but it drew immediate scorn from most of the scientific world.

Even so, theories of ancient flight persist. Dreams of flying have gripped the imagination since ancient people first gazed up at the birds, admiring their grace, yearning for the freedom implicit in their flight. Hardly a culture has been without its myths and legends of god or human taking wing in some form. But is truth shrouded in such legends? There are scattered tales and artifacts suggesting that perhaps, somewhere, some ancient pioneer gave shape to those imaginings and actually flew. As yet, however, the reality of a long-lost knowledge of aviation remains inseparable from myth, a riddle yet to be unraveled. □

A Fiery Secret Weapon

"It made such a noise in arriving that it seemed like thunder in the sky. It was like a dragon flying through the air."

Thus did one witness describe the wonders of Greek fire, the Byzantine Empire's mysterious flaming weapon that awed all who saw its devastating power. This withering, liquid incendiary (called Greek because Greeks had founded the Byzantine Empire) allowed soldiers and sailors to shower fire on their enemies and blast easily through wooden defense works. Armed with it, the Byzantines turned back fierce Muslim attacks in the seventh and eighth centuries and repulsed later assaults by the Russian Empire.

Greek fire's most remarkable feature was that it burst into flame on contact with water. Pumped through bronze nozzles mounted on the decks of warships, it made a singularly formidable naval weapon.

Like modern military establishments, the Byzantine Empire guarded the secret of its deadly weapon, and even today, chemists can only guess at the formula. Possibly the withering mixture contained petroleum, sulphur, nitrates, lime, and bones, and perhaps even urine. □

Turning Up the Heat

In a manner of speaking, the world's first central heating owed its existence to oysters.

Around 80 BC, an ingenious Roman epicure named Gaius Sergius Orata took an interest in harvesting oysters as a commercial enterprise. In this early attempt at seafood farming, Orata sought a year-round source of warm water, known to promote the growth of the succulent mollusks. He devised a system in which furnaces circulated hot air beneath a series of tanks raised on brick pillars. One thing led to another, and soon Orata had invented the Roman hypocaust system, which was used to heat public baths as well as the private villas of the wealthy.

The hypocaust system entailed the erecting of pillars on a concrete and tile floor. Atop the pillars rested a second, well-insulated floor made of bricks, a layer of clay, and a top layer of stone or marble. One or two furnaces fed by wood or charcoal supplied heat that was funneled through a large pipe or a series of flues into the cavity between the two floors. Furnaces at the public baths were used to heat water at the same time that they warmed the floors. In a subsequent refinement, tile flues were used to distribute heat along the walls *(below)*. □

Harnessing Horsepower

Inventions that seem both small and simple in retrospect can sometimes shape the course of history. A case in point is an efficient horse harness—a device that took more than 1,000 years to make its way to Europe from its origins in China.

Until the eighth century, Europeans had devised nothing better for utilizing horsepower than a throat-and-girth harness—a two-strap affair whose top band went around the horse's throat. Its effect was to start choking the horse as soon as the animal exerted itself. The harness also had serious ramifications for human beings: They had no viable way of using horses to transport goods. This meant, for instance, that ancient Rome, with all its power, had to rely on grain shipped in from Egypt to feed itself. Growing grain in Italy was no problem, but getting it to Rome overland was an insurmountable dilemma.

The only ancient civilization to devise a sensible harness was China, where, in the fourth century BC, some unknown wizard invented the trace harness *(above)*. The load-bearing strap of this contraption went across the horse's breast, allowing the animal to pull and breathe at the same time.

Trace harnesses were introduced to Europe by way of Central Asia when the Avars invaded Hungary in AD 568. Over the next 200 years, they spread across the continent, revolutionizing land transport. □

An Ancient Harvest

In 1834, American inventor Cyrus McCormick developed the first truly efficient mechanical reaping machine, sparking a revolution in agriculture. However, a strikingly similar piece of farming equipment existed in ancient Gaul nearly 2,000 years earlier.

Carved stone reliefs from the first century AD show this early harvester, which resembles an outsize comb mounted on two wheels and is pushed along by a mule or a donkey. Farmers used it to harvest their wheat.

By all accounts, the device was quite efficient. Nevertheless, Gallic farmers abandoned it and reverted to the backbreaking method of harvesting with sickles. Most probably, the early reaper fell prey to the general breakdown of society brought about by the fall of the Roman Empire. □

Rolling On

Far ahead of Westerners in hauling as well as in riding, the Chinese invented the wheelbarrow during the first century BC.

For the first few hundred years after this event, the inventors were coy about spreading the news of their creation, since its military importance was considerable: Early Chinese wheelbarrows could carry hundreds of pounds of supplies each, could transport soldiers, and could be arranged as movable barriers against cavalry charges.

Ancient Chinese wheelbarrows were called such things as wooden ox and gliding horse, conveying some idea of how useful they were: A wheelbarrow could cut in half the number of workers needed for any building project. Unfortunately, the laborsaving bonanza was unknown in Europe until the late twelfth or early thirteenth century. Even today, the world's most versatile and efficient wheelbarrows are found in China. □

Ignoring the Wheel

Beyond question, the wheel is among the most significant technological breakthroughs of all time. By about 1000 BC, it had come into use throughout the Old World, but because wheeled carts did not reach the Americas until the Spanish conquest some 2,500 years later, historians had been assuming that the people of the New World had no independent knowledge of the wheel. In the 1940s, however, they learned otherwise.

In Veracruz, Mexico, at burial sites dating from the first century AD, archaeologists unearthed a number of small clay animal figures, each one possessing a set of completely functional wheels. Some, such as the jaguar shown at right, could also be used as whistles. Other wheeled figures from several different time periods have subsequently been uncovered, showing that the objects were made over a span of several centuries. Their presence in graves indicates that they may have had some spiritual significance.

Why, then, did the people of the New World—who sometimes built elaborate, paved roads to link their cities—fail to make any practical use of the wheel?

Some scholars theorize that the wheel had little workaday utility: Draft animals such as horses or oxen were unknown, making wheeled carts impractical. On the other hand, a lack of draft animals would hardly have stood in the way of the development of wheelbarrows, handcarts, and other such conveyances. And even if carts proved to be unattractive, alternate uses for the device, such as the potter's wheel and spinning wheel, could have been developed. Yet, so far, none has been uncovered. □

Egypt's Edison

The intellectual center of the world at the time, Alexandria, Egypt, in the third century BC produced one of history's great inventors—an individual who might have missed his calling in life had he not been a dutiful son.

The inventor's name was Ctesibius, and his career began when he was apprenticed in the family barbershop. For his father's convenience, the budding inventor devised an adjustable mirror, employing a lead ball in a tube as a counterweight. He found that when the mirror was adjusted, the lead ball compressed the air within the tube and created a loud noise. The discovery intrigued young Ctesibius, who rigged up a cylinder and plunger to carry out further sound experiments. In time, he created the first musical organ. Its design incorporated most of the basic features of modern organs, which produce their distinctive sounds when compressed air is introduced into a set of pipes, each pipe having a different pitch. In order to direct the flow of air, Ctesibius devised the world's first musical keyboard.

Because water pressure was used to force air through its pipes, Ctesibius's instrument was called the hydraulus, or water organ. The heart of the device was a large, inverted funnel immersed in water. Under steady pressure from the water at the funnel's mouth, air was drawn off into the pipes to produce sound. A bellows replenished the supply of air in the funnel. (Later organ makers, building on Ctesibius's work, dispensed with water pressure in favor of powerful bellows.)

Ctesibius's fascination with hydraulics led him to further inventions, including a highly accurate water clock, one of the age's great mechanical marvels. Some 2,300 years after he first tinkered with a barber's mirror, the versatile father of the musical organ is still viewed as a founder of the modern science of hydraulics. □

This Roman clay model of Ctesibius's water organ was found in ancient Carthage.

34

HEALERS

For many ancient societies, medicine and magic were almost indistinguishable. Thousands of years ago, for example, Egyptian physicians battled not injury and disease, but the demons that invaded their patients' bodies. They invoked Thoth, god of wisdom and sorcery, and chanted an exorcism: "Flow out thou who breakest bones, destroyest the skull, diggest in the bone-marrow and makest the seven holes in the head ill."

But pragmatism existed side by side with magic, and great pioneer physicians, with little guidance but trial and error, observation, and logic, discovered drugs and procedures that successfully combatted the body's ills. These doctors knew nothing of microorganisms, but they concocted salves that healed wounds and prevented infection. Indian surgeons examined human cadavers in order to learn anatomy, so their techniques were especially advanced. They even dared to undertake cataract operations and invented plastic surgery. Hippocrates, the Greek who founded rational medicine in the fifth century BC, built on the contributions of the Egyptians and the Indians.

In the China of the second century BC, divines of the native Taoist religion performed medical experiments of a complexity not to be equaled elsewhere for hundreds of years. Inoculation and endocrinology probably began with them. And a number of useful modern drugs owe their existence to plant-wise peoples who have lived in the South American rain forest for thousands of years.

Using copper or bronze implements such as these, early Peruvian surgeons operated on the skulls of hundreds of injured warriors.

Ancient Brain Surgery

One day in the early 1860s, an American diplomat and amateur archaeologist named E. G. Squier was browsing through a private archaeological collection in Cuzco, Peru, when the skull of a pre-Columbian Indian caught his eye. Squier's attention was drawn to a small rectangular hole in the bone: It could, he concluded, only have been cut by a human hand. Squier bought the skull and packed it off to Paul Broca, a prominent French physician and anatomist.

Late Stone Age tombs in France had yielded skulls with similar artificial holes. Anthropologists assumed the holes had been made during religious or magical rituals performed after an individual's death; the operation was called trepanation. But when Broca examined the Peruvian skull, he made a startling discovery. The hole, he announced, could not have been cut after death because an infection had left characteristic pockmarks in the surrounding bone. He estimated that the patient must have survived for at least a week after trepanation for the infection to have developed.

Following Broca's lead, anthropologists took a new look at the Neolithic French finds and discovered that many of these skulls, too, had been trepanned during life and not after death. Extensive evidence of the ancient surgical procedure also turned up in other European countries, as far east as Russia, although the pre-Columbian Peruvians seem to have

performed trepanation on a scale that was unequaled at any other time or place. More than a thousand trepanned skulls have been found in Peru, a number greater than in all the other countries of the world combined.

Most of the Peruvian skulls are from adult males, and most bear the marks of terrible blows to the head. Almost certainly, the men were warriors injured in battle by maces or projectiles from slingshots. Surgeons apparently trepanned their skulls not in rituals, but for purely therapeutic reasons, such as removing bone pressing on the brain or relieving swelling. The Peruvians, in short, practiced medicine, not magic.

Not so the earlier Neolithic surgeons, whose motives appear to have been linked more to ritual than to healing. Few of the Eu-

ropean skulls show signs of injury, and in France, most of the subjects were women. Why this was so remains a mystery—as does the meaning of some intriguing discs archaeologists have gathered in Neolithic tombs.

Called rondelles, the discs are made of polished, perforated cranial bone. They appear to be amulets or talismans that were worn around the neck to ensure good fortune or ward off evil spirits. Each rondelle was cut from the skull of a dead person but only from an individual who in life had undergone trepanation: The rondelle encompasses an arc of bone taken from the edge of a trepanned hole. What magical or religious power Neolithic peoples believed to suffuse trepanned bone can only be guessed.

Magic and therapy may have merged in some trepanations. Primitive peoples commonly blamed demons for illness. Thus, cutting a hole in the skull must have seemed a logical way to rid the body of a resident devil, especially in diseases such as mental illness that appeared to arise in the head. Over time, though, trepanation's medical uses came to predominate in Europe. By the fifth century BC, Hippocrates and other medical authorities were recommending it as a treatment for head injuries.

Because of their sheer numbers, Peruvian skulls have provided much information about the procedure. For making a hole, surgeons had a choice of four techniques: scraping, boring, cutting, and incising. Each required a special instrument, usually of copper or bronze. Using such implements, Paul Broca tried the procedure on

cadavers and found that it took as little as a half-hour—mercifully short for a badly-wounded, comatose warrior, but no doubt endlessly long for a conscious patient with access to no anesthetic except alcohol or hallucinogenic herbs.

Typically, the operation involved making a single hole one to two inches across. However, multiple openings were often made, and some patients returned for repeat surgery. One skull has openings from seven trepannings. Considering the dangers of infection and uncontrolled bleeding, the survival rate was high: About 50 percent of the Peruvian patients survived, judging by the degree to which their skulls had healed.

Ancient European patients could have faced trepanation with a good deal of confidence, for more than 80 percent of them survived—no doubt because, unlike the Peruvian warriors, they went under the knife in good health. But pathologist Arthur C. Aufderheide of the University of Minnesota has noted that a neurosurgeon of 1900 would have been pleased to have his patients pull through as often as even the Peruvians did. Fully 75 percent of a turn-of-the-century brain surgeon's patients were likely to die, usually from infection. Ancient peoples evidently did not have to contend with infectious organisms as virulent as those in the crowded modern world. □

Disease to Cure Disease

In the eleventh century AD, a Taoist hermit living on a mountain in the Chinese province of Sichuan learned that the prime minister, Wang Dan, had sent a desperate summons throughout the empire: Anyone who knew how to prevent or cure smallpox was to come to him. His eldest son had just died of the disease, and he feared the rest of his family might succumb.

Answering the summons, the old hermit journeyed to the imperial capital, bringing with her a number of smallpox scabs. She placed them on bits of cotton that she inserted into her patients' noses—and thereby demonstrated the esoteric Taoist practice of inoculation.

The story of the hermit, which appeared in a mid-sixteenth century text on China's imperial medical

tradition, may blend measures of myth and reality. Other tellings of the tale describe the hermit as either a monk or a nun. Even so, inoculation—the controlled introduction of a virus to stimulate the body's manufacture of protective antibodies—is without doubt a Chinese innovation, and it may have sprung from the work of Taoist alchemists. Unlike their Western counterparts, these early scientific researchers sought the elixir of eternal youth not in a laboratory, but within their own bodies. Perhaps, in their search for this elusive substance, they stumbled on the technique of inoculation.

By the late sixteenth century, Chinese physicians knew of a relatively safe version of the practice. The worst cases of smallpox are

caused by *Variola major;* a second smallpox virus, *Variola minor,* is not so lethal. Physicians distinguished between the symptoms of the two strains and used scabs from people infected with the milder type for inoculation. And, instead of taking scabs produced by a full-blown case of smallpox, they used scabs from people who had recently been inoculated. They thereby obtained a weakened virus—one incapable of causing the illness but still strong enough to trigger antibody formation.

Another technique for ensuring a safe supply of viruses involved having the physician wrap the scabs in paper, seal them in a tightly corked bottle, and carry them around with him for a month. During that time, about 80 percent of the hardy viruses would die from the doctor's body heat, rendering the scabs safer for use. □

China's Early Endocrinology

Endocrinology, the medical specialty dealing with hormone-producing glands, enjoyed a landmark year in 1890. That was when Western doctors came up with a revolutionary treatment for thyroid hormone deficiency. The science took another giant step in 1927, when two researchers announced that they had discovered a rich supply of sex hormones in the urine of pregnant women.

But such breakthroughs in the West were old news in China. Some 2,000 years earlier, Chinese physicians routinely cured goiter, a condition in which the thyroid gland fails to manufacture enough of the hormone thyroxine, essential for the body's metabolism. The cause of goiter is a lack of iodine, and the Chinese treatment was simple: Their cure involved the use of seaweed, a rich source of iodine. By the fifth century they had devised ways to concentrate the active ingredient into pills and a wine-based tincture. The Chinese observed that goiter was common in some mountainous areas and surmised, correctly, that the soil and water must somehow be deficient.

A Chinese pharmacopoeia of the early seventh century reported a still more sophisticated treatment called organotherapy. Thyroid glands from sheep were chopped and combined with fruit in pill form. A cruder variation required patients to be dosed with raw glands. Organotherapy supplied both iodine, which the body concentrates in the thyroid gland, and thyroxine itself—a special boon in cases where disease had diminished or destroyed the gland's ability to produce the hormone.

As remarkable as this therapeutic achievement was, it was matched by another—the treatment of sexual disorders with sex and pituitary hormones extracted from urine. At least as early as 125 BC, Chinese alchemists are known to have produced from concentrated urine a hard, white crystalline substance called autumn mineral. These pioneer endocrinologists could alter the effect of the autumn mineral by varying the proportions of male and female urine. Impotence, menstrual disorders, even cases of hermaphroditism and sex reversals were treated with urine extracts.

Their effectiveness was probably unpredictable, however, owing to the uneven quality of the medicine. The alchemists developed a variety of techniques for producing autumn mineral. All were major undertakings that required many participants, since 150 gallons of urine yielded a mere two or three ounces of autumn mineral.

But modern research has revealed that only one of the methods would have yielded a hormone-rich substance. In that process, evaporation of the urine left a powdered residue containing hormones and many impurities. Heating the powder in a closed vessel vaporized the hormones—which then condensed on the cooler surface of the vessel's lid. □

The Healing Power of Honey

An Egyptian papyrus of medical lore dating back to 3,600 years ago lists close to a thousand remedies—and in more than half of them honey is an important ingredient. It was particularly valued in salves, usually in combination with a vegetable or animal fat.

To the chagrin of some modern skeptics, experiments have shown that honey deserved the confidence that Egyptian apothecaries placed in it—a confidence shared by practitioners of folk medicine in many cultures down to the present day. It can soothe a wound and prevent a bandage from sticking. But beyond such mundane virtues, honey has a peculiar and complex chemistry that actively combats infection and speeds healing.

Honey is a potent killer of harmful bacteria. It has an enzyme from bees' laryngeal glands that combines with glucose and oxygen to form the disinfectant hydrogen peroxide and an antibiotic called gluconolactone. Honey is also hypertonic—it readily absorbs water—thus it can keep a wound dry and draw off fluid bacteria need to live.

Moreover, honey has been shown to promote the growth of healthy tissue in some instances. In 1983, for example, Israeli physicians reported on an experiment in which skin wounds on one group of mice were simply cleaned with a saline solution, while wounds on a second group were salved with ordi-

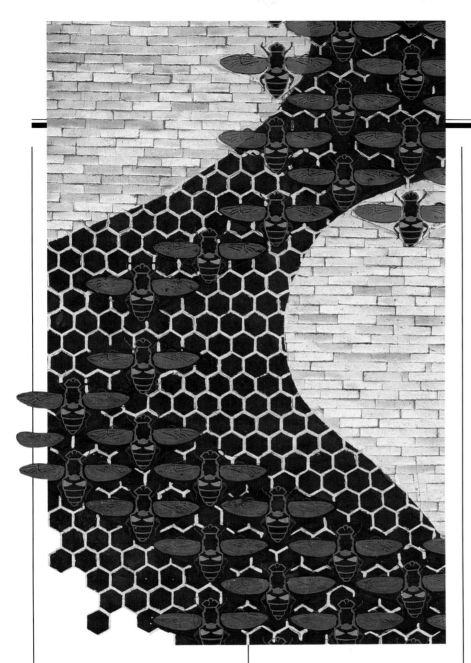

Building New Noses

No feat of ancient medicine out-shines what Hindu plastic surgeons accomplished for patients disfig-ured by mutilation or accident. Among other achievements, these physicians, practicing as long as 2,600 years ago, invented a meth-od of rebuilding noses that is still used in the twentieth century.

There was no lack of patients for reconstructive surgery in ancient India. In addition to missing nos-es, ripped ears were a major prob-lem. It was customary for everyone, male and female alike, to have pierced ears, and the sheer weight of the large earrings commonly worn could tear the earlobe, as could a vicious yank on an earring during a fight.

Earlobe reconstruction involved surgically lifting a flap of skin from the patient's cheek. The flap was then pulled backward and su-tured to the ear to form a new lobe. The *Sushruta Samhita*, the Hindu surgical compendium, ad-vised that after the operation, the patient "should be careful not to disturb the bandage and avoid physical exercise, over-eating, sex-ual intercourse, exposure to, or basking in the glare of fire, fati-guing talk, and sleep by day." When downy hair began to grow on the new lobe, the surgeon knew that the graft had taken nicely and could soon sport an earring.

Noses were a more complex matter. Amputation was a common punishment for theft, adultery, and any number of far more trivial acts. No body part was sacrosanct, but a person whose nose was ◊

nary commercial honey. The honey-treated mice grew new skin at double the rate of the first group.

More recently, Nigerian physi-cian S. E. E. Efem tried honey on fifty-nine patients suffering from horrible skin ulcers that had defied conventional treatment for as long as two years. In every case but one, he reported, honey worked where all else had failed. Within a week, swelling and infection subsided,

and healthy skin began to grow.

Since it can kill bacteria, honey defies decay. In the ruins of the ancient town of Paestum in Italy, archaeologists have unearthed some honey, still golden and sticky after 2,500 years in a tomb, where it was left as an offering. The hon-ey had been preserved by its own purity, the same quality Egyptians of long ago found so effective against pain and disease. □

amputated looked hideous and suffered intense humiliation. To the ancient Indians, the nose symbolized one's reputation, so its loss meant a loss of face, literally and figuratively. No longer deserving respect, a noseless person became a social outcast.

The first beneficiary of nose restoration was, according to Indian tradition, a certain Lady Surpunakha, whose nose was amputated on the orders of a prince in 1500 BC. Taking pity on her, the king instructed his physicians to rebuild the lady's nose.

One reconstructive technique described in the *Sushruta Samhita* had the physician use skin from the cheek as the stuff of a new nose. A second version favored skin from the middle of the forehead, but otherwise the procedure was the same. Using a vine leaf the size of the severed nose as a template, the surgeon cut a flap of

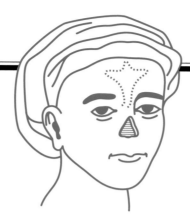

skin with a narrow stem-shaped end called a pedicle, which remained attached to the face. He made shallow cuts in the flap to shape the tissue, then rotated it to keep the skin side facing outward, pulled it over the nasal area, and stitched it in place.

To create a functional organ, two little pipes—probably made of bamboo or clay—were inserted at the lower end of the new nose to make breathing easy and help mold a pair of nostrils. The cotton bandage placed over the area was

sprinkled with sesame oil or clarified butter, which helped shield the surgical wound from germs.

Even if the new nose was imperfect it nevertheless restored a patient's reputation and place in society. The rewards of rhinoplasty thus more than repaid patients for the pain they had to endure. □

From Ancient Lore to Mainstream Medicine

At least 3,500 years ago, Egyptian and Sumerian apothecaries whipped up medications containing parts of the willow tree. The Greeks and Romans relied on extracts of willow for earaches, gout, corns, inflammations, and eye infections, and American Indians brewed a medicinal tea from willow bark. Colds, asthma, and what Elizabethan botanist John Gerard described as "the spitting of

Bloud"—probably from pneumonia—called for decoctions of willow bark and leaves.

It was not until the nineteenth century that chemists discovered the old remedy's active ingredient—a bitter-tasting compound dubbed salicin after the willow's Latin name, *Salix.* Once the tree's secret was out, scientific tinkerers went to work on the compound, hoping to improve on nature and

produce a version without such unpleasant side-effects as nausea and stomach cramps. One of their laboratory creations was aspirin, which went on the market in 1899 and was soon hailed as a miracle drug for its power to relieve pain, fever, and inflammation.

Folk medicine brims with plants that, like the willow, ease pain and cure ills. Even peoples regarded as primitive by Westerners steeped in rationalist tradition have highly sophisticated pharmacopoeias, refined from experience that has been passed down orally for untold generations. Ethnobotanist Walter H. Lewis and his wife, Memory Elvin-Lewis, a microbiologist, have studied such groups in their native environments and report that although the Jívaro of the Amazon jungle neither read nor write, they use more than 500 different species of medicinal plants. Troublesome teeth, for instance, are coated with the juice of a mulberry tree and, within ten days, the teeth crumble and fall out painlessly.

Western medicine long ago adopted two Jívaro finds—quinine for malaria, and curare, a paralyzing poison, as a muscle relaxant. The Jívaro are one of a score of Amazonian tribes that use curare to kill or stun prey—and, on occasion, their enemies. The substance is extracted from any of several species of climbing vines, the most potent of which is the moonseed. The active ingredient is an alkaloid that prevents nerve impulses from reaching the muscles. In large doses, it kills. In small doses, it simply eases muscular tension, and surgeons find it invaluable in abdominal surgery. Other drugs, reputed to prevent conception for months, to boost a woman's fertility, or to speed the healing of broken bones, make the Jívaro's plant lore a fascinating and potentially rewarding field of study.

To be sure, modern medicine has not always been open to such preparations. Holy men of ancient India treasured rauwolfia, which they called the moonshine plant, for the relief it gave people suffering from the "moon disease," or insanity. Besides sedating the mentally ill, it was used for snake bite, fever, diarrhea, and dysentery. Holy men chewed its root during meditation, and a mild extract calmed cranky babies.

Rauwolfia was still a popular folk remedy in 1931, when Indian researchers announced that a drug extracted from the plant not only tranquilized disturbed patients but also lowered blood pressure. Yet Western medical scientists continued to ignore the Indian experience. Then, in 1952, rauwolfia was tested in the West. Within two years, the age-old tranquilizer had helped launch a revolution, and drug therapy became standard treatment for mental illness. □

Ancient Salves: Cures and Quackery

The drugs of the ancient world's pharmacopoeia compounded magic and reason in unequal measures. Some substances did benefit patients and are still prescribed today. But the vast majority—they numbered in the thousands and included animal, vegetable, and mineral products in astonishing variety—were sometimes harmful, often ineffectual, and frequently repulsive.

For instance, excrement—from flies, crocodiles, pelicans, even humans—was relied on for complaints ranging from baldness to cataracts. Such substances, repellent to the modern mind, were chosen for a supposed magical potency often reinforced by incantation. Thus an Egyptian physician treating blindness poured liquid extracted from a pig's eye into the patient's ear (in the erroneous belief that a conduit connected ear to eye) as he chanted, "I have brought this which was applied to the seat of yonder and replaces the horrible suffering."

Their peculiarities notwithstanding, some remarkably offensive or seemingly irrational preparations did cure or prevent disease. The Chinese treated eye ailments with bat dung, and patients suffering from at least one condition—night blindness—probably improved. Analysis shows that bat dung has a high level of vitamin A, the active ingredient in an extract of liver prescribed by modern ophthalmologists for night blindness. The ancient Egyptians were even closer to the modern mark than the Chinese in their prescription for the same ailment: "Ox-liver placed over a fire of grain or barley stems and suffused with the vapours they emit, the resulting liquid to be pressed on the eyes."

Infections may have yielded to another Egyptian innovation, a salve of "rotten bread" for wounds. Medical historians speculate that the salve had antibacterial molds comparable to penicillin.

A millipede's chemical defense against predators—a liquid with benzoquinone, an antiseptic—was a favorite ingredient of ancient Greek nostrums for wounds. Because the millipede yields up this substance only when disturbed, Greek physicians first had to alarm the creature. The liquid was then added to the salve. □

Leeching for Health

In ancient times, the principal cause of disease was thought to be an inharmonious balance of the body's essential fluids, or humors. A reasonable treatment, therefore, involved getting rid of excess blood or some other body fluid that seemed to be in oversupply.

Bleeding was sometimes induced with a knife or needle and a suction cup, but another handy and relatively painless implement was the leech, a voracious little bloodsucking invertebrate. A wall painting in the tomb of an Egyptian scribe named Userhat, who died in 1308 BC, appears to show a man hunching on a stool as a practitioner applies leeches to his forehead. What ailed this patient is unknown, but over the years the leech has been employed to treat a long list of maladies.

One of the oldest surviving medical prescriptions dates to the second century BC, when the Greek physician Nicander suggested the use of leeches for venomous bites. Other practitioners prescribed them for epilepsy, headache, pleurisy, insanity, infected wounds, and gout, along with disorders of the eye and ailments of the spleen and other internal organs.

The medicinal leech, a species that inhabits Old World streams and ponds, was the favorite of physicians, who often kept a supply on hand. The inch-long creature has a round mouth housing three cutting plates, each armed with as many as 100 teeth. After piercing its host's skin, the leech feeds steadily for fifteen minutes or so. When its digestive tract has been filled to capacity—it holds as much as two ounces of blood—the leech lets go.

For most patients, from the earliest days to the more recent past, the leech probably did neither harm nor good. Modern surgeons, however, have found that in some respects their ancient counterparts may have had the right idea: Leeches have a decided benefit in delicate procedures such as the reattachment of severed ears or fingers. The blood supply to the reattached member is assured by surgical repair of arteries. But the smaller veins—which carry blood to the heart—must usually be left to heal themselves; until they do, the blood stagnates in the reattached part. When leeches are allowed to remove the blood, pain and swelling are lessened and healing enhanced. The animals also inject an anticoagulant that causes a continued ooze of blood for several hours.

Leeching is, of course, a less than perfect treatment. Many patients are queasy at the thought of it, and a leech harbors a potentially infectious bacterium. Even so, this ancient treatment has so thoroughly proved its benefits that a leech farm in Wales does a lively business supplying tens of thousands of the creatures yearly to surgeons all over the world. □

Living Sutures

The kit of a skillful surgeon in ancient India may literally have been acrawl with a cunning technical aid—a handful of large black ants.

In a medical treatise compiled some 2,000 years ago, the scholar Sushruta indicated that surgeons used ants to suture intestinal wounds. "According to others," he wrote, "large black ants should be applied even to the perforated intestines, . . . and their bodies should be separated from their heads after they had firmly bitten the perforated parts. . . . After that the intestines with the heads of the ants attached to them should be gently pushed back into the cavity and reinstated in their original situation therein."

Modern anthropologists have turned up evidence that peoples in Africa, South America, and Bhutan even today suture wounds with large ants. In South America, soldiers of the species *Eciton burchelli,* an army ant, are used. These creatures have powerful, hooklike mandibles that easily pierce flesh, and dislodging them is a painful and arduous process. Even if the ant is killed in mid-bite, its mandibles maintain their viselike hold. □

43

The Shining Leg of Capua

More than two millennia ago, a man who must have been something of a dandy stumped about the Roman city of Capua on a handsome and most unusual leg. His own was missing from just below the knee, perhaps lost to a war injury, an accident, or an infection that ended in amputation. Whatever the cause, he declined to make do with a simple peg leg, as people of the time ordinarily did. Instead, the device that he wore had a realistically modeled wood core and a decorative sheath of gleaming bronze.

The Capua leg went to the grave with its owner around 300 BC and remained undiscovered and unnoted until the late nineteenth century. Even then, the leg drew only casual attention—although, as far as anyone knew, no other prosthetic device built in the classical era ever resembled the form, as well as the function, of the bodily member that it replaced. No false foot was found in the grave, and, although iron rods pierced with holes were attached to the top of the bronze sheath, it remains uncertain exactly how the leg was held in place.

Scholars believe that this prosthesis was the work of a craftsman, not a doctor. Physicians of old seem not to have concerned themselves with artificial body parts; they are unmentioned in any surviving classical medical text.

Somehow the Capua leg came to rest at the Museum of the Royal College of Surgeons in London. Around 1910, a facsimile of the leg was made—a fortunate thing, since German bombs destroyed the original in a 1941 air raid. □

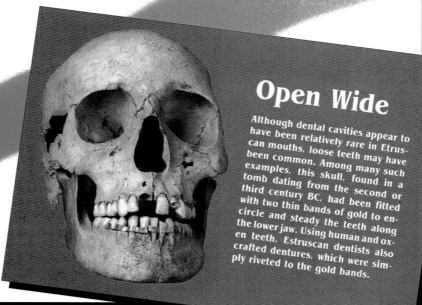

Open Wide

Although dental cavities appear to have been relatively rare in Etruscan mouths, loose teeth may have been common. Among many such examples, this skull, found in a tomb dating from the second or third century BC, had been fitted with two thin bands of gold to encircle and steady the teeth along the lower jaw. Using human and oxen teeth, Estruscan dentists also crafted dentures, which were simply riveted to the gold bands.

Clearing the Clouds from Ancient Eyes

Far from being a strictly modern sight-saving miracle, cataract surgery was performed successfully in ancient times.

A cataract is a clouding of the eye's lens that prevents light entering the pupil from reaching the retina at the back of the eyeball. Since the light has to reach this destination in order to create a visual image in the brain, untreated cataracts can eventually cause blindness. Many ancient Indians escaped this unhappy fate, however, because of a Hindu operation now called couching.

Couching is described in *Sushruta Samhita,* a treatise that records Hindu surgical practices prevalent thousands of years ago. The aim of the procedure was to move the clouded lens to a position where it could not obstruct vision. To perform the operation, a surgeon needed a working knowledge of the eye's anatomy, no small measure of boldness, and ambidexterity: The *Sushruta Samhita* advised operating on the left eye with the right hand and on the right with the left.

The surgeon sat on a low stool facing the patient, who was seated on the ground. To prevent the patient from thrashing about in pain, his hands were tied together, and the surgeon's assistant held his head firmly. After inserting a lancet between the iris and the corner of the eye, the surgeon moved the instrument's tip from side to side and upward, listening for a characteristic sound and watching for a drop of liquid emerging from the eye. These signs indicated that the lens was impaled. "If the patient ▷

can see objects," the treatise counsels, "the doctor should draw the lancet out slowly, lay cotton soaked in fat on the wound, and let the patient lie still with bandaged eyes." The fat formed a barrier to bacteria and reduced the risk of infection.

Whether couching was a Hindu invention is impossible to determine. A passage in Hammurabi's Code, which predates the *Sushruta Samhita* by more than one thousand years, hints that Babylonian surgeons were familiar with the operation. Wherever it originated, couching persisted into classical times. But, unlike their Hindu counterparts, Roman surgeons of the first century AD favored penetrating the eye above the iris, rather than beside it, and pushing the lens downward from the pupil. If it resumed its original position when the lancet was withdrawn, the surgeon used the instrument's tip to cut the lens into pieces. The Roman writer Celsus says in *De Me-*

dicina that tiny pieces are "more easily stowed away singly and form smaller obstacles to vision."

Around AD 1000, Arabic surgeon and writer Ammar al-Mausili announced that he had made a radical advance in treating cataracts. With a syringelike instrument, he could actually extract the lens instead of couching it and thus prevent any recurrent visual obstruction. It seems, however, that the Romans may have preceded Ammar with this innovation. In 1975, archaeologists found a small cache of ophthalmological instruments at Montbellet, France, once part of Roman Gaul. Along with three small bronze couching needles were two other devices in which a needle was housed in a tiny tube marked with an eye at its tip. The correspondence between Ammar's description of his device and the Montbellet syringe was quite precise, leading medical historians to credit Roman surgeons with being first to use the technique. □

ENGINEERS

The world as it looks today is in many respects a tamed place. Rivers have been dammed, great sections of marshland filled, forests turned into farmland, deserts irrigated. But all this man-wrought transformation began a long time ago—much further back in the past than most people appreciate.

The first alteration of the landscape no doubt occurred tens of thousands of years ago. That exercise of the human will may only have been a mound of earth, scraped together and heaped high to commemorate some momentous event or to venerate a newly fallen chieftain. Or it may have been a pile of stones, raised to honor some fearful but now-forgotten god. Time and wind and rain have scrubbed away such early monuments. But the die had been cast, and although it had yet to be named, engineering had been born. Indeed, go forward through the centuries to the third millennium BC, and those mounds have become mountain high and stuffed with treasure, the piles of stones have turned into pyramids, and the species responsible has abandoned its caves and crude huts to build entire cities of handmade brick, with paved streets, neat rows of houses, and plumbing.

Tunnels were burrowed, canals dug, roads laid to last as long as empires—much of this thousands of years before the Christian era began. Few challenges seemed too large to ancient engineers, few obstacles too high, so they gave the world a Stonehenge, a Great Pyramid, and, in the Peruvian Andes, stonework so intricate it still inspires awe *(above)*.

Who were these master builders? No one knows for certain; their names went largely unrecorded or were later lost. But much of what they built remains, if only as splendid ruins—and sometimes as splendid mysteries.

Raising the Pyramids

It weighs some 6,500,000 tons, soars 481 feet above the surrounding desert, and covers more than thirteen acres. Around 2600 BC when it was built, it was honeycombed with booby-trapped passages, chambers, and galleries. In fact, the Great Pyramid of Khufu boasts so many impressive statistics that to call it great seems an understatement—all the more so since it was built without benefit of the wheel or beasts of burden or sophisticated tools or equipment.

Mindful of the challenges the builders of the Great Pyramid must have faced, historians, archaeologists, and Egyptologists have served up a multitude of theories over the centuries to explain its construction. Some of those theories demand a greater leap of faith than others.

In the nineteenth century, for instance, there arose the notion of the "pyramid inch," a divinely inspired dimension that supposedly encoded in micro form a wealth of cosmic information. This arcane measure was the brainchild of Scotland's

Charles Piazzi Smyth, a professor of astronomy at the University of Edinburgh. A devout Presbyterian, Smyth had unbridled enthusiasm for the Great Pyramid's possible spiritual implications. Applying his pyramid inch, which amounted to .999 inches, to the pyramid's inner and outer dimensions, Smyth deduced calculations for the earth's density and equatorial diameter and the distance from the earth to the sun. In addition, by equating each pyramid inch with one year, he found interesting chronologies embedded in the architecture. Among them were the dates for the Hebrews' exodus from Egypt, the birth of Jesus, and, by projection, the end of the world. Writing in the 1860s, Smyth put the final cataclysm at 1881.

In the twentieth century came the claim of a French chemist named Joseph Davidovits that the pyramids were not so much built as poured. In 1974, Davidovits pro-

posed that instead of being quarried and hauled, the stones used to build the pyramids were cast as needed on the spot, employing a process similar to the one used today to make Portland cement. According to Davidovits, crushed limestone was mixed with a special "geopolymeric" binder to create a fluid, epoxylike substance. This mixture was then poured into wooden molds, where it supposedly hardened into solid rock. Other researchers, citing an abundance of archaeological evidence, dispute Davidovits's claim that the pyramids are "plastic megaliths," even as newer theories crop up.

Among the latest is that of Thomas J. Crowder, a manpower-planning specialist and amateur Egyptologist, who argues that the pyramids were built with the aid of hydraulic power harnessed from a second Nile River, one that flowed underground. Crowder believes that Egyptian priests stumbled across this hidden

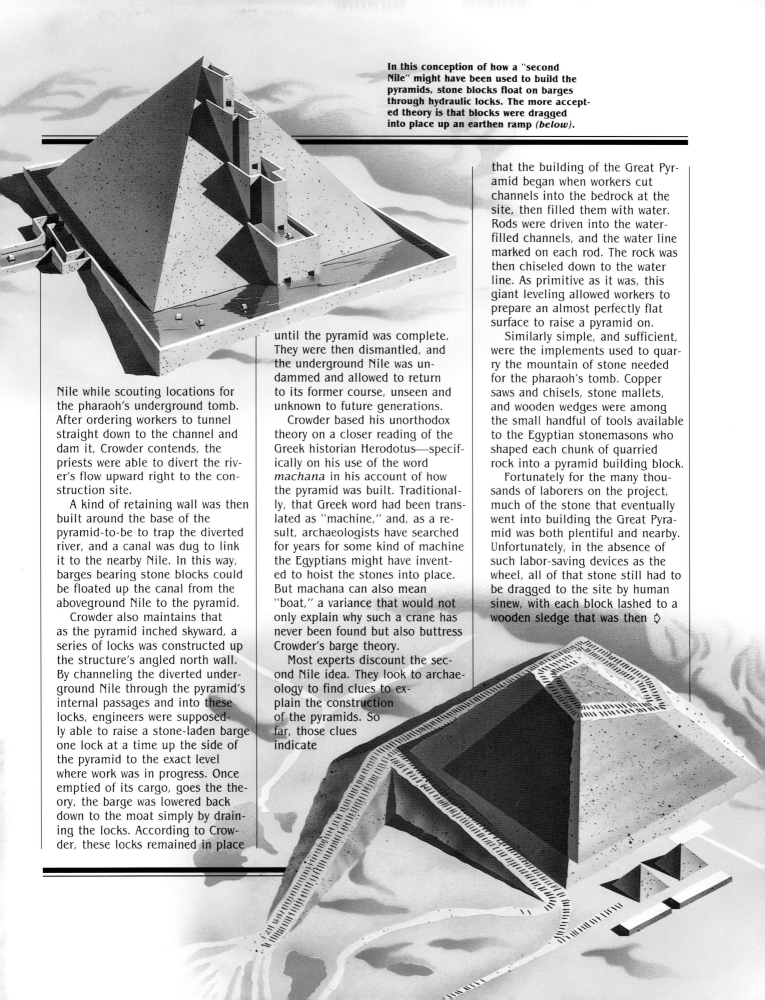

In this conception of how a "second Nile" might have been used to build the pyramids, stone blocks float on barges through hydraulic locks. The more accepted theory is that blocks were dragged into place up an earthen ramp (below).

Nile while scouting locations for the pharaoh's underground tomb. After ordering workers to tunnel straight down to the channel and dam it, Crowder contends, the priests were able to divert the river's flow upward right to the construction site.

A kind of retaining wall was then built around the base of the pyramid-to-be to trap the diverted river, and a canal was dug to link it to the nearby Nile. In this way, barges bearing stone blocks could be floated up the canal from the aboveground Nile to the pyramid.

Crowder also maintains that as the pyramid inched skyward, a series of locks was constructed up the structure's angled north wall. By channeling the diverted underground Nile through the pyramid's internal passages and into these locks, engineers were supposedly able to raise a stone-laden barge one lock at a time up the side of the pyramid to the exact level where work was in progress. Once emptied of its cargo, goes the theory, the barge was lowered back down to the moat simply by draining the locks. According to Crowder, these locks remained in place

until the pyramid was complete. They were then dismantled, and the underground Nile was undammed and allowed to return to its former course, unseen and unknown to future generations.

Crowder based his unorthodox theory on a closer reading of the Greek historian Herodotus—specifically on his use of the word *machana* in his account of how the pyramid was built. Traditionally, that Greek word had been translated as "machine," and, as a result, archaeologists have searched for years for some kind of machine the Egyptians might have invented to hoist the stones into place. But machana can also mean "boat," a variance that would not only explain why such a crane has never been found but also buttress Crowder's barge theory.

Most experts discount the second Nile idea. They look to archaeology to find clues to explain the construction of the pyramids. So far, those clues indicate

that the building of the Great Pyramid began when workers cut channels into the bedrock at the site, then filled them with water. Rods were driven into the water-filled channels, and the water line marked on each rod. The rock was then chiseled down to the water line. As primitive as it was, this giant leveling allowed workers to prepare an almost perfectly flat surface to raise a pyramid on.

Similarly simple, and sufficient, were the implements used to quarry the mountain of stone needed for the pharaoh's tomb. Copper saws and chisels, stone mallets, and wooden wedges were among the small handful of tools available to the Egyptian stonemasons who shaped each chunk of quarried rock into a pyramid building block.

Fortunately for the many thousands of laborers on the project, much of the stone that eventually went into building the Great Pyramid was both plentiful and nearby. Unfortunately, in the absence of such labor-saving devices as the wheel, all of that stone still had to be dragged to the site by human sinew, with each block lashed to a wooden sledge that was then ◊

hauled over log rollers using ropes made of plaited reeds. The polished limestone blocks that eventually faced the pyramid had to be floated up the Nile from a quarry ten miles south of Cairo, then dragged the final half-mile from the river to the work site. The granite destined to frame the pharaoh's burial chamber made a similar, albeit longer, journey from its quarry 600 miles upriver at Aswan.

All that dragging did not end at the work site, since each stone still had to be hauled up the side of the pyramid and heaved into final position. The archaeological evidence suggests that one or more ramps were built for this purpose, the ramps eventually reaching to the very top of the pyramid. Once the structure's sandstone cap was in place, the masons worked their way down again, finishing the pyramid in its limestone veneer and dismantling the ramps as they went along.

In all, as many as 150,000 laborers may have poured out their sweat on the Great Pyramid in the name of their god-king, working every year, for as long as thirty years, during the three to four months of late summer when the Nile flooded and they were idled from their jobs in the fields.

Even before those workers had nudged the Great Pyramid's last stone into place, other structures were taking shape on the plateau at Giza. Eventually the Great Pyramid would stand as the centerpiece of a magnificent complex of temples and tombs that would one day rank among the Seven Wonders of the ancient world.

Today, the ruins of that complex are the last of the Seven Wonders that remain, a mecca for tourists and a perennial source of mystery, shrouded as much in myth as they are in the desert haze. □

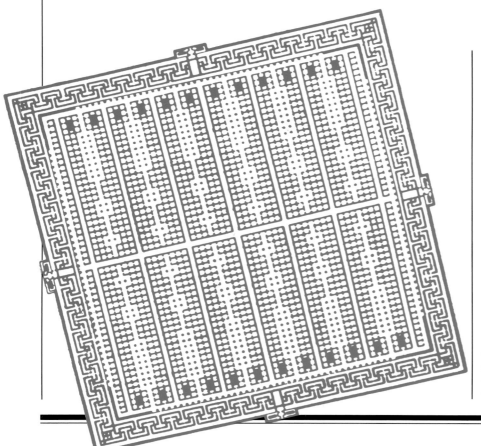

Egypt's Royal Puzzle

What looks like the work of a master weaver is actually the floor plan of one of ancient Egypt's grandest structures. This complex labyrinth, built in about 2000 BC for the pharaoh Amenemhet III near his pyramid at Fayoum, had two levels, 3,000 rooms, and an enigmatic tangle of dark passages. The historian Herodotus noted that it cost more in money and labor than "all the works and buildings of the Greeks put together."

The maze housed tombs of kings—and of sacred crocodiles—but no one is sure why the sepulchres required such an intricate setting. The labyrinth may have reflected no more than a royal fondness for puzzles. □

Petra: The City of the Dead

Even today, the road to the ruins of Jordan's rose-tinted city of Petra can be traveled only on foot or on horseback along a path that is no more than three feet wide in places. The path winds beneath towering cliffs of pink sandstone that are an impressive prologue for the drama to come: After one last turn, the road becomes a valley whose rocky western wall has been sculpted into a ninety-foot-tall temple, with porticoes, porches, and windows that back onto nothing at all, just like a theater set.

The mysterious temple is called the Pharaoh's Treasury, although no pharaoh ever set foot in it. It was built for some forgotten reason about 2,000 years ago by a nomadic desert people called the Nabataeans. An urn, carved into the rock above the temple and bearing the scars of hundreds of bullets, helps explain the Treasury's name. The urn, says a legend, held a pharaoh's treasure, making the stone vessel a tempting target for passing Bedouins who hoped a lucky shot would pay off in a shower of gold.

Startling as it is, the Pharaoh's Treasury is only one of a number of carved curiosities found near the ruins of Petra. Nearby, for example, stands the palace, and cut into a mountain overlooking the valley looms the Deir, or monastery *(above).* Like the Pharaoh's Treasury, both are mostly facade, with only a single room behind their elegantly carved pediments, columns, and scrollwork.

In this same eerie complex are

the remains of a Roman theater, its thirty-three tiers of seats hewed from a wall of rock that was already pocked with hundreds of Nabataean tombs when the Romans incorporated Petra into their empire in AD 106. Some of the tombs open onto the theater's uppermost row. From the stage, the scene is one of grim contrast, with rows of seats for 3,000 living spectators and, above and all around them, the resting places of the dead.

More tombs line the road to the city of Petra itself, once the crossroads of the region's great trade routes and home to more than 20,000 people. But a shift in those trade routes sidetracked Petra sometime in the third century, and a devastating earthquake silenced the city forever in AD 350. □

Successive Suez Canals

The present Suez Canal is not the original. Such a waterway was started by the Egyptians around 1800 BC and much later was finished by conquering Romans. The Byzantines neglected it during their period of hegemony in the region, but the Arabs dredged it open again in the seventh century AD. Their labor was wasted, however, since the Ottomans filled it in for military reasons in the year 775. Thereafter, no water route linked the Mediterranean and the Red Sea until the modern canal was completed in 1869. □

Malta's Mysterious Echo Chamber

The word in Greek means "subterranean chamber," but this scarcely describes the marvels of Malta's Hypogeum, a vast complex of more than twenty natural and man-made caverns. Some 4,500 years ago, the Hypogeum was probably a sanctuary—and was certainly a tomb.

In this lightless temple deep underground, worshipers may once have huddled, surrounded perhaps by the bones of their own ancestors, while the voice of an unseen oracle resounded from chamber to chamber. Research has revealed that the Hypogeum is a superb echo chamber that will transmit any deep, low voice from one end of the vault to the other. The speaker has only to sit in a small niche off the so-called Oracle Room and talk, and the words rumble along a ridge cut into the rock below the ceiling and bounce eerily from wall to wall.

That ceiling ridge would seem to denote a prehistoric knowledge of acoustics, and its uncanny sound effects must have been compelling to the prehistoric Maltese who gathered there in order to seek the counsel of the oracle. But the chiseled molding is not the Hypogeum's only archaeological embellishment. Elsewhere within it are decorative spirals painted in red ocher on the ceilings and, in one room, traces of a black-and-white checkerboard pattern on the wall. Many of the rooms feature elaborately carved pillars, doorways, and window niches.

All these carvings—indeed, the entire Hypogeum itself—had to be hewed from solid limestone by workers using only the antler picks and stone mallets of the third millennium BC. The backbreaking task took centuries. Eventually, the Hypogeum encompassed three levels—the lowest thirty feet below the ground—and a disorienting maze of rooms, passages, and stairways. The rooms, some archaeologists believe, constituted a temple devoted to the worship of a goddess. In time, however, the temple apparently became a tomb; it is believed to have held the remains of 6,000 to 7,000 people. Later still, the Hypogeum was inexplicably abandoned. Its dead kept their secret until 1902, when workers cutting cisterns for new houses accidentally broke through the roof of the Hypogeum and flooded its chambers with daylight for the first time in centuries. □

Greeks directed by the engineer Eupalinus built a tunnel more than half a mile long through rock on the island Samos in the sixth century BC. Work started from either side of the mountain, and, although they had only the crudest surveying equipment, the tunnelers managed to meet almost exactly in the middle.

Blueprints in Stone

Scholars have long known that the architects of classical Greece made meticulous plans of the temples and monuments that would become their claims to fame. None of those designs was thought to have survived, however, until 1979, when a set of ancient "blueprints" for the Temple of Apollo at Didyma turned up right under some archaeologists' noses. The plans were etched into the marble walls of the temple itself. Covering hundreds of square yards, they depicted individual parts of the temple in exact 1:1 scale.

Ironically, the plans survived because they were never brought to full fruition. Begun some 2,000 years ago, construction of the temple at Didyma crept along for 600 years, then halted short of completion. Had the temple been finished, final polishing of its marble would have obliterated every trace of the inscribed blueprints. □

The Romans, by the first century AD, had already built some 50,000 miles of paved roads—a number of them so durable that they are still in use. By contrast, the U.S. Interstate Highway System, when it is finished, will only encompass about 42,000 miles of roadway.

A menacing deity with both human and jaguar features glowers from a 3,500-year-old adobe wall at Huaca de los Reyes in the Andes Mountains of Peru.

A New World Older than Anyone Knew

Historians have long believed that no ancient American society rivaled in achievement or complexity Mesopotamia and Egypt, the great cultural cradles of the Old World. But in the 1980s, archaeologists discovered otherwise.

Working in the fifty or more narrow river valleys that crisscross the Andes along the length of Peru, they found evidence of architecture on a grand scale—towering pyramids and temples, secular buildings, plazas, and private homes—all in planned communities dating back to between 5,000 and 3,500 years ago. This is about the same time that the pyramids were being built in Egypt, and the city-states of Sumer were reaching their peak in Mesopotamia.

"This idea of the Old World being ahead of the New World has to be put on hold," according to Yale archaeologist Richard Burger, one of the antiquarians working on the Andean project. The experts do not contend that the old Peruvian civilization ever matched all the achievements of the ancient Middle East, where writing arose and crucial inventions such as the wheel were created. There is no evidence that the river valley Andean people had a written language or used the wheel—nor did their descendants, including the creative Inca. Even so, the scholars say, the new finds indicate that in the areas of planning, engineering, organization, political sophistication, and creative artistry, the vanished civilization of Peru compared favorably to the Old World cultures.

The Andean finds, adobe structures that have been admirably preserved by the cold, dry mountain climate, include a stepped pyramid more than ten stories tall and an equally lofty U-shaped temple. There were also large secular buildings, storehouses, and plazas—one of them two-thirds of a mile long—flanked by residential areas. Dramatic friezes, their myriad colors still intact, adorn some buildings. The communities apparently lived and lived well on crops grown on nearby irrigated farms.

Many of the ruins, scattered among scores of sites, had only been partially excavated as the 1990s approached, and it seemed likely that the Andean project would yield still more wonders. From what they had already learned, however, archaeologists reasoned that the people who built the Andean towns were politically cohesive and relied on economic cooperation—factors that could explain their ability to mobilize the talent and labor to plan and build on a monumental scale.

Along with casting doubt on the idea of Old World supremacy, the Andean finds have called into question the long-held notion that the Maya, who flourished in Central America, had created the seminal culture of the western hemisphere. The largest of the Andean monuments predate the rise of the Maya by nearly two millennia. □

The Stone Puzzles of the Inca

Although they had neither the wheel nor draft animals and had only the simplest of tools, Incan craftsmen were surpassingly skillful at working with huge blocks of stone. As a result, Incan walls and buildings are masterpieces of construction, with each stone so precisely and painstakingly fitted to adjoining stones that very often even a razor blade cannot be slipped between the joints. Moreover, this remarkably tight fit was achieved without the use of any mortar whatever.

Without mortar, ordinary stonemasons might have relied on gravity, and on the great weight and size of their raw materials, to hold

their handiwork together. Incan stonemasons, however, were anything but ordinary. Although they worked with stones weighing as much as 200 tons and standing as tall as twenty-eight feet, they apparently refused to place their trust in even so faithful a force as gravity. Instead, they carved each stone into a multisided block, leaving a slightly convex projection on each face. A corresponding concave depression would then be chiseled out of the adjacent faces of blocks that were already in position in a wall.

It was a lengthy and laborious process of trial and error. Each block had to be repeatedly heaved into place, tested for fit, and then removed—until, finally, it matched up exactly with each of its neighbors. The end result was that each course of stones locked into the ones above and below it with uncanny, jigsaw precision, virtually guaranteeing that the wall or building would be able to stand any test of time.

Many of the Incan structures have survived for more than four centuries in a country where earthquakes quickly turn conventional masonry into rubble. The durability of Incan stonework was put to a severe test in 1950 when an earthquake struck the former Incan capital of Cuzco. Buildings swayed, the ground itself heaved and buckled, and when it was all over, 90 percent of the city's edifices had been damaged or destroyed.

Not one Incan-built wall suffered a single crack. □

The Stones of Tiahuanaco

For many centuries, it was the cultural and ceremonial capital of central South America, a city so admired that local Indians later believed it had been built by the gods or a race of giants. In truth, however, the city of Tiahuanaco, which lies about six miles from Lake Titicaca in present-day Bolivia, was the handiwork of an indigenous Andean people.

The people of Tiahuanaco never had a written language and thus left no written account of themselves. Only Indian legends and the silent stones of the ruined city itself bear witness to a population that may once have numbered 40,000, many of them skilled artisans and knowledgeable farmers. The ruins speak of a brilliant civilization that 2,000 years ago built a city that was a model of urban planning, whose engineers devised a drainage and sewage system that was centuries ahead of its time

and transformed huge blocks of stone into buildings that were at once majestic and mysterious. Among these structures are the Temple of the Sun, whose walls contain many large stones weighing up to 150 tons, and the Gateway of the Sun, which was hewed from a single block of hard andesite.

Yet the people of Tiahuanaco had no harnessed animals and no wheels, not even a roller, and not a single tool made out of anything but stone or bronze. Moreover, there were no quarries or scattered boulders nearby with which to

build such a city. So where did the stones of Tiahuanaco come from, and how did they get here?

A Jesuit priest writing in the days of the Spanish conquest claimed that the stones "were carried through the air to the sound of a trumpet." Actually, they were dragged to their destination and dragged for some distance: ◊

Archaeologists have determined that the quarries that furnished the stones lay anywhere from six to 200 miles away. Some of the stones may have been ferried across Lake Titicaca on totora-reed boats to a port fourteen miles from Tiahuanaco, then hauled overland to the construction site. Once there, the stones were painstakingly chiseled and polished down to an accuracy of one-fiftieth of an inch and fitted together with consummate skill.

That skill is just as apparent at Tiahuanaco's satellite city, Lukurmata, where a temple complex contains stones whose corners are perfectly squared, implying a remarkable knowledge of geometry on the part of some forgotten engineer or stonemason. Some of the stones also have markings on them, perhaps to show workers where and how to place them. If the markings were, in fact, directions, it is possible that the blocks were prefitted and the buildings, in effect, prefabricated.

The temples of Lukurmata and Tiahuanaco, like the cities themselves, feature an ingenious drainage system, one that continues to keep the temple floors dry some 2,000 years after it was installed.

Unfortunately for the people of Tiahuanaco, their empire proved to be shorter-lived than their drainage system. Sometime around AD 1200, the empire slipped into irreversible decline; within fifty years, once-thriving Tiahuanaco was a dead city. To this day, no one can explain its demise. It has since been devastated by earthquakes, pillaged by treasure hunters, and, ironically, used as a quarry, its stone buildings and sculptures scavenged for reuse in building local churches and haciendas. □

Superfarms of the Andes

On the long plain stretching into Peru and Bolivia from 12,000-foot-high Lake Titicaca, the land is mostly pasture now, marked with corrugated strips of alternately high and low ground. Called *waru waru* by the local Indians, these undulating patterns of raised earthen platforms and shallow canals have been all but erased by time and the elements.

Rediscovered in the 1960s, the rippled patches at one time blanketed some 200,000 acres and were believed to be the work of the Inca who farmed there four or five centuries ago. More recent archaeological studies, however, have revealed that the system is in fact an agricultural design, perfected more than 2,500 years ago, that has the ability to outperform modern farming techniques.

At the heart of the system are the earthen platforms *(opposite, above)*, about 3 feet high, 30 to 300 feet long, and 10 to 30 feet wide. These elevated earthworks are separated by canals of similar dimensions and built out of the excavated soil. Over time, the platforms were fertilized periodically with organic silt and nitrogen-rich algae scooped up from the bottom of the canals during the dry season. Even today, more than 500 years after the fields fell idle, the sediment in the old canals is much richer in nutrients than the soil of the surrounding plains.

But the platform-canal system was not merely a way of enriching infertile ground. It also appears to have created a climate that both

extended the high-altitude growing season and helped crops survive hard times. During the area's frequent periods of drought, for example, the canals provided vital moisture, while the higher level of the platforms raised plants above the worst effects of the region's frequent floods. Moreover, the canal water may have acted as a kind of thermal storage battery, absorbing the sun's heat during the day and radiating it back into the freezing night, to create a blanket of relatively warm air over the growing plants.

In 1981, archaeologists began to reconstruct some of the ancient raised fields, using tools, techniques, and crops similar to those used by the original farmers. Over the first five years of the experiment, the raised fields consistently yielded three times more potatoes—a time-honored Andean staple—than did conventional plots.

The resurrected technology also performed well in the harsh climate of the high Andes. A severe frost that devastated nearby farms in 1982 did little damage to the experimental fields. The following year the crops on the elevated platforms survived an equally ruinous drought, then rode high and dry through a 1986 flood that swamped surrounding farmlands.

Impressed by these results, the government of Peru and international development agencies are paying farmers to repair the waru waru and to put them back into production. Farmers elsewhere in Latin America are also experimenting with the old technique of raised-platform farming. □

Sanctuaries in the Clouds

High in the Andes, a mile or more above the elevations of permanent settlements, archaeologists have discovered scores of ruined structures that present-day South American Indians call *huacas*, or holy places. Scattered along the spine of the Andes from Peru to Chile, the ruins are mostly rows of stones or low walls, although some are more elaborately equipped with altarlike platforms and outdoor shelters. One has been found at an elevation of 22,000 feet, nearly two miles above the level where airplane pilots must don oxygen masks. It is believed to be the world's highest structure.

No one knows who built the sanctuaries or precisely how they were used. Ritual offerings of dolls, statues, coca leaves, and food—and even evidence of human sacrifice—have been found at some sites, seeming to confirm the religious significance of the shrines. Some researchers see a link with Incan sun worship in the orientation of the structures; they also detect the skilled hand of Incan engineers in the high-altitude constructions.

But others associate the shattered huacas with rituals that predate the Inca. In this view, the difficult climb to such heights, the exhausting labor, and the vanished ceremonies that were once performed there were efforts to gain favor with meteorological gods—of a so-called water cult that persists even today among the people of the high, dry Andes. □

The mummified remains of this Incan child, sacrificed to the sun 500 years ago, were discovered in 1954 at a shrine on the peak of 17,712-foot El Plomo Mountain (background).

Chimor's Quest for Water

The Chimu of pre-Columbian Peru were scientifically unsophisticated by many measures, but their struggle to survive in one of the world's driest coastal deserts spurred them on to prodigious feats of hydraulic engineering.

Some of their knowledge of water management was inherited from their predecessors, the Mochica people, who inhabited Peru's Moche Valley during the first millennium AD and built a network of so-called great trenches to irrigate their fields. By the time the Chimu came on the scene around AD 1100, however, shifts in the earth's crust had permanently separated many of those early canals from the rivers that fed them.

In an effort to thwart the effects of terrestrial buckling, Chimu engineers devised sophisticated gravity-fed canals that hugged the contours of the land and provided just enough slope to maintain a constant flow of water. Movable sluice gates were installed in order to further control the flow of water from the main canals to the distribution lines.

Eventually, the Chimu canal system would comprise hundreds of miles of waterways. Earthen aqueducts, some of them almost 30 feet high and close to 2,000 feet long, were constructed to carry water across canyons. Elaborate terraces were built up along mountainsides to bring the canals across the Andean foothills.

The construction and maintenance of this network was funded by a labor tax levied on the people of Chimor, while the manpower was recruited from the kingdom's large lower class. Work gangs used stone and bronze tools to build the canals, chiseling through solid rock in some places. An ingenious ceramic surveying device *(below)*, remarkably similar to today's the-odolite, allowed the system's architects to plot the best routes through terrain that would challenge modern engineers equipped with the latest technology.

As it turned out, however, even the contour canals were no match for tectonic uplift, the inexorable rising of the earth's crust. Like the great trenches before them, the canals were in constant need of repair. In addition, unusually heavy rainfalls—the result of cyclical El Niño climate disturbances that as recently as 1982 dumped ninety inches of rain on the area in a single week—destroyed large sections of the canals, necessitating massive reconstruction.

But rebuilding the canals also gave the system's engineers the opportunity to redesign them. As a result, many were straightened and lined with stones to improve their hydraulic efficiency and reduce the effects of erosion. Some were also rebuilt with trapezoid channels—a design that minimized the friction of the flowing water.

Despite these innovations, tectonic uplift continued to strand some of the canals, eventually forcing their abandonment. In a desperate effort to replenish the system's water supply, the Chimu decided to tap the Chicama River, located some fifty miles north of their capital city of Chan Chan. They built a new waterway, now called the Intervalley Canal, to funnel the river's water into the existing canal system.

Over the next century, as many as 5,000 people may have toiled away whole lifetimes on the project, even rebuilding some sections of the unfinished canal four times in order to correct for tectonic uplift. But the rising of the terrain outpaced these efforts, and the builders finally called off the construction of the Intervalley Canal sometime around the year 1300. Work never resumed. Even though the canal had almost been completed, not one drop of water ever trickled through its stone-lined channel. □

Europe's Glass Fortresses

No one knows for certain how it happened, but dozens of ancient forts in Europe were at some point subjected to such intense heat that their stone walls melted and fused into a solid, glassy mass.

Most of these so-called vitrified forts are located in Scotland, although a few have been found in England, France, and Germany. Some, such as Scotland's Tap O' North, are huge, with walls twenty feet thick enclosing thousands of square yards, and are placed strategically on hilltops. Others, including the ring forts of Rahoy and Langwell, are tiny enclosures encompassing fewer than two hundred square yards. Many of these fortresses date from as early as the seventh century BC, although others were built centuries later.

Regardless of location, size, or age, all these forts have one thing in common: They were once engulfed by flames that reached blast-furnace temperatures of at least 2,000 degrees Fahrenheit and virtually melted the rock.

Some archaeologists have speculated that the glass forts were produced by mischance. According to this theory, the forts' walls may have been framed with timbers that were accidentally ignited by sparks from domestic fires. But given the large number of vitrified forts, it is difficult to believe that the prehistoric people who built them could have been so habitually careless with fire.

A more likely scenario is that the walls were built around a core of timbers and then intentionally torched, perhaps by invaders who piled brush and trees against the ramparts and set them on fire. However, as experiments have shown, such fires would have had to rage for many hours, if not days, to generate the hellish heat needed to vitrify stone—time ◊

This reconstruction of a Chimu surveying instrument shows how canal-building Peruvians may have calculated the slope of the land to achieve the most efficient water flow. The device consisted of a ceramic bowl pierced by a hollow sighting tube passing through a calibrated, cross-shaped opening *(inset)*. An artificial horizon was established by aligning water with the three dots in the bowl, which was leveled in a larger, sand-filled vessel atop a tripod *(far left)*; when the sighting tube was in the center of the cross-shaped opening it was parallel to the artificial horizon. Chimu surveyors marked a rod at the height of the level sighting tube, then moved the rod a known distance along uneven ground and sighted the mark. The ground slope corresponded to the tube angle indicated by the calibrations inside the bowl.

enough, say detractors of this theory, for all but the dullest-witted defenders to douse the flames, and time enough for survivors of such a battle to redesign their forts to make them less vulnerable to fire.

On the other hand, the fires may have been set by the builders of the forts themselves, perhaps to strengthen their defenses by fusing piled stone into a solid, glassy shield. This would explain why some forts appear to have been designed with vitrification in mind and why that design persisted for a thousand years or more. But it still leaves open the question of how the forts were vitrified, a riddle even modern scientists have so far been unable to solve. □

The Megalithic Mysteries

Europe in general, and Britain and France in particular, are dotted with prehistoric megalithic monuments—hulking slabs of stone, rising solitary in the landscape in many cases, but sometimes arranged in circles, lines, or clusters. Among the most mysterious and surely the most widely known of the megalithic sites is Stonehenge, the haunting ring of stone that has dominated England's Salisbury Plain for almost five millennia.

According to a number of legends, magic played a role in Stonehenge's creation: The wizard Merlin raised the stones through sorcery, one fanciful story goes. But the truth, archaeologists now surmise, is actually more remarkable than any of the numerous fictions. Stonehenge, they assert, represents the sweat of generations of ancient Britons, with the work spread over some 1,200 years and across the backs of hundreds of laborers at any one time.

Studies have revealed that the monument was built in three stages, the first beginning around 3000 BC, when surveyors pegged one end of a 160-foot rope to the ground and tied a pointed stake to the other end to make an enormous compass. By stretching the rope taut and dragging the stake over the turf as they walked along, the surveyors were able to draw what is today Stonehenge's great outer circle. In their wake came teams of laborers who used deer-antler picks and ox-bone shovels to turn the scribed line into a ditch rimmed on either side by banks of excavated earth and chalk.

Inside the innermost bank, the workers dug a second circle consisting of fifty-six pits, each two to six feet across and some two to four feet deep. These so-called Aubrey Holes, named for their seventeenth-century discoverer, were later found to contain cremated human remains, leading some researchers to the obvious conclusion that the holes had been burial pits. Other people claim, however, that stone or wooden markers inserted in the holes could be used to calculate eclipses of the sun and the moon. The Heel Stone, a thirty-five-ton hunk of sarsen, was also heaved into place at this time, one hundred feet outside Stonehenge's entranceway, where it stands to this day as a lone sentinel.

The second phase of construction got under way around 2000 BC, when about eighty more standing stones were erected in two rows to form a half circle within the perimeter of Stonehenge's outer circle. What distinguishes these stones, however, is not their size—they weigh a paltry four tons compared to the thirty-five-ton Heel Stone—but their composition. They are made of volcanic bluestone, a type of rock found only in Wales, more than 130 miles away, and only in a one-square-mile area of the Prescelly Mountains.

According to archaeologists, after the stones were cut free from their Welsh quarry, they were tied to wooden sledges and hauled about fifteen miles to the sea over a path of log rollers. The stones were then transferred to rafts and ferried along the Welsh coast and up a series of rivers, eventually reaching the river Avon and the edge of the Salisbury Plain. There they were unloaded and dragged the final ten miles or so to the construction site.

But even that culturally jarring feat pales in comparison to the amount of energy that was expended in the third phase of construction, which began with the removal of the bluestone pillars around 1500 BC. Afterward, more than eighty huge sarsen stones, some weighing fifty tons, were hauled about twenty miles from the quarry site at Avebury to Stonehenge, a task that is estimated to have taken 1,000 people seven full years to accomplish.

Many, if not all, of those stones had already been roughly shaped before the journey to Stonehenge.

The shaping process probably involved setting fire to a line of fat-soaked twigs laid atop a stone, then splashing the hot strip of rock with cold water. This, together with synchronized bashing with stone mauls, was often enough to cause the stone to split apart. Final shaping and polishing took place at the construction site, where stonemasons used sarsen mauls to pound away any imperfections and shape the mortises and tenons that would join the horizontal lintels to their corresponding uprights. At the estimated rate of six cubic inches per hour, this job alone would have consumed half a million man-hours of labor. Even so, the stones still had to be sanded smooth —by using other sarsens as gigantic files—and even then the work was far from over. For each up-

right, a deep hole had to be dug with three straight sides and the fourth side sloped to form a ramp. As many as 200 people then tilted each stone into its hole, easing it down the ramp and using log levers to pry it upright.

The process of capping each set of uprights with a lintel was no less exacting. Each seven-ton lintel was laid on the ground alongside the uprights, then levered upward inches at a time at each end while workers shoved logs underneath. Once the tower of logs had risen to the thirteen-foot level of the uprights, the lintel was shifted sideways so that its mortises slipped over the projecting tenons of the uprights.

When it was finally completed, sometime after 1600 BC, Stonehenge boasted five trilithons, or three-stone groupings, each consisting of two uprights crowned with a single lintel, surrounded by an unbroken ring of uprights and lintels. The bluestones that had been removed earlier were also replaced, with some of them forming a horseshoe inside the trilithons and others composing a circle between the trilithons and the outer ring of stones.

Nearly 1.5 million man-hours of labor had gone into building Stonehenge, and whole generations of early Britons had lived, labored, and died within its lengthening shadow. Today, almost 5,000 years later, the end result of all that labor still stands, still commanding admiration and awe. □

Shaping the Earth

Just seventeen miles from Stonehenge stands a mystery to rival those riddles in stone: a manmade mountain, 130 feet high and 4,500 years old, known for centuries as Silbury Hill.

Old stories say that the mountain owes its name to a certain King Sil, who, after his death, was propped up on a horse made of gold and then entombed in an estimated 36,000,000 basketfuls of earth—a task that may have kept some 500 people busy for fifteen years or more.

The project was not only gargantuan, it was also fairly precise. From a base covering five acres, workers skillfully constructed the mound in stairstep fashion, like a wedding cake, then smoothed it over with still more dirt.

Despite tales of the gold horse that lay within, the hill was left untouched until the modern era; plunderers were no doubt discouraged by the need to bore through so much earth. Not until 1776 was a shaft sunk into Silbury Hill. But neither King Sil nor his golden steed was found on that occasion. A second tunnel in 1849 fared no better, nor did an even more ambitious effort in 1968. In fact, all of the digging has yet to produce a single convincing clue to explain why so many people might have worked so hard for so long to create a mound that had no defensive use nor, apparently, any other utilitarian purpose.

There are many theories about what the mound's builders might have intended—a giant sundial, perhaps, or a huge symbol of an eye or a monument to some long-forgotten deity. For now, however, Silbury Hill, the tallest prehistoric structure in Europe, reveals no more about its makers than their capacity for epic feats of labor. □

Sri Lanka's Life-Sustaining Wewas

The problem facing the people of ancient Sri Lanka was one of too much too soon: too much rain in too short a time. During the two yearly monsoon seasons that lasted a total of seven months, most of the island virtually drowned in rain. The remainder of the year, drought threatened to destroy the vital rice crop.

The solution was an ambitious system of dams, canals, and storage tanks—called *wewas*—designed to trap the monsoon rains for timed release during the dry season. This approach was not easily achieved, since Sri Lankans of the first century AD had only the simplest of tools.

Nevertheless, the system was built—and rebuilt and enlarged and repaired over many generations. By the time the twelfth-century king Parakramabahu I *(right)* officially decreed that not one drop of water should reach the sea without first serving humanity, his tiny kingdom was already studded with thousands of wewas.

The tanks were fed by tapping and trapping almost every natural source of

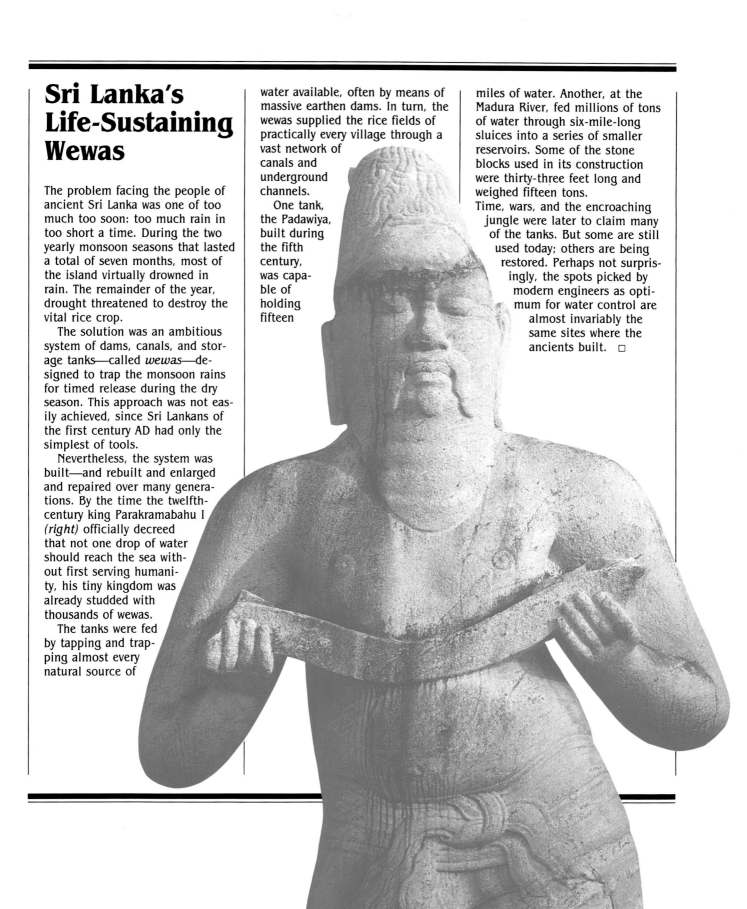

water available, often by means of massive earthen dams. In turn, the wewas supplied the rice fields of practically every village through a vast network of canals and underground channels.

One tank, the Padawiya, built during the fifth century, was capable of holding fifteen

miles of water. Another, at the Madura River, fed millions of tons of water through six-mile-long sluices into a series of smaller reservoirs. Some of the stone blocks used in its construction were thirty-three feet long and weighed fifteen tons.

Time, wars, and the encroaching jungle were later to claim many of the tanks. But some are still used today; others are being restored. Perhaps not surprisingly, the spots picked by modern engineers as optimum for water control are almost invariably the same sites where the ancients built. □

The Bronze Age Manhattan

It should never have been there, reasoned archaeologists, sure that no full-fledged civilization could have existed in Pakistan's Indus River valley 4,500 years ago. But there Mohenjo-Daro was, an entire city, centuries ahead of its time and remarkably preserved beneath the very layer of silt that may have contributed to its downfall.

The city was discovered by accident in 1922, when an Indian archaeologist, intent on probing the remains of a Buddhist temple, dug deep and found, in addition to the temple, the relics of a prehistoric civilization. Teams of archaeologists descended on the area and gradually unearthed the outlines of a carefully planned metropolis *(above)*, complete with paved streets, stately brick civic centers, and rows of brick townhouses served by indoor plumbing and an extensive sewage system.

The antiquarians could thank Mohenjo-Daro's location for the city's superb state of preservation; it had been built on the mound that inspired its name—which in the local Sindhi dialect means "Hill of the Dead." The hill was thought to be bewitched, causing anyone who dared climb it to turn a bright blue, and fear of this fate had been enough to keep away the curious for centuries.

In its heyday around 2000 BC, Mohenjo-Daro was home to some 40,000 people, and together with its sister-city, Harappa, located 350 miles away, embodied the strength of an empire that flourished for five centuries.

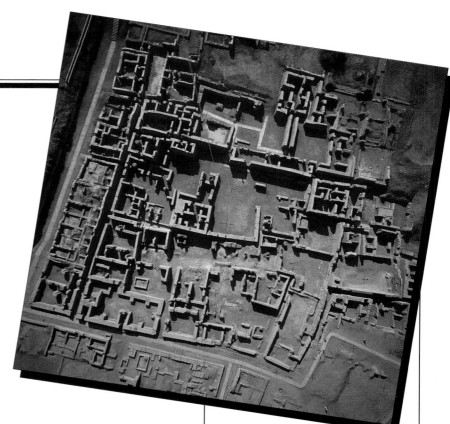

The heart of Mohenjo-Daro was its citadel, a walled complex of assembly halls and administrative offices. Nearby stood a huge communal bath, along with a civic granary that featured an ingenious air-circulation system that was apparently designed to keep stored grain from spoiling.

Below the citadel a dozen arrow-straight streets carved the city into a north-south grid that was then sliced into blocks by somewhat narrower east-west streets. It was this layout that prompted archaeologists to dub the city the "Bronze Age Manhattan," so closely did the grid resemble the straightforward arrangement of the New York City borough.

Shops, food stands, and look-alike, two-story houses—all built of brick, like almost everything else in Mohenjo-Daro—crowded the streets. Inside the houses, bedrooms, passageways, and guest rooms clustered around central courtyards. Many of the houses also had indoor brick-lined wells, and almost every house had its own bathroom, which included a brick-paved shower stall and a brick, sit-down toilet.

Water for these facilities was hand-carried, of course, in the absence of any system for piping it into the houses. However, there was a system of chutes and clay pipes to carry the runoff from the bathrooms into brick-lined sewage drains that ran alongside each main street. Manholes with removable stone covers were located at each intersection to make it easier for sanitation workers to clean and maintain the entire system.

Given the city's seeming passion for cleanliness and order, it is ironic that water may have played a part in Mohenjo-Daro's decline.

Archaeological evidence suggests that the residents fought a protracted battle against floods. Indeed, parts of Mohenjo-Daro may have been rebuilt as many as eight times, and its citizens were apparently as exacting as they were tenacious. With each rebuilding, the city appears to have been reconstructed in brick-for-brick detail.

But its citizens' determination proved unavailing in the end.

Sometime in the eighteenth century BC, Mohenjo-Daro faded from history—perhaps, ultimately, at the point of an invader's sword. Archaeologists have uncovered in the city's ruins a number of skeletons whose skulls bear the telltale scars of sword cuts.

Time and nature did the rest, silting over the city and burying it beneath the rubble of its own extraordinary brickwork. □

The Monster Stones of Baalbek

Near the modern Lebanese city of Baalbek—a place the Greeks and Romans called Heliopolis, or City of the Sun—there once ran an ancient trade route linking Damascus and Tyre. At this site, Roman engineers in the first century AD raised a spectacular temple complex that seemed designed to dazzle passing caravans with the empire's power and splendor. The complex was dominated by the magnificent Temple of Jupiter, a stone colossus surrounded by a forest of fifty-four columns of immense size and height. Beneath the temple lay an even greater wonder: a huge foundation called the Grand Terrace, comprising an area of more than five million square feet and containing more stone—all precisely cut and fitted—than the Great Pyramid of Khufu. Not one ounce of mortar was used in its construction; yet, in twenty centuries, the Grand Terrace has not settled a single millimeter.

The secret of the Grand Terrace's remarkable stability may lie in one of its retaining walls, which contains three of the world's biggest blocks of cut stone. Stood upright, each would be as tall as a five-story building, and each weighs more than 600 tons.

Together, these three stones compose the Trilithon—and one of the world's oldest mysteries: To this day, no one can convincingly explain how the builders of Baalbek managed to move these monstrous slabs of rock from their quarry almost a mile away, let alone how these dauntless workers might have lifted the stones twenty feet above the ground in order to nudge them into position. It was a job that even today would tax the most sophisticated equipment.

The mystery is only deepened by the presence of a fourth, even larger, stone, cut but then abandoned in the quarry *(left)*. At almost 1,100 tons and seventy-two feet long, the so-called Monolith is the largest piece of hewn rock on the face of the earth. To budge it an inch would have required an army of more than 16,000 workers, all pulling in unison. Moreover, as far as anyone today knows, no machine of its time could have lifted the Monolith. Indeed, the technology to move so massive an object would not appear for another 2,000 years, with the development of an enormous tracked crawler of the sort NASA used to transport the Saturn V rocket from its assembly building to its launching pad at Cape Canaveral. □

The Venice of the South Pacific

Dangling off the eastern coast of the mountainous volcanic island of Pohnpei in the South Pacific is a necklace of ninety-two artificial islets. They rest in a shallow lagoon, interlaced with waterways and separated from the ocean surf by a pair of giant sea walls. The islets make up a Venicelike city called Nan Madol, which various legends have said was built by Spanish pirates or was once the capital of a vast oceanic empire or is all that remains of the mythical lost continent of Mu.

In fact, Nan Madol was built some 800 years ago, not by pirates or by advanced beings now extinct, but by native Pohnpeians. It was, moreover, both a center of ritual and a royal enclave, seat of a dynasty of powerful island monarchs called *saudeleurs*—one of whom is remembered chiefly for his fondness for dining on head lice and for his insistence that those subjects who refused to share their cargo of vermin with their king should be put to death.

However barbaric the ruler's dining habits might seem, his engineers were quite sophisticated. At its peak in the sixteenth century, Nan Madol was home to as many as a thousand people, who lived in a style altogether different from that of the island's modern inhabitants. Chief among those early citizens, of course, was the saudeleur himself. He made his home on Pahnkadira Islet, a residential compound the size of three football fields, complete with servants' quarters, bathing pools, and the temple of Nan Zapue, the thunder god.

Like all of Nan Madol's islets, Pahnkadira rests on a stretch of coral reef that was walled in with basalt columns quarried on Pohnpei. Once the walls were in place, the resulting enclosed pool was filled with coral gravel to form a dry platform above sea level. The platform, in turn, was paved over with stones. Some of the Nan Madol islets built in this way rise as high as twenty feet above the surrounding waters, and the walls that enclose them tower as high as thirty feet.

To build the walls that made the islets possible, basalt blocks weighing from five to ten tons each were fractured loose from Pohnpei quarries in a process that involved heating the rock at its base with huge fires, then cooling it rapidly with seawater. Giant slabs were then hauled and floated into place offshore, where they were stacked like logs to form the islets' retaining walls *(opposite)*.

In the residential section of Nan Madol, islanders lived in pole-and-thatch dwellings whose size was determined by the status of the owners. The saudeleur, for example, lived in a house that measured almost 1,500 square feet. Other nobles made do with half as much space, while servants squeezed into tiny huts measuring a mere 60 square feet.

The saudeleur was equally exalted in death. Many of the rulers were buried in the royal mortuary on Nandauwas Islet behind elegantly upswept walls that rose as high as twenty-five feet around a maze of courtyards and crypts.

Nan Madol's glory ended sometime in the 1600s, when, according to tradition, the reigning saudeleur was defeated by an invader from a neighboring island—no less an invader, in fact, than the alleged son of the thunder god. A century or so later, Nan Madol was deserted, and by the time the first Europeans stepped ashore in the 1820s, it was little more than a ghost town, with only its dead to keep watch amid the eerie ruins of its basalt majesty. □

The Great Zimbabwe

Geologist Karl Mauch could hardly believe his eyes as he and his party, exploring in what would later become the British colony of Rhodesia, stepped from the bush one day in 1871. Scattered across the hill and valley in front of him was a network of ruins—edifices expertly worked in stone in a land where primitive mud huts were the norm. The mystery of the place was almost palpable. "Profound silence brooded over the scene," Mauch would later recall of the slumbering enigma called Great Zimbabwe.

Beneath that pall of silence and at the heart of the ruins, Mauch found a huge enclosure with granite walls thirty feet high and twenty feet thick in places *(below)*. This stone enclosure was known to the natives as Mumbahuru, or "the House of the Great Woman," and it did not take Mauch long to succumb to his own wishful thinking and leap to the conclusion that the great woman must be the legendary queen of Sheba. Great Zimbabwe, by the same stretch of the imagination, must have been the capital of her kingdom of Ophir and the site of the fabled mines of the queen's consort, Israel's King Solomon.

But Mauch was wrong, as were the legions of later explorers and historians who concocted other myths of a lost white civilization in the heart of black Africa. The truth, as archaeolo- ◊

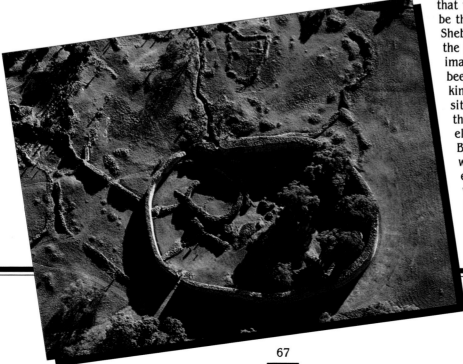

gists learned by 1906, was that Great Zimbabwe had once been the trading and religious capital of a black African empire, and parts of it were built as early as the second or third century AD by the ancestors of the very natives who first led Karl Mauch to the site.

Over a period of more than a thousand years, Great Zimbabwe grew from a typical Iron Age settlement of poled huts into a simple walled enclave and finally into a bewildering sixty-acre sprawl of huts, ceremonial shrines, passageways, and granaries. Nowhere in this complex was there a straight wall or a right angle, and nowhere

was any mortar used to bind granite block to granite block *(below)*. Moreover, all of the blocks, including the 15,000 tons of granite used in the so-called Great Enclosure, were laid in bricklike courses, fitted together with precision, and sometimes capped with decorative, chevron-shaped border treatments.

The ruins of the complex are clustered in two main groups, with a smattering of smaller sites in between. The first group is a jumble of natural rock and man-made structures inaccurately dubbed the Hill Fortress. (It was built not for defense but only to impress.) Also called the Acropolis, the complex

stands atop a boulder-strewn, 300-foot-high hill. It is reached by climbing a narrow, twisting stairway that squeezes between outcrops of rock and often allows only one person at a time to pass. Stone walls, punctuated by stone towers, creep from rock to rock and climb uphill and down, creating a labyrinth of enclosures.

Nearby, at the edge of a cliff overlooking the valley, is a cave that acts as a giant amplifier, augmenting the voice of anyone speaking inside and projecting it to the valley below. The cave lends some credence to an ancient tribal legend that tells of an African god-king who ruled from a rocky hilltop. No mere mortal dared look this king in the eye, since the penalty for such effrontery was instant death. The king's cowering subjects were only allowed to hear their master's voice, a voice that was said to echo and reecho, striking terror into all who heard it.

If that king did reign at Great Zimbabwe, he may have made his home across the valley from the Hilltop Fortress in the Great Enclosure itself, a massive, oval-shaped structure that dates to the fourteenth century and was apparently the palace of a great chief. Dominating the Great Enclosure, and built of the same mortarless granite, is a strange conical tower thirty feet high and fifty feet wide at its base. Although it may have had some forgotten religious significance, its function is unknown today. Moreover, that mystery is likely to endure, since the tower is literally rock solid, with no windows or doors to provide access and no distinguishing features of any kind to provide even the slightest clue to its use. □

Marked by a flashlight transformed by time exposure into a glowing trail, a road built a thousand years ago by the Anasazi Indians of New Mexico stretches toward the dawn.

Roads to Nowhere

They were built a thousand years ago by people who knew nothing of the wheel and had never seen a horse. Yet the Anasazi Indian roads of New Mexico were not simple footpaths but a 500-mile network of carefully planned and superbly engineered causeways.

Now worn faint by wind and time, some of the roads were thirty feet wide. Others had stone curbs. And most of them ran arrow straight through mile after dusty mile of barren desert, regardless of the surrounding terrain. Even where a short detour might have offered the road builders a flat surface for their labors, the Anasazi cut steps and ramps into cliffs if necessary to keep their avenues relentlessly linear.

The likeliest-seeming purpose of the highway system would be to link the main Anasazi settlement at Chaco Canyon to its thirty or so satellite communities. But although all the roads do radiate from Chaco Canyon, and some of them do connect with outlying villages, a few lead only to isolated lakes, springs, and mountain peaks. Even more mysterious, in certain places there are two parallel sets of roads.

Most enigmatic of all is the Great North Road, which climbs out of Chaco Canyon and makes a fifty-mile beeline due north across rolling sagebrush country, only to come to a dead end at the edge of another, even more isolated, canyon. With one possible exception, there were no villages along the road's route. Its only apparent purpose was to strike north, and its only apparent destination was a particular mound on the rim of a

particular canyon. But why that mound? And why due north? And why, moreover, should this road to nowhere be littered in places with broken pottery?

The answers may lie in the many Anasazi legends that tell of ritual journeys to sacred mountains and canyons. Similar tales speak of straight roads that lead to *sipapu,* small holes that the Anasazi believed were channels to the spirit world. Clues may also rest with Anasazi rituals in which pottery was ceremoniously shattered to honor the dead.

Some researchers have concluded that a number of the Anasazi roads—the Great North Road in particular—were never meant to go anywhere, at least in the temporal world. Instead, the roads may have been bridges designed to link the real world of Chaco Canyon to an unseen landscape of the spirit. □

The Cuzco Cat

In the fifteenth century AD, Pachacuti, the first Incan conqueror and ninth of a dynasty of kings, decided to rebuild the 400-year-old capital at Cuzco, located high in the Peruvian Andes. Monumental buildings were raised around broad plazas, and the banks of the Huatanay and Tullumayo rivers were paved with flagstones.

On a crag known as Sacsahuaman, which overlooked the city, the builders and their legions of workers fashioned a granite fortress from carefully tailored interlocking stones, assembled without mortar. The three zigzag walls were made of precisely fitted blocks weighing as much as 300 tons, among the largest ever used in human construction.

But Pachacuti's engineers were engaged in more than precocious stonework. To achieve their sovereign's grand design for Cuzco, they used the terrain as a giant canvas on which to depict a sacred animal; the new city took form within the stylized body of the beast. The two rivers flowing through Cuzco defined a feline body; their junction south of the city, a tail. Cuzco's broad central plaza was the creature's heart. The granite fortress on Sacsahuaman became a ferocious head, its angled walls the zigzag teeth of a growling jaguar, drawn in stone. □

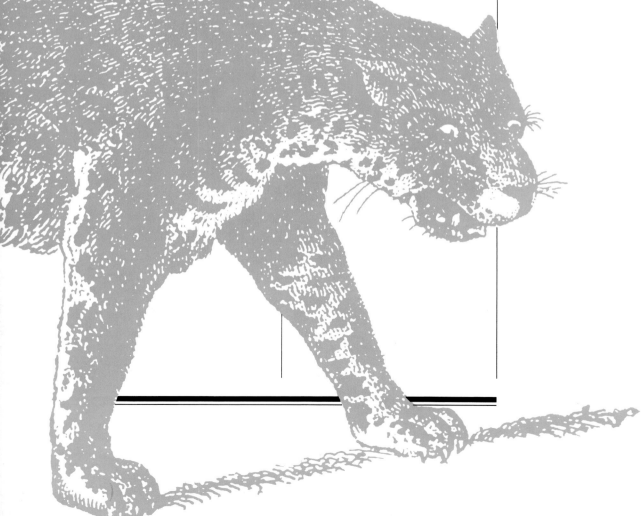

ARTISTS

The urge to create works of art has been a driving force in human development since the dawn of time. Archaeologists the world over have uncovered artifacts showing that so-called primitive peoples everywhere felt a deep need to express themselves in some tangible way. What so often surprises us today about their output is its scale and the excellence of its execution, despite the fact that the earliest artists were severely restricted in the tools they had at their disposal.

For the Cro-Magnon, the first modern humans in Europe, the walls of caves became canvases on which they painted panoplies of animals, some of which they depended on for food and clothing. For other prehistoric peoples it was the earth itself that was shaped and manipulated, and in the process of rearranging nature, they produced some of the largest renditions of human and animal forms ever.

Art was magic and power. Anyone who could draw an animal to near perfection must have been seen as a special person, a conjurer. Indeed, the first artists are thought to have been shamans or priests—individuals who could evoke through their work the very spirits of the beasts that they rendered.

Soon, art became a regular part of ceremony and ritual, a way of engendering mystery and supporting belief, and the artists' output in the centuries ahead steadily increased as demand for it grew. And then, with a further blossoming of skills and improvements in technology, art took on another major function. It became the means by which important individuals could impress their gods and fellow mortals in hope of ensuring that their memory would live on through the ages, as with the terra-cotta army of Qin Shi Huangdi *(above)*. Although the names of the patrons have in most instances been lost to time, their monuments survive, now tributes less to any individual's greatness than to human ingenuity and creativity.

Art Ahead of Its Time

"We have invented nothing!" Pablo Picasso reportedly exclaimed as he emerged from France's famed Lascaux Cave. Inside, he had examined some of the most remarkable art in the world. What remains humbling to this day is that it was produced 17,000 years ago.

When the first of the caves containing such prehistoric art came to light in 1868 in Altamira, Spain, incredulous viewers dismissed the paintings as being no more than twenty years old, "the expression of a mediocre student of the modern school." But later discoveries of other painted caves in Spain and France forced a radical reversal of opinion; critics were soon marveling over the artists'

incredible achievements. Only one of these caves would outrival Altamira for pure brilliance, however, and that was Lascaux, accidentally stumbled upon in 1940 by a boy searching for his lost dog.

Here, approximately 600 paintings, almost 1,500 engravings on stone, and many inscrutable dots and geometric forms bedazzle the eye. Across the ceilings and walls flows a cavalcade of animals—aurochs (ancestors of today's oxen), bison, reindeer, horses *(below)*,

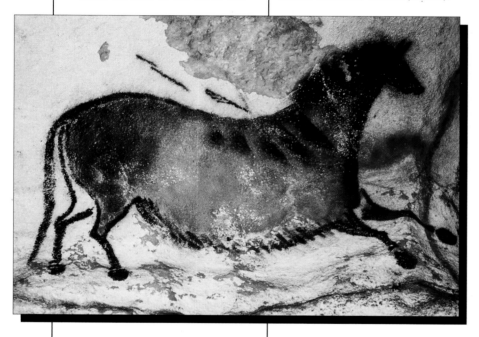

and other creatures, depicted running, galloping, charging.

Working in semidarkness, with only the light of guttering torches and fat-burning lamps to see by, sitting or standing on rickety scaffolding or out-of-the-way perches, and using the most primitive of tools (often a fingertip for a brush), the geniuses of Lascaux carefully outlined and then colored

in their menagerie. Even after the lapse of millennia, the paintings preserve much of their original brilliance. The reason for this goes beyond the fact that they were sealed away in darkness for so long. Modern analysis of the paints shows that the artists had a deep knowledge of how to prepare pigments for maximum clarity and stability. They ground such naturally occurring substances as iron and manganese oxide with primitive mortars to produce reds, blacks, and yellows, then mixed the powders with water before applying the colors to the walls. But they were not above experimentation, and they tried a variety of other binding agents as well, everything from blood, urine, and fish glue to fat, egg white, and vegetable juices. To bring out just the right tones, they at times subjected the pigments to high heat. The entire process, in some ways, presaged modern chemistry.

More amazingly, the artists grappled with the problem of three dimensionality. They cleverly used natural irregularities in the rock surface to help give the paintings depth; thus a bulge in the wall might become the haunch of an aurochs or the swollen belly of a pregnant bison. By overlapping animals of different sizes, they created a further illusion of depth. And they took pains to provide just the right amount of distance between the front or hind legs of some of their beasts to make it appear as though there were real space between them. In all this, the cave artists were well ahead of their times—so much so, in fact, that many of their techniques would not be duplicated for millennia to come. □

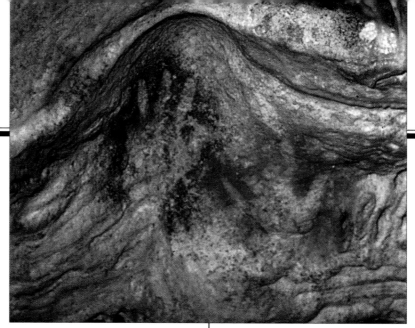

A Show of Hands

The hands of a vanished people seem to wave from the walls of more than twenty caves in northern Spain, Italy, and southwestern France. Stenciled by Cro-Magnon some 25,000 years ago, they are ghostly impressions left by some of the first modern humans. But why the hands are there and what they mean is a puzzle.

Of the caves, the one called Gargas in the French Pyrénées has the most handprints—more than 150 of them—and these range in size from infant to adult. Remarkably, the majority represent left hands. But the truly astonishing aspect of the hands is that almost all of them—including those of small children—seem to be missing parts of their fingers.

Made during the late Ice Age, most of the outlines were sprayed on with earth pigments: ocher for red, manganese dioxide for black. The coloring, either in powdered or liquid form, was probably blown through a tube—possibly a hollow reed or stem—onto the hand as the palm was pressed to the moist wall. This method, experts say, may account for the prevalence of left hands, since the right hand—typically, the more dexterous one— would have held the tube.

What is not clear at all is why so many of the hands appear to be mutilated. Usually missing are the top two joints of at least two fingers. Close study suggests that the joints were actually gone, not merely bent under.

One theory held that because the Cro-Magnon lived during the Ice Age, frostbite, which can lead to gangrene, may have caused the digits to drop off. Even leprosy was considered as a possibility. But a study of strange holes poked in the mud walls and ceiling of a circular chamber in the Gargas Cave indicated otherwise. When the investigator examining the holes made casts of them, he found they had been created by fingers—but instead of displaying the rounded ends of normal fingertips, many of the holes terminated bluntly in scar-tissue lumps.

Here was evidence that the fingers had been deliberately truncated, perhaps as part of a ritual. The Bushmen of Africa and certain North American Indians once practiced a similar type of mutilation, either as a good-luck birth ritual or to appease hunting gods. It is even possible that the amputations may have been carried out to reflect a primitive but permanent kind of sign language. The deformed hands may have been intended to symbolically represent the shapes of particular kinds of beasts important to the Cro-Magnon's livelihood or even to stand for individuals' specific animal totems or nature guardians. □

The Magical Skull of Doom

Few objects have stirred as much controversy or speculation as the crystal Skull of Doom. Life-size in its dimensions and lifelike in its execution, it has defied efforts to pinpoint its place of origin, determine its method of manufacture, or explain the strange phenomena supposedly associated with it.

The skull is said to have turned up in the 1920s under an altar in the ruins of the Mayan city of Lubaantun in British Honduras (now Belize). But doubts have been raised about its being a pre-Columbian work. Although other crystal skulls from Central America exist, none matches this one for quality of workmanship or sophistication. Moreover, the crystal from which it was made seems to have come not from Central America, but from California, where rock crystal formations of the same ◊

high quality and same size occur.

Some specialists consider the skull the product of a later culture. But then how could it have been found in a Mayan ruin, they ask? Skeptics believe the skull was a plant, buried under the altar by the British explorer-archaeologist Frederick Mitchell-Hedges, so that his adopted daughter Anna Mitchell-Hedges could come across it on her birthday as she assisted him in his excavations.

Others have suggested that the skull was never in Lubaantun or that Anna was not there on the supposed discovery day. They claim Mitchell-Hedges purchased the skull from an English owner in the 1940s and manufactured the story about Anna finding it in the Lubaantun temple, perhaps as a way of gaining publicity for it and enhancing its allure. Furthermore, they label as pure invention Mitchell-Hedges's claim that the skull was "used by

the high priest of the Maya to concentrate on and will death;" that it was "the embodiment of all evil;" and that "several people who have cynically laughed at it have died" or "have been stricken and become seriously ill."

Yet as controversy continues to swirl around it, the Skull of Doom, as Mitchell-Hedges called it, remains an object of fascination. Frank Dorland, a noted art restorer who studied it closely over a six-year period, claimed that the skull sometimes changed color or filled with a cottony haze; that it produced an "elusive perfume" and

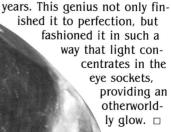

strange tinkling sounds; that images of mountains, temples, and other objects appeared within it; and that an aura once surrounded it for several minutes. Others who saw the skull when it was in Dorland's keep reported similar phenomena, as well as such physiological reactions to it as a quickening of their pulse, a tightening of their arm and leg muscles, and even a strange tugging of their eyes.

Part of the awe the skull generates in those who behold it comes from its exquisiteness. Only the detachable lower jaw reveals faint tool marks. Whoever produced the skull had to have been a master of the first order. Just polishing it would have required weeks or even years. This genius not only finished it to perfection, but fashioned it in such a way that light concentrates in the eye sockets, providing an otherworldly glow. □

Las Bolas Grandes of Costa Rica

Even with today's tools and techniques, crafting a flawless sphere from stone by hand is a remarkably difficult challenge. And yet near-perfection in that pursuit was achieved perhaps 1,600 years ago in Central America by the carvers of Las Bolas Grandes, "the Great Stone Balls."

Ranging in diameter from eight feet to only a few inches and weighing as much as sixteen tons, the globes fairly litter the landscape of the Diquis River delta of southern Costa Rica. At least 186 of them survive whole and probably hundreds more lie buried, awaiting discovery; hundreds of others have already been irrevocably lost—through bulldozers clearing land, exposure to the elements, and native Costa Ricans who smashed the spheres in the belief that they concealed gold.

Brought to the attention of science in the 1930s when jungle was cleared for banana plantations, the spheres have undergone rigorous analysis. It is thought that the artisans who produced the stone balls used wooden templates as a means of guiding their efforts. Since almost all the spheres were made from an especially hard granite, shaping them demanded an enormous amount of patience. The process probably involved shaping the stone into a rough ball before smoothing its surface

with an abrasive, perhaps sand.

However primitive their methods may have been, the artisans succeeded in turning out almost perfectly proportioned spheres. Indeed, a writer who has closely studied Las Bolas Grandes has characterized them as "perhaps the finest examples of precision stone carving in the ancient world." One sphere, measuring approximately six and a half feet in diameter, deviates in its circumference by only half an inch—or

about two-tenths of one percent.

Who carved the balls and why are questions that may go forever unanswered. It is not even possible to date them effectively, since they occur in association with artifacts that span several pre-Columbian cultures. Theories as to their use range from grave markers to a form of money. A mystery too is where the Indians got the granite that they used; the nearest source lies many miles away and shows no signs of quarrying. □

The Puzzling Lines of Life

Among the oldest and most fundamental of all man-made designs are the spirals, concentric circles, and complex labyrinths with which ancient peoples decorated a variety of objects large and small.

These patterns turn up on everything from Sumerian seals, Babylonian clay tablets, and Cretan coins to Etruscan wine jugs, Roman mosaic floors, and a pillar in the ash-buried city of Pompeii. They are particularly numerous in northern Europe, where in the form of carvings they cover rocks, megaliths, and burial monuments, including one of the world's oldest surviving structures, Ireland's 5,000-year-old Newgrange tomb *(pages 86-87).* They occur also in the New World and in Asia. Clearly, they had a hold on the ancients' psyche.

Their meaning, though, remains obscure. Some scholars have claimed that they seem to have been created less to please the eye than to jog the brain. Indeed, in whatever culture they are found, spirals and labyrinths frequently share one perplexing element; they have indirect paths leading to—or from—the center.

Scholars have spared no effort

These Cretan coins are embellished with labyrinth designs; a similar motif marks a large rock from the British Isles.

The Earth Artists

to unlock their hidden significance. One offers 104 different theories purportedly explaining them. Among the more likely explanations of spirals is that they were symbols of fertility, a metaphor for the female uterus and the process of procreation, or that they represented the bowels of the earth or perhaps the very caves in which the earliest humans worshiped and sometimes lived. In some instances, they may even have been primitive astronomical instruments with which ancient priests studied the equinoxes, the solstices, and the movements of the moon, hoping to gain mastery over the elements.

The more elaborate labyrinths are thought to represent both burial and spiritual rebirth or perhaps hypothetical maps of the underworld. Basically puzzles to which there is only one solution, labyrinths may also have illustrated the notion of exclusivity. Those who knew a labyrinth's secret could follow a direct route to or from the center. For the uninitiated, this was not so easy, many a wrong turn being made before reaching the goal. Consequently, labyrinths were to become linked in later days with Christianity, their circuitous lines portraying the difficult and often frustrating path to righteousness or heaven that devout individuals hoped to take on their journey through life. □

Some of the most remarkable monuments ever created are those drawn directly on the earth or sculpted from it by ancient peoples. These works include huge animal-shaped mounds, mystifying lines, geometric or anthropomorphic designs, and colossal figures, including the two-thousand-year-old, 393-foot Atacama Giant, scraped into a mountainside in Chile. Indeed, many of these macroforms or earthworks are so grandiose in scale that they can be seen whole only from the air or from a great distance away.

Enigmatic vestiges of cultures swallowed up by time, they occur both in the New World and the Old. Earthworks are particularly prevalent in England, the American West, and South America.

The best known perhaps are the so-called Nazca Lines of Peru, stylized drawings of monkeys, birds, lizards, spiders, flowers, and geometric shapes that range from 100 feet to five miles in length. Stretching across arid reaches of the Atacama Desert, they were made more than 1,500 years ago by Indian artists who removed the darker covering of weathered stones in order to reveal the lighter surface underneath.

The fame of the Nazca Lines has tended to overshadow other equally impressive earthworks in Chile. Here loom 300-foot-long warriors, among them the Atacama Giant, as well as llamas, spirals, circles, condors, a flying man, and a curious candelabra-like shape.

Various theories have been put forth to explain the South American earthworks. The most fanciful is that they were made not by Indians at all, but by extraterrestrials who laid them out as spaceship landing sites. Far more likely is the theory that they had magical significance for their creators, perhaps related to the mysteries of the hunt or fertility. Some scholars think that they may have served as sacred paths linking shrines, as astronomical aids, or even as a kind of colossal calendar.

There are many less-known but equally impressive earthworks in the United States, particularly in desert areas of the Southwest. More than 270 have been found along the 160-mile stretch between Bull Head City and Yuma, Arizona, and their number continues to grow as new ones are discovered in remote parts of the desert. Often using the same stone-clearing technique as their South American counterparts or aligning rocks into patterns, the North American Indians shaped huge humans, serpents, mountain lions, and other animals, as well as abstract designs. One serpentine earthwork that may be more than 5,000 years old meanders for a mile and a quarter across southeastern California.

By evaluating such physical evidence as tools found at the various sites and the physical aging of the rocks themselves, Jay von Werlhof, an archaeologist, has estimated some of the earthworks to be 10,000 years old. For clues to their meaning, he interviewed local Indians to whom the drawings continue to be sacred. His investigations suggest that they may have been created by shamans or medicine ◊

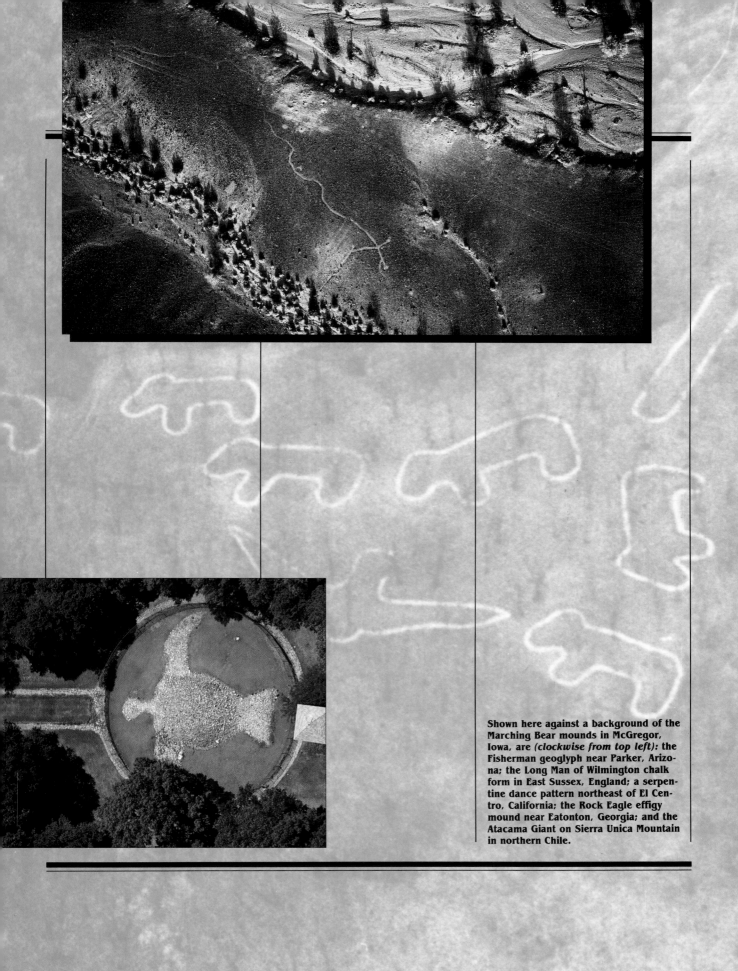

Shown here against a background of the Marching Bear mounds in McGregor, Iowa, are *(clockwise from top left):* the Fisherman geoglyph near Parker, Arizona; the Long Man of Wilmington chalk form in East Sussex, England; a serpentine dance pattern northeast of El Centro, California; the Rock Eagle effigy mound near Eatonton, Georgia; and the Atacama Giant on Sierra Unica Mountain in northern Chile.

men for the protection of the tribe or as a means of attracting the attention of the gods and getting them to intercede on the tribe's behalf in times of crisis. It is even thought that the Indians may have walked or danced along the lines formed by the figures as a means of absorbing the essence of whatever animal or symbol the earth artists had portrayed.

Earthworks are by no means limited to the American Southwest; they occur in the Midwest and South as well. Lacking the desert for a canvas, the earth artists in these other regions took to building effigy mounds in the shape of turtles, panthers, birds, bears, and other creatures. One of the most spectacular of these creations is the Great Serpent Mound near Chillicothe, Ohio. Constructed by the so-called Adena people, whose culture flourished between 1000 BC and AD 200, the snake coils over the landscape for nearly a quarter of a mile. At Eatonton, Georgia, rocks blanket a mound fifty centuries old that rises 10 feet from its surroundings to form an eagle 102 feet long, with a 120-foot wingspan. And at McGregor, Iowa, ten bears march one behind the other, each 3 feet high and from 80 to 100 feet long. Although only 25 other effigy mounds survive in Iowa today, the state once had 375 of them.

In England, earthworks of another sort dominate the landscape. On the green slopes of the chalk downs of southern England, some fifty earthworks were made by artists who cut through the turf to reveal the white strata underneath. The most impressive is the Long Man of Wilmington in East Sussex, second only to the Atacama Giant in scale. Carved into a hillside, the figure stands 231 feet tall, with square shoulders 46 feet broad, a waist 23 feet wide, and legs 100 feet long—each limb as wide as a country lane. No one knows precisely how old the Wilmington giant is; but there is speculation that it may date back 2,500 years.

A similar giant, this one boldly naked and wielding a club, measures 180 feet and overlooks the Dorset village of Cerne Abbas. But experts widely disagree on its age: Some say it dates to 2,000 years ago, while others maintain that it is only about 300 years old. □

China's See-Through Mirrors

For centuries, people have been amazed by the solid metal "magic mirrors" of China. When held up to light, the mirrors seem to allow the light to pass through, projecting the image of raised decorations on the back onto a white wall. Yet the image does not show on the mirror's face.

Dating from the Western Han period of 206 BC to AD 9, these mirrors and their decorations were cast from bronze and their slightly convex faces made very thin by careful grinding, scraping, and polishing. The mirrors baffled generations of Chinese after the secret of their manufacture seemed to die with their creators. One eleventh-century scholar, who had three of these so-called light-penetration mirrors, pondered their mystery in an essay but could not understand "why other mirrors, though extremely thin, do not let light through."

The magic mirrors caused a considerable stir when they finally came to the attention of Westerners in 1832. Some of the best scientific minds of the day tried to figure out how they worked, but the investigators wound up being as stymied as the Chinese had been. A century would pass before the mystery was solved.

The secret lay on the face. There, casting and polishing had produced slight variations—invisible to the naked eye—that corresponded to the raised designs on the back. When light struck this irregular surface, it bounced off all the many minute ups and downs, reproducing the decoration as a magnified reflection. □

This intriguing Chinese "magic mirror" (left) is from the first century BC. Above, the mirror's image is reflected onto a flat surface.

The Underground Army

China's first true emperor, Qin Shi Huangdi—who ruled from 221 to 206 BC—willed into existence wonders the likes of which the ancient world had never seen before. Not only did he order much of the Great Wall of China built, he also had monuments glorifying himself produced on such a scale that they bedazzle the mind to this day.

Not content with one palace, he erected 270 of them in his capital, Xianyang. Seven hundred thousand convict laborers worked on his primary residence alone; its vast terraces were spacious enough to have held 10,000 subjects at a time. His mausoleum, begun when he was only thirteen years old, was executed on a similar scale and became part of a complex measuring nearly four square miles. In the words of a historian writing a century after its completion, the tomb was "fitted with models of palaces, pavilions and offices, as well as fine vessels, precious stones and rarities." Even more miraculous, "all the country's streams, the Yellow River, and the Yangtze were reproduced in quicksilver, and by some mechanical means made to flow into a miniature ocean."

Although Qin Shi Huangdi's palaces have long since moldered into dust, his mausoleum survives under a 150-foot mound of earth. One day it will be explored, but in the meantime, archaeologists with an interest in the site have much else to occupy their time.

In 1974, well diggers working in the vicinity of the burial mound found bits and pieces of statues representing humans and horses—and set off one of the most stunning excavations of modern time. As archaeologists carefully troweled away the earth in what proved to be an enormous pit, they began laying bare the first traces of an entire army—life-size figures of terra-cotta warriors and horses.

Subsequent test digs in the surrounding area revealed two other pits with more soldiers buried in them. All three pits had once been roofed over and covered with dirt to conceal the underground force that symbolically guarded the mausoleum.

Work concentrated on the first pit, in which more than 1,000 figures have since come to light, with an estimated 5,000 others yet to be ◊

excavated. Three rows of 70 fierce-looking warriors stand in the foreground. Behind the rows of warriors stretch thirty-eight columns of infantrymen divided into eleven groups. The clay figures are dressed in armor, and in their hands they once held spears, swords, and crossbows. The metal weapons, which fell to the ground when the wooden handles rotted away, remain as sharp and shiny as on the day that the figures were consigned to darkness.

Only preliminary work has been carried out on the other two pits, but it is enough to suggest that they hold military treasure of their own. The second pit is believed to contain another 1,000 soldiers, plus 80 chariots drawn by 400 horses. The third pit, with far fewer figures, may represent headquarters for the guardian army.

The miracle of this clay army is not just its size, but the quality of its execution and the minute attention to detail given it by the anonymous sculptors. The uniforms and headgear vary by rank and were originally brightly painted. Down to the shape of a mustache or the cold stare of an obvious veteran, each face is unique, suggesting that the figures were modeled on actual soldiers.

The production of such imposing statues—the warriors stand six feet tall—required great technical skill. Even today, creating such figures would take tremendous effort, with a framework of metal or wood necessary to support them and keep them from becoming distorted during firing. Although the work on the site will go on for years, the emperor's army is already known as the Eighth Wonder of the Ancient World. □

A Race of Stone Giants

Few places in the world are as remote as Easter Island. Yet somehow, men, women, and children of the fourth century AD found their way from Polynesia to this 69-square-mile dot in the Pacific, 2,300 miles west of Chile and 1,300 miles east of Pitcairn Island, and established a culture remarkable for its achievements. Not only did the Easter Islanders evolve a form of writing uniquely their own, develop a sophisticated system of solar observation, and bring rock and cave painting to a high art; they also produced over a 900-year-period the estimated 1,000 stone heads, or *moai*, for which the island has become so famous.

Carved out of soft, yellowish volcanic rock and crowned with huge cylindrical topknots of red stone, the finished moai faced inland on massive altars, called *ahu*, that marked the burial sites of kings, chiefs, and other important personages. Early European voyagers, who first encountered the island in the eighteenth century, saw hundreds of the stone heads standing along the coastline. Yet the number of statues was once far greater. Either for unknown religious reasons, a shift in belief, or because of growing competition and aggressiveness among the various groups of moai builders, many of the giants had already been toppled. And by the mid-nineteenth century, the rest of the statues had been sent crashing to the ground.

Today, nearly thirty of the monoliths once again stand upright, put back in place by archae-

ologists. The rest lie where they fell or were left unfinished. The vertical ones rear twelve to twenty-five feet high. Of the fallen monoliths, the largest, measuring thirty-two feet long and weighing 80 tons, had to be transported five miles from the quarry to its present site, then raised and crowned with a 12-ton stone topknot. What would have been the biggest statue of all is still attached to the volcanic rock from which it was being cut; it is sixty-nine feet long and is estimated to weigh about 270 tons. Had it been erected, it would have loomed as high as a six-story building.

Confronted by the awesome dimensions of the stone giants, explorers at first doubted that the Easter Islanders could have carved them with the primitive stone tools at their disposal, much less have moved the statues from the quarry to the distant sites they occupy. In the years since, some enthusiasts have sought to explain the heads as the work of a lost civilization, perhaps Atlantis (pages 130-131)—or even of interplanetary visitors.

Several more mundane theories have been put forth to explain how the Easter Islanders raised their statues. The most likely explanation is that once the carvers freed a figure from the stone, they placed it on a sledge, face down, and inched it along with the aid of a wooden device—attached by ropes to the neck—that lifted the head and thrust it forward. The islanders then raised the statue by piling rocks under it and levered it into an upright position with the aid of logs.

As the quest for power and prestige grew among the islanders, the need to erect ever bigger statues apparently accelerated. Those groups with the most imposing moai doubtless had control over many of the island's resources, particularly its agriculture. But as the population grew, reaching a peak of perhaps 15,000, resources began to fail. Once densely forest-ed, the island was all but stripped bare of its trees as more and more land was turned over to farming. Deprived of wood, the islanders lost the means to transport and raise their statues, as well as the opportunity to build ocean-going canoes that might have enabled them to emigrate elsewhere as crowding grew intolerable.

When Peruvian slavers captured 2,000 of the inhabitants between 1859 and 1862, including the king, his son, and numerous priests, and took them to South America, the Easter Islanders and their culture were dealt a blow from which they would never recover. The eventual return of a few who survived their South American servitude spread diseases for which the remaining inhabitants had no resistance. By 1877, the once-proud Easter Islanders had dwindled to no more than 150, and with the eventual deaths of these—the last holders of the ancient traditions—the secrets of the moai went to the grave. □

The Enigma of Scotland's Stone Balls

Perfectly carved stone balls at least thirty centuries old have been turning up for years in Scotland, tantalizing scholars with the mystery of their origin and function. To date, well over 350 balls have been discovered, mostly between the towns of Aberdeenshire and Angus.

Measuring from one inch to three and a half inches in diameter, some are incised with spirals, concentric circles, and other geometric designs; some are unadorned; some have knobs. Few show hard wear, but several are conspicuously smooth, suggesting that they were much valued and often handled.

All sorts of theories have been put forth to explain these ancient spheres. They were at first thought to be weapons, perhaps lashed to handles with leather thongs, like maces, or tied to the ends of thongs and used as bolas. But the grooves cut in them are too shallow for thongs to have been attached securely. Another theory suggested that the balls may have been used in some type of competitive game. However, few of them show any extensive damage. Indeed, the smoothness of so many has led some researchers to conclude that the balls may have been portable symbols of power, not unlike coats of arms. Since they are relatively small and fairly light in weight, they may have been carried by leaders in leather pouches worn at the waist and passed down from generation to generation. If so, this would explain why the balls have never been discovered in any graves. □

SKY WATCHERS

Scanning the heavens with high-technology telescopes and spacecraft, modern astronomers have fashioned an understanding of the universe far beyond what was thought possible only a few decades ago. Yet, in a sense, the achievements of these scientists are less remarkable than those of ancient sky watchers—the priests, shamans, and philosophers of long-vanished societies. Somehow, through observation, intuition, and methods now lost in time, these scholars amassed a wealth of knowledge about the movements of the sun, moon, planets, and stars and how they might be linked to the rhythms of humankind, of sowing and reaping, life and death.

History does not say when or why humans first began noting and recording patterns of motion among celestial bodies. Certainly they were driven partly by an early realization that time was a dimension of life and that, in the apparent chaos of a primitive world, there was order to be found among the stars.

Whatever their motives, it appears that—in nearly every region of the world and with tools and techniques of their own devising—the ancients reached a sophisticated understanding of a number of complex celestial phenomena a long time before the beginning of the historical record. Some of them may have learned how to predict eclipses; others may even have grasped the notion that the earth is not flat, but round.

Since the 1960s, a new branch of scholarship called archaeoastronomy has emerged to trace the full extent of this considerable ancient knowledge. By studying the artifacts and lore of early human communities, archaeoastronomers hope to discover how these societies learned about the heavens and how and why they used their insights in agriculture, philosophy, and religion. But the researchers are dogged by a frustrating certainty: Much of what they seek has been lost beyond retrieving. The astronomers of old will keep many of their secrets through eternity.

A Sunbeam for the Dead

Thirty miles north of Dublin stands one of the great astronomical wonders of prehistoric Europe. On a long, low ridge overlooking the narrow Boyne River, ancient farmers built a mound more than 260 feet in diameter and 30 feet high. Its southern edge, facing the river, is banded with a wall of sparkling white quartz. At the middle of this wall, guarded by a massive, intricately carved stone, is an entryway: For the mound is more than a heap of stones; it is a shell enclosing an early masterpiece of megalithic architecture.

The entrance opens onto a passage sixty-two feet long, a buried avenue flanked by forty-three stones—most of them taller than a man and weighing ten to twelve tons each. At the end of the passage lies a complex structure of huge rocks, some carved with symbolic designs, forming a cross-shaped chamber that rises into a vault some twenty feet above the floor. On the floor of each arm of the cross lies a basin stone—a large, flat rock with a shallow indentation carved into it. In this area bodies of the dead were placed, corpses now broken and scattered by time and marauding animals. The roof stones are grooved to carry water away from

the chamber, and their seams are sealed with puttylike burned soil.

Newgrange, as the structure is called, is the largest and most elaborate of a trio of New Stone Age tombs put down by early Irish farmers in this bend in the Boyne. This house of the dead predates the completion of England's Stonehenge by 1,000 years and Egypt's pyramids by several centuries. But Newgrange is more than a tomb; it appears to have been meant as a kind of cathedral to the life force embodied in the sun.

During a restoration of the mound that began in 1960, two Irish archaeologists, Michael and Claire O'Kelly, discovered a vertical opening between roof slabs above the entrance to Newgrange. Set in the gap was a decorated, open-ended structure they dubbed the roof box. In 1969, acting on a hunch, the O'Kellys stationed themselves in the tomb's interior passageway at dawn on December 21. This day marked the winter solstice, when the sun stops its retreat from the northern hemisphere and the dark winter days begin to lengthen into spring.

Four minutes after sunrise, they noted, "the first pencil of direct sunlight shone through the roof box and right along the passage to reach across the tomb chamber floor as far as the front edge of the basin stone in the end chamber. As the thin line of light widened . . . and swung across the chamber floor, the tomb was dramatically illuminated." The solar beam began to narrow; seventeen minutes after the sun appeared in the roof-box aperture, it vanished. The subterranean light show, the O'Kellys discovered, began about a week before the winter solstice and continued for a week afterward. For that short interval each year, sunlight entered Newgrange so that only the dead could see it.

Although many

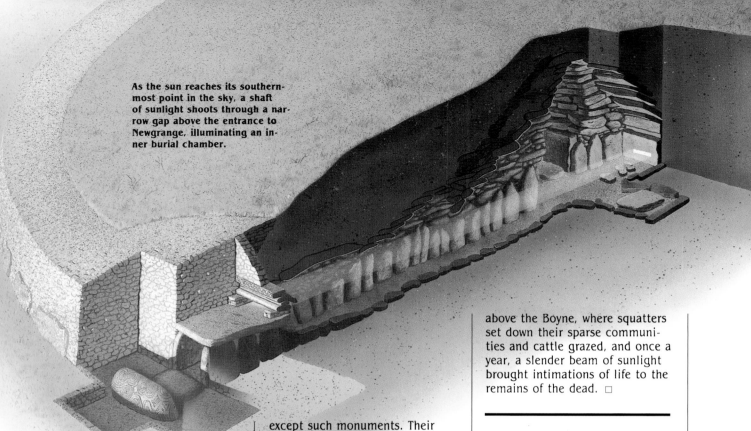

As the sun reaches its southernmost point in the sky, a shaft of sunlight shoots through a narrow gap above the entrance to Newgrange, illuminating an inner burial chamber.

scholars thought it likely that this precise solar alignment was mere chance, others believed it must have been deliberate. Convincing proof of this did not come until 1988, however, when Tom P. Ray, an astrophysicist at the Dublin Institute for Advanced Studies, investigated Newgrange and found that the central passage, though slightly winding, would have been aligned with the midwinter sunrise of 5,150 years ago. It would have permitted a single beam of light to enter the chamber not four minutes after, but at the exact moment of sunrise. Obviously, the architects of the day did not achieve such close tolerances only by accident.

Ray's discovery was significant for researchers seeking to understand the Neolithic people of Ireland, who left behind nothing except such monuments. Their culture seems to have first appeared about 10,000 years ago, when human agriculture began, then vanished before the first written histories of civilization. Archaeologists now think that the workers who built the tombs were drawn from a very small population—perhaps as few as 3,000 people. The complexity, workmanship, and precision of the structure shows that this ancient society had planning and building skills far beyond what had formerly been attributed to them.

But all of these abilities, it appears, focused on tomb building, and the compulsion to celebrate the deceased bore the seeds of ruin for the living. Newgrange seems to have been the product of an intensifying obsession with death. Ultimately, the building of such tombs so depleted the wealth of the builders that their economy collapsed and the land was left to lie fallow. A thousand years after its builders' time, Newgrange was simply an overgrown mound above the Boyne, where squatters set down their sparse communities and cattle grazed, and once a year, a slender beam of sunlight brought intimations of life to the remains of the dead. □

Round Earth Roundup

Christopher Columbus's conclusion that the world is round would have come as old news to the ancients.

"The earth is a globe," said Pythagoras, the Greek philosopher of the fifth century BC. Two centuries later another Greek, Aristarchus of Samos, affirmed the earth's shape and added that it spun on its axis and, with other planets, revolved around the sun. Also in the third century BC, Eratosthenes, custodian of the library at Alexandria, used his knowledge of astronomy to measure with considerable accuracy the earth's circumference and diameter.

Ancient writings indicate that the sages of India knew of the world's spherical shape by the fourth century BC, and the Chinese even earlier than that—perhaps as long as 3,000 years ago. □

Moon among the Stones

On a ridge above Loch Roag in Scotland's Outer Hebrides, columns of rock stand like mournful giants. They are the Callanish stones, among the most remote of the hundreds of stone circles erected as early as 5,000 years ago across the British Isles and Brittany. But Callanish is something more: Of all the megalithic sites, it most powerfully evokes ancient understanding of the skies.

The pillars were emplaced about 2000 BC by the New Stone Age inhabitants of the Isle of Lewis, who arranged them in a rough Celtic cross—a cross circled by a ring—oriented toward the south *(right).* The design centers on a five-ton gneiss megalith more than fifteen feet high, ringed by thirteen slightly shorter companions. To the north, an avenue flanked by two lines of standing stones extends some 250 feet. A shorter single line of stones marches southward from the circle, which is intermittently surrounded by individual slabs of rock, seemingly set down at random. Closer scrutiny suggests, however, that Callanish's shape is in no way random but was shaped by a grand astronomical design.

According to most modern researchers, the Callanish stones were set up partly to mark the extreme northern and southern points of the moon's rising and setting. In an erratic imitation of the sun's steady year-long journey between solstices—the northernmost and southernmost points in

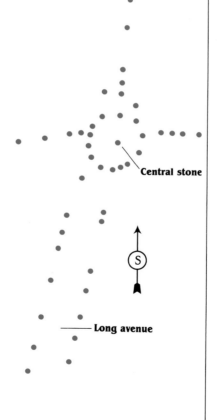

Central stone

S

Long avenue

its apparent track across the sky—the moon's path shifts slowly toward the north and south, reaching a maximum position at precise intervals of 18.61 years. Because the moon's path extends no farther north or south than these maximum points, the phenomenon is sometimes given the misleading label of "lunar standstill," although the moon continues its rapid daily crossing of the heavens.

The complex orbital variations that produce this effect were first explained by Sir Isaac Newton in the seventeenth century and later elaborated by Europe's brilliant eighteenth-century astronomers. But it now appears almost certain that this lengthy lunar cycle—so long that even the long-lived humans of today must stretch to experience four of them in a lifetime—was known to a Neolithic race whose average life span would scarcely permit cognizance of more than one cycle.

Callanish was apparently designed to reveal this dazzling lunar vision, which can be seen only at far northern latitudes in midwinter and midsummer—and only for a short interval every eighteen and a half years. One alignment of stones radiating from the center of the cross, for example, denotes a point on the far southwestern horizon where the midsummer moon sets

Every 18.61 years, the midsummer full moon rises and sets almost due south of Callanish, barely grazing the southern horizon on its short track across the sky *(top).* Evidently, the stones were arranged *(above)* to mark this setting of the moon.

during one such extreme. Then, the full moon in its passage across the sky barely grazes the crests of the hills to the south across the loch, vanishing, reappearing, then vanishing once again. Seen from the long avenue, this horizon-skimming moon moves through the ranked megaliths like a shining spirit, alternately hidden and revealed by the columns.

Seeing the moon among those pillars set one modern observer on a lifelong quest to decipher the stones. In 1934, Alexander Thom, an engineering professor at Oxford University and an ardent sailor, steered his small sailboat into Loch Roag, where he saw on the ridge above a tableau that would alter his life: the stones of Callanish silhouetted against the disk of the moon rising to the east. He hurried ashore and approached the columns, noticing as he did that the short line of standing rocks above the horizontal member of the cross aimed directly at the north star—the center of the sky's apparent rotation. The eerie moonrise and the seemingly deliberate orientation of the stones moved him deeply. "From that minute," Thom wrote later, "I knew I had to deal with a highly developed culture, and everything I have uncovered since lends support to that."

Although Thom was among the first to conclude that Callanish was built to show the lunar standstill, he was not the first to attribute astronomical precision to such monuments; others had made that connection more than two centuries earlier. But he was the most determined. After critics derided his astronomical case for Callanish, Thom devoted much of his spare time to quantifying what he had witnessed there. With his engineer son, Archibald, Thom tramped the remote reaches of the British Isles, making careful surveys of megalithic monuments and interpreting their alignments in astronomical terms.

Decades of study led him to conclude that the megaliths' builders had been far more than primitive farmers. To mark the lunar standstills, they must have been capable of systematic observation over generations. Although Thom's view has its detractors, it may explain why the Callanish megaliths are arranged the way they are.

But it does not explain why Stone Age farmers spent years cutting, transporting, and erecting such huge and heavy slabs of rock. Working at Stonehenge in the early 1960s, Gerald Hawkins, a British-born astronomer then lecturing at Boston University, concluded that such megalithic sites were designed as rudimentary comput-

ers, used to predict two of the most fearsomely portentous of heavenly events: solar and lunar eclipses. Hawkins's theory was echoed and extended by Thom, who interpreted Callanish and many other stone rings and cruciforms as the work of Neolithic scientists capable of such predictions.

Indeed, the sun, moon, and earth are aligned during the extreme lunar standstill, so that the 18.61-year lunar cycle coincides with what modern astronomers call eclipse seasons—periods when eclipses are likely to occur. The ponderous computer would have invested early leaders with the power to predict intervals when these events—dreaded by the ancients as signs of impending doom—might occur. The brooding stones may have been a kind of early warning system against those fearsome nights when darkness would swallow the full moon over the moor at Callanish. □

Oenopides of Chios, a Greek philosopher of the fifth century BC, is credited with being the first to calculate the angle of the earth's tilt on its axis. He computed the slant at 24 degrees with respect to the plane of earth's orbit, only .5 degrees from the currently accepted angle of 23.5 degrees.

Astronomy of the Unseen

Sirius, the primary star in the constellation Canis Majoris, is the brightest in earth's sky. Known as the Dog Star, it has long figured in human cosmology and myth. In 1836, German astronomer Friedrich Bessel discovered that something tugging at Sirius caused an almost imperceptible wobble in the star's orbit. Apparently, the Dog Star was circled by a fainter star every fifty years.

The unseen companion, labeled Sirius B, was not viewed until 1862, when an American telescope-maker named Alvan Clark saw it through his 18.5-inch refractor, then the world's most powerful telescope. More than half a century later, astronomers at California's Mount Wilson Observatory established that Sirius B was a new type of super-dense star they called a white dwarf: a stellar left-over that had collapsed into a ball of highly compressed material.

But the most puzzling aspect of Sirius B was announced in 1950, not by astronomers but by two distinguished French anthropologists just back from what is now the Republic of Mali. According to Marcel Griaule and Germaine Dieterlen, the white dwarf, though quite invisible to the naked eye, had been the celestial keystone of an African tribe's cosmology for centuries.

Griaule and Dieterlen had gone to live with the Dogon tribe in its sub-Saharan corner of French

Sudan in 1931. By 1946, the tribe had come to trust Griaule enough to reveal their cosmology to him. As the Frenchman watched, Dogon holy men and women used sticks to scratch a rough oval diagram of the heavens in the dirt. Before long, Griaule could make out in the drawing the Dog Star, and around it, in elliptical orbit, a companion star, along with another unseen body that has not yet been detected by astronomers. According to the Dogon, the egg-shaped orbit represented fertility: the "egg of the world." The companion star circled Sirius A in a period of fifty years, they explained, and was so small that they named it *po* for their tiniest

seed, a grain called *digitaria exilis.*

Digitaria, as Griaule labeled the companion star, was said to be made of a metal the Dogon called *sagala,* brighter than iron and so heavy that "all earthly beings combined cannot lift it."

Griaule found that the verisimilitude of the Dogon cosmos goes well beyond Sirius. They rightly believe, for example, that Jupiter has four large moons, Saturn is ringed, the earth revolves around the sun, and stars spin, as they do in the real universe.

How could tribal myth that predated telescopes have come so close to astronomical reality? Some researchers treat the celestial knowledge of the Dogon as an enigma that can only be resolved by invoking extraordinary and improbable means such as divination or psychic viewing. Others, though, note that the Dogon are neither as primitive nor as isolated as certain reports have made them out to be. Their villages of tightly clustered mud huts lie along overland trade routes that once linked West Africa with ancient Egypt and border the Niger River, a major regional conduit of commerce. They live just south of Timbuktu, the seat of a university that, 400 years ago, was one of Islam's great intellectual centers. And the Dogon have been able to attend French schools in the area since 1907. All these factors lead many scholars to attribute the tribe's knowledge of the skies to cultural interchange, transfers among various cultures— or even outright fraud.

Cultural interactions may well explain some of the details of their cosmology. But the congruence between the real Sirius star system and the mythic one constructed by the Dogon continues to bemuse investigators.

To the tribe, however, there is no mystery. Many years ago, they say, amphibious beings called *nommo* from the Sirius star system brought the Dogon special knowledge of the heavens, then returned home. With very few exceptions, only the Dogon believe this. But no one else has quite explained how, in their rough celestial diagrams, the Africans can describe stars they have still not seen. □

A Cryptic Disk

One evening in 1971, wealthy amateur philologist Leon Pomerance looked up at a simulation of the star-strewn sky of ancient Crete. With him was Kenneth Franklin, an astronomer who in 1955 had shared in the discovery of the planet Jupiter's radio emissions and who now worked at the American Museum's Hayden Planetarium in New York. For this occasion, Franklin had programmed the planetarium's projector to display the star patterns that would have appeared 4,000 years ago. Pomerance had noted this sequence of constellations before but not on a conventional star chart. Rather, he had discerned the peculiar lineup of stars on the weathered face of one of prehistory's most inscrutable objects: the Phaistos Disk.

Discovered in 1908 by Italian archaeologist Luigi Pernier, the disk was part of a trove dug from ruins of the city-palace of Phaistos, a center of the Minoan civilization that thrived in Crete from about 3000 to 1100 BC. The Phaistos Disk is a terra-cotta plate six inches across, marked with some forty-five different pictograms of people, animals, and designs, repeated in various combinations along a spiral band that coils to an end in the plate's center.

The disk's symbols—among them dot clusters, a bird, a bear, a serpentine squiggle, and a profiled human head—are completely unlike those of Linear A and Linear B, the known hieroglyphic systems ◊

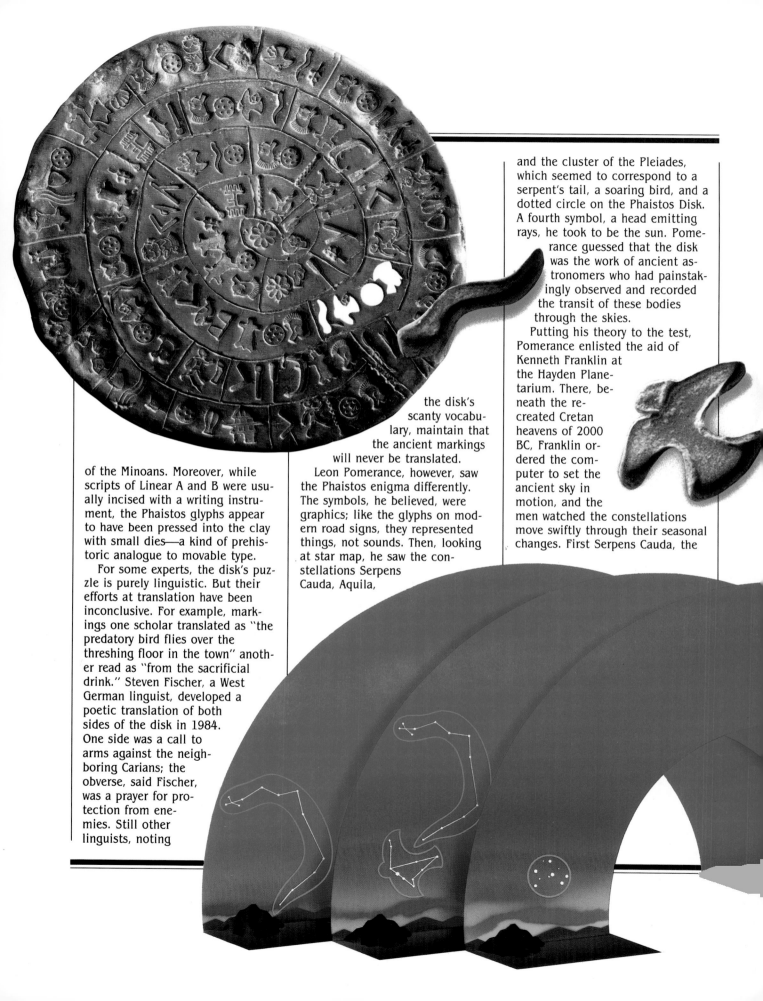

and the cluster of the Pleiades, which seemed to correspond to a serpent's tail, a soaring bird, and a dotted circle on the Phaistos Disk. A fourth symbol, a head emitting rays, he took to be the sun. Pomerance guessed that the disk was the work of ancient astronomers who had painstakingly observed and recorded the transit of these bodies through the skies.

Putting his theory to the test, Pomerance enlisted the aid of Kenneth Franklin at the Hayden Planetarium. There, beneath the recreated Cretan heavens of 2000 BC, Franklin ordered the computer to set the ancient sky in motion, and the men watched the constellations move swiftly through their seasonal changes. First Serpens Cauda, the

the disk's scanty vocabulary, maintain that the ancient markings will never be translated.

Leon Pomerance, however, saw the Phaistos enigma differently. The symbols, he believed, were graphics; like the glyphs on modern road signs, they represented things, not sounds. Then, looking at star map, he saw the constellations Serpens Cauda, Aquila,

of the Minoans. Moreover, while scripts of Linear A and B were usually incised with a writing instrument, the Phaistos glyphs appear to have been pressed into the clay with small dies—a kind of prehistoric analogue to movable type.

For some experts, the disk's puzzle is purely linguistic. But their efforts at translation have been inconclusive. For example, markings one scholar translated as "the predatory bird flies over the threshing floor in the town" another read as "from the sacrificial drink." Steven Fischer, a West German linguist, developed a poetic translation of both sides of the disk in 1984. One side was a call to arms against the neighboring Carians; the obverse, said Fischer, was a prayer for protection from enemies. Still other linguists, noting

Serpent's Tail, emerged in what would have been late November, followed by Aquila, the Eagle, which seemed to fly toward the west. As the simulation progressed, the seven-star Pleiades rose in April, just before the sun. The year unfolded, and the stars made their turnings: By October, the Eagle had reversed itself and flew eastward, upside down. Pomerance had seen this sequence before, pressed into the surface of the Phaistos Disk. The mysterious plate, he concluded, was a kind of early almanac, probably used by farmers to chronicle planting and harvesting.

This interpretation won cautious endorsement from some authorities, but there is no consensus. Today, what may be one of the first human records of seasonal changes in the sky waits in the Heraklion Museum on Crete for confirmation, perhaps by a companion object dredged from the Aegean or discovered within Minoan ruins. □

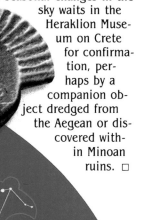

An Ancient Computer

For 2,000 years, the wreckage of a Greek merchant ship lay undisturbed beneath the gale-swept waters of the eastern Mediterranean, its ghostly hulk shrouded in silt. Littering the seafloor along its 150-foot length were relics of its riches: storage jars, statuary, unidentifiable bits and oddments consigned to the deep. Then, in 1900, sponge fishermen diving for their catch in a bay off a barren islet called Antikythera chanced on the ship's wreckage—and transformed forever modern notions about ancient Greece.

The Antikythera find was archaeology's first great underwater discovery, and as such it caused a great stir in scholarly circles. Artifacts from the ancient wreck made their way to the Greek National Archaeological Museum in Athens, where they were scrutinized, catalogued, and assembled. Smaller pieces were set aside as possible missing parts. Among these were four heavily corroded lumps of bronze, which were examined by museum archaeologist Valerios Staïs. He noticed that what had at first appeared to be simply scratches on the metal were in fact an inscription. Looking more closely, he saw that the bronze fragments were actually clusters of geared wheels—the remnant of some kind of machine.

Further study of the pieces led Staïs to conclude in 1902 that the device dated from the first century BC and that it appeared to be a navigational tool, perhaps an early astrolabe, an instrument used to determine the positions of celestial bodies. There speculation

about the artifact stood until 1951, when Professor Derek de Solla Price of Yale University began what would become the definitive study of the Antikythera Mechanism, as it had come to be called. Attempting to re-create the device, Price and his Greek co-workers used x-rays and gamma-rays to probe the internal structure. The mechanism, he discovered, contained layer upon layer of various-sized gears. After long calculations of possible gear ratios, Price arrived at an astonishing conclusion: Some ancient Greek inventor had designed a mechanism that mimicked the actual movements of the sun, moon, and planets, past, present, and future. The Antikythera Mechanism was a 2,000-year-old analog computer.

As hypothetically reconstructed by Price, the original mechanism consisted of a rectangular box about twelve by six by three inches, with the bronze machinery contained by wooden sides. The front and back were covered by bronze doors on which the inventor had inscribed detailed instructions. Three dials displayed the device's "readout." The first contained two concentric bands, one showing the signs of the zodiac, a sixteen-degree-wide belt straddling the apparent path of the sun, and the other the names of the Greek months. A pointer revealed the position of the sun in the zodiac for every day of the year. A second dial displayed an eighteen-year cycle of solar eclipses, while a third kept track of the different phases of the moon.

Inside the box, some thirty- ◊

In this schematic re-creation of the Cretan sky in about 2000 BC, rising constellations mimic the order of symbols on the Phaistos Disk. On the eastern horizon *(rear)*, the Serpent's Tail rises in late November; followed in December by the Eagle *(center)*; and, in the spring, by the Pleiades *(front)*.

nine bronze gears were meshed on parallel planes and set in motion by a handle that needed to be turned once a day. These were linked through a kind of toothed turntable that acted as a differential gear train, permitting two shafts to rotate at different speeds. Operating on the same principle that allows the traction wheels on modern automobiles to turn at different rates on curves, the differential gear had long been assumed to be an invention of the seventeenth century.

Fascinated by Price's hypothesis, physicist Allan Bromley, a professor at the University of Sydney, enlisted the help of clockmaker Frank Percival to construct a working model of the Antikythera Mechanism. Using techniques that would have been available to the ancient Greeks, in 1987 the pair assembled a functional replica that largely verified a majority of Price's theories.

Still, the identity of the machine's original creator is lost in time. Some scholars believe that the Antikythera Mechanism originated on the island of Rhodes, where cultural conditions two thousand years ago might have been right for the emergence of the necessary skills. There, without any fanfare, a consummate mechanical artisan who had a strong knowledge of the heavens somehow fashioned the ancient computer of Antikythera, the device that Price called one of "the greatest basic mechanical inventions of all time."

Rising from its watery grave after two millennia, the mechanism belied the prevailing view that ancient Greece was a land of brilliant theoreticians who, pampered by slaves, disdained the physical. These Greeks, it seems, had a mechanical genius after all. □

Sun Stones

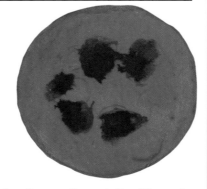

Gazing through smoky crystal or translucent jade, Chinese astronomers observed sunspots—black blotches caused by relatively cool areas in the sun's atmosphere— at least 1,600 years before the Italian astronomer Galileo saw them through his telescope.

Many ancient Chinese histories and memoirs refer to sunspots, and historians believe that observing the sun through the filters of semitransparent stones was an early Chinese practice. Some scholars theorize that haze from dust storms in the Gobi also provided Chinese astronomers with a natural filter for solar study. □

The Crescent and the Star

A photographic re-creation of the Crab supernova near the crescent moon before sunrise on July 5, 1054, simulates the sky as seen by the Anasazi pictogram artist from Chaco Canyon.

The now-vanished civilization of the Anasazi Indians flourished in the American Southwest about 1,000 years ago. On the baked plateaus of the high desert, ruins of their stone cities and mysterious roadways *(page 69)* offer mute witness to Anasazi craft and tenacity. And the rocky, earth-hued mesas hint at another of their talents: astronomy.

Modern archaeoastronomers interpret certain signs on the desert rocks to mean that the Anasazi were systematic sky watchers who understood much about the heavens. On a ledge near the top of a towering butte *(above)* in New Mexico's Chaco Canyon, for instance, three large sandstone slabs formed an aperture through which sunlight played in enigmatic ways along two spirals carved in the rock face behind the stones. For perhaps 1,000 years, until the late 1980s when erosion caused the slabs to shift, shafts of light accurately demarked the summer and winter solstices— the longest and shortest days of the year—as well as the March and September equinoxes, the times when day and night are of equal length. Scholars believe that the Sun Dagger, as the phenomenon has come to be called, was a calendar devised by the Anasazi.

Testament to the astronomical acumen of the Anasazi does not, however, rest with the Sun Dagger alone: Chaco Canyon's stones also hint that these sky watchers saw and chronicled the death of a star.

On a cliff beneath the ruins of an Anasazi town called Penasco Blanco, an overhanging rock bears on its underside three painted designs: a crescent, a rayed disk, and a hand. Directly below them on the sandstone wall is painted a dot circled by two rings, still recognized by modern Pueblo Indians as the sign for the sun.

Found in 1972 by archaeologists from the University of New Mexico, the symbols, which appear to mark the post of the former Anasazi sun watchers, echo markings found ◊

at other such posts in the southwestern Indian territories. To some astronomers, the symbols evoke nothing more remarkable than the occasional proximity of Venus and the moon. But, because the crescent is relatively rare in southwestern rock art, several experts believe that the painted objects—those at Chaco Canyon especially—must commemorate a spectacular celestial event. The rayed disk, they speculate, might denote an exploding star. The Chaco Canyon images were painted during the most active era of Anasazi civilization, about a millennium ago. At that time, across the world in China, astronomers reported the appearance of a "guest star," probably the bright explosion, or supernova, marking the death of exceptionally massive stars. According to the Chinese, the guest star appeared on July 5, 1054, a day when the predawn sky blazed with a new object five or six times brighter than Venus—the brightest star besides the sun ever seen by humans. Its remnants are the Crab nebula, a vast and still-expanding cloud of gas in the constellation Taurus.

Might the Chaco Canyon pictograms record that same titanic explosion? Some researchers think they must. Hoping to verify it, NASA astronomer John Brandt, in 1979, asked a colleague at the U.S. Naval Observatory in Washington, D.C., to reproduce the southwestern night sky as it would have been in July 1054. In those long-ago heavens, the astronomers discovered, the moon, an inverted crescent, was barely two degrees (about four lunar diameters) away from the Crab nebula, almost exactly as shown on the rock at Chaco Canyon.

If this evidence can be trusted, nearly 1,000 years ago an Anasazi sun watcher took up his post on the cliff below Penasco Blanco just before sunrise. As he watched the eastern horizon, the moon rose with a star of astonishing brilliance suspended almost in the curve of its upside-down crescent. Fascinated by the bright stranger in the skies, the observer commemorated its appearance with an indelible portrait in rock. □

ANCIENTS AT PLAY

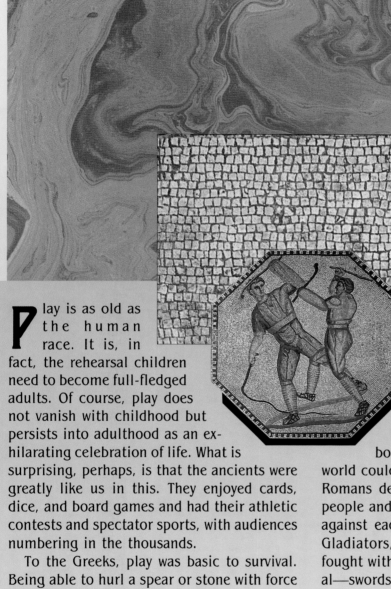

Play is as old as the human race. It is, in fact, the rehearsal children need to become full-fledged adults. Of course, play does not vanish with childhood but persists into adulthood as an exhilarating celebration of life. What is surprising, perhaps, is that the ancients were greatly like us in this. They enjoyed cards, dice, and board games and had their athletic contests and spectator sports, with audiences numbering in the thousands.

To the Greeks, play was basic to survival. Being able to hurl a spear or stone with force or defend one's self in combat was the mark of a good citizen, and there was only one way for a man to achieve such prowess—through athletics. The Greeks believed that in competing they were honoring the gods. It was no accident, then, that they founded the Olympic Games and kept the event going for more than eleven centuries, until the Christian emperor Theodosius I finally closed the games in AD 393.

But if Greek play was essentially a healthy expression of mind and of body, the play of others in the ancient world could be colored by violent urges. The Romans developed a taste for gore, pitting people and beasts or gladiator and gladiator against each other in battles to the death. Gladiators, the sports heroes of the day, fought with a regular armory at their disposal—swords, lances, barbed pikes and forks, metal nets. Boxers wore iron spikes on their fists. Across the seas, in a world yet unknown to Europeans, the Maya gave their own games a similar bloody cast; in fact, they took one ball game so seriously that the losers were decapitated as a way of placating the gods.

Deadly Child's Play

At one end of the arena stood a great bull with forbidding horns; at the other, an unarmed human waited expectantly. As the bull charged, its intended victim stood his ground without visible fear until, an instant before he would surely be impaled, he grasped the tips of the horns and vaulted over the bull, turning a somersault over the animal's back before landing on the ground behind it.

No documents survive to provide a description of this deadly pastime, practiced by the Minoans on Crete sometime during the middle of the second millennium BC. But an abundance of detailed wall decorations, showing massive bulls and diminutive humans *(below)*, have led scholars to the startling conclusion that the ancient bull leapers were not muscular adults but specially trained boys and girls who were agile and light enough to be lifted over the menacing horns.

Some historians suggest that bull leaping may have been a ritual contest, perhaps a form of fertility or coming-of-age rite. Others say it was just a sport, performed during religious festivals. Whatever the intent, it was not a blood sport, at least not in the sense of modern bullfighting. No weapons were used, and the only danger was to human beings. Indeed, some Cretan paintings show the bull-leaping acrobats being gored. □

The Golden Wreath

The spirit of peace and the love of sport for its own sake that are invoked in the modern Olympics were not always evident during the nearly twelve centuries of the ancient Olympics. In fact, these original games, held at the magnificent Greek city and sports complex of Olympia, were riddled with professionalism, bribery, chicanery, and political intrigue.

Such imperfections were rooted, perhaps, in the very word *athlete*, Greek for "prize seeker." The Greeks took this literally and provided ample rewards for their Olympic heroes. Although the offi-

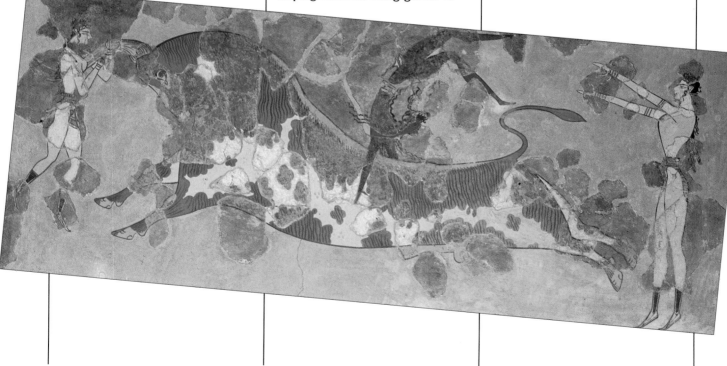

Figures of Greek athletes parade across a "victory cup" from the fifth century BC. Winners at sports festivals received as many as six of these vessels filled with valuable olive oil.

cial prize for winners was a wild olive wreath, victors were showered with more substantial rewards—cash, free housing, and other privileges—by their home states. Also-rans received nothing for their pains.

In this climate, it is not surprising that professionalism appeared in the Olympics within a few centuries after the first recorded games were held in 776 BC. Greek states bought and sold athletes, and the athletes changed allegiances to accommodate the highest bidder.

Celebrity-athletes were paid high fees to compete at local events. One record payment came to nearly 300 pounds of silver. In Athens a champion sprinter was awarded 1,200 drachmas for a race, enough to buy a luxurious home or a flock of 100 sheep and a half-dozen slaves to tend them. In time, professionalism became so commonplace that athletes in both Greece and Rome set up trade unions.

Although some historians argue that only a handful of cheating incidents occurred during the ancient games, the Greeks themselves said otherwise. Most cheating was punished by stiff fines, which were paid by sponsoring states and used to erect bronze statues of the gods. Athens, for example, paid for six such statues when its Olympic athlete Kallipos was caught bribing his opponents to let him win the pentathlon in the second half of the fourth century BC.

The most celebrated incident involved the Roman emperor Nero, who traveled to Greece to compete in the Olympic chariot races in AD 67. His was a difficult race. First, he fell out of his chariot. Helped back in, he still was unable to finish. Nevertheless the emperor was declared victorious—with the help of a 250,000-drachma bribe that induced the judges to proclaim that Nero deserved the wreath because he would have won if he had been able to finish. After Nero's death, however, the decision was ruled invalid and his name stricken from the record of victors. Simple chicanery was probably more the rule. For example, all Olympic athletes covered their bodies with olive oil, but wrestlers were required to dust themselves with powder so that their opponents could get a firm grip. But some of them, according to the playwright Aristophanes, would secretly wipe an oily hand over the areas of their bodies most likely to be clutched by an opponent.

The ancient games occasioned their share of political intrigue and at least once were a cause of war. In 420 BC, during the Peloponnesian War between Athens and Sparta, the Eleans—who controlled Olympia—sided with Athens and barred the Spartans from the Olympics. One Spartan charioteer, named Lichas, competed anyway, claiming to be from neutral Thebes. He won but was discovered and publicly whipped. The Spartans responded by attacking the Eleans.

In the end, the Olympics themselves fell victim to politics and changing times. In AD 393, not long before the old Roman Empire—heir to the lost grandeur of Greece—collapsed in the face of marauding hordes from the north, Rome's first Christian emperor, Theodosius I, abolished the games as a pagan holdover. By the time the Olympics were revived 1,500 years later, Olympia's temples, magnificent statuary, and elaborate sports facilities were no more. □

An Olympic Superstar

Milo of Crotona, who lived in the sixth century BC, may well have been the the world's first sports celebrity. He was certainly among the most enduring through legends of his athletic prowess and enormous strength.

Milo's fame was built around his domination of wrestling, in which he won five Olympic crowns and twenty-five victories in other championship contests before he retired. The story is told that he began training for each Olympic competition by carrying a newborn calf on his shoulders every day until the animal was fully grown.

This champion of wrestlers demonstrated his strength before 40,000 spectators at one Olympic festival by carrying a four-year-old heifer around the stadium, then killing it with one blow of his fist. After it had been cleaned and cooked, he ate the entire animal in a single day. Milo's regular daily diet included twenty pounds of wheat, another twenty of bread, and eighteen pints of wine.

Like numerous sports celebrities in later times, Milo married into a prominent family. His bride was the daughter of Pythagoras, the philosopher and mathematician, who also lived in Crotona. The father-in-law chose well, it is said, for the muscular Milo once saved the philosopher's life by supporting the entire roof of Pythagoras's house when it threatened to collapse. After owner and guests had safely fled, Milo relaxed his muscles, then strode unharmed from the falling debris.

This giant's death fostered a legend just as grand as his life. One day, the story goes, Milo was walking in the hills outside Crotona when he came upon a huge tree that had been cut down and partially split by a woodsman. The woodsman's wedges were still jammed in the trunk, prompting Milo to think that he could finish the job himself by thrusting his fingers into the split and prying outward. But nature conspired to defeat this master of the arena. As the split widened, the wedges fell out and the log snapped together, trapping Milo's fingers. By the time he was found, the great wrestler had been killed and partially eaten by wolves. ☐

Bare Facts

Greek men felt no shame at displaying their naked bodies, and all contestants in the Olympic Games competed in the nude. Indeed, the Greeks always looked on their readiness to strip in public as one of the traits that set them apart from uncouth barbarians.

No certain explanation has been offered for the code of athletic undress, but a cautionary tale by the poet Homer may account for it. In this story of competition, the contestants wore shorts—until one champion lost a race when he tripped over his dropping drawers.

A more plausible explanation might have been the great pride Greek men took in their bodies. Following the example of the Spartans, who dominated the Olympics, the athletes covered their bodies with olive oil, which kept dirt from getting into the pores and highlighted muscles. They also believed that the oil—carried in a special flask and wiped away after a contest with a curved metal scraper called a strigil (below)—made their skin more supple. ☐

Olympic Revels

The ancient Olympic Games were a grand festival, with myriad distractions for spectators and athletes. Vendors hawked food and other commodities, ranging from religious statues to horses. Acrobats, jugglers, sword swallowers, and conjurers entertained between events. And, since all Greeks loved a good tale, poets and writers declaimed their works from the porticoes of the Temple of Zeus. ☐

Aztec Gambling Fever

The Aztecs were among the most ardent high-stakes gamblers the world has ever known. Their favorite vehicle was a board game called Patolli, in which players cast dicelike marked beans to determine the progress of six colored markers over a cross-shaped playing surface *(above, right)*.

A game of Patolli was a raucous occasion of joking, shouting, drinking, and desperate wagering. Indeed, it was not uncommon for players and spectators to bet all they owned—clothing, jewelry, home, lands, mistresses, children, and even their own freedom.

Such frantic gaming was spurred by far more than lust for winnings. In fact, it was an expression of religious belief, and heavy betting was almost mandatory in Aztec society; a reluctance to risk all was considered a lack of faith in the gods. Gambling was one way a man could learn how the gods felt about him—a consistent winner was evidently favored, but a loser was not. At every cast of the marked beans, players invoked the gods—most often Macuilxochitl, the god of games and feasting *(above, left)*, and Ometochtli, god of pulque, the fermented drink that was consumed in great quantities during Patolli play.

Patolli was so bound up with Aztec religion and culture that, for many players, it became a symbol of their own lives. For example, the Aztec calendar was based on a fifty-two-year cycle; there were fifty-two squares to be traversed during a game, and a victorious player could thus believe that the next fifty-two-year cycle would be a lucky one. But if victory assured the continuation of a happy life or the improvement of an unhappy one, defeat represented an end to joy or the continuation of despair—and if a player lost his freedom, it could well mean death in a society that sometimes offered up slaves as sacrifices to the gods.

Disturbed by the religious implications of Patolli, early Christian missionaries did all they could to stamp it out. But the Aztecs continued to play in secret. Their descendants still play it today, but only as a harmless board game. □

In 2300 BC, the game Wei-qi was played in China's provinces to decide major issues such as the choice of rulers. This, the oldest known board game, is still popular today—known to its many fans as the game of go.

Bloody Spectacles

The most famous of all Roman games—fights to the death between combatants known as gladiators—began as a variation of an Etruscan funeral custom. In this ancient rite, men were sacrificed in mock combat so that the honored dead would have an armed escort for the journey into the next world.

The first gladiatorial contests in Rome were held at the city's cattle market in 264 BC to mark the funerals of certain aristocrats. There, slaves were forced to fight each other, apparently to honor the dead and divert the mourners. Because of the large crowds that were drawn to these battles, the contests were soon shifted to the far more spacious Roman Forum. Thus began a 600-year reign of wanton butchery staged to entertain an enthusiastic populace.

Gladiators were most often slaves and prisoners. They protected themselves with armor and shields and fought with weapons ranging from swords and javelins to three-pronged spears called tridents. Fearlessness and a lust for combat were demanded; anything less was rewarded with a whipping or prodding with a hot iron—means of forcing a reluctant gladiator into the arena.

At first, private citizens sponsored the contests; eventually, the state took over the games, which became ever more extravagant. Julius Caesar, for example, used the gigantic Circus Maximus in Rome to stage a full-scale battle, each army complete with 500 infantrymen, 60 cavalrymen, and 20 elephants. In order to accommodate the ever-grander contests, work began in the first century AD on the mammoth Colosseum, an architectural marvel that still stands in the heart of Rome.

To satisfy the public's increasing thirst for novelty, women and dwarfs were featured in gladiatorial combat. Forests were uprooted and replanted in the Colosseum to provide a properly primeval setting for contests between men and imported lions and tigers. Wild animals were unleashed to put criminals to death—in executions so horrible and humiliating that condemned prisoners sometimes took their own lives in order to avoid entering the arena.

Bloodlust was not all that brought Romans to such spectacles. There were also lotteries, with prizes ranging from elephants and ships to houses. And the armor of fallen gladiators was customarily tossed to the mob in the Colosseum's lower tiers, an act that frequently touched off frenzied battles over the spoils.

In time, the games went far beyond mere casual entertainment and became a principal part of the Romans' lives. By the middle of the first century AD, no fewer than ninety-three days were set aside each year as game days, when Roman citizens put in short workdays, then spent the remainder of their day at the arena. By the fourth century, the number of such days had nearly doubled.

Historians have been unable to agree on an explanation for Rome's infatuation with organized slaughter. Some speculate that the games had religious implications; others that they helped celebrate military victories or unify the people. As for the Romans themselves, they held that watching such grisly spectacles elevated the spirit. □

Rare Roman Pity

Seldom in the bloody history of the Roman games were spectators moved by compassion for the thousands of human beings and beasts who died for their entertainment. On one notable occasion, however, the mob took pity on its suffering victims—a dying herd of North African elephants.

The year was 79 BC, and the animals had been pitted against a band of the Getuli, a nomadic African people who carried javelins and shields on their hunts. It was a gory, one-sided contest, although one elephant, driven to its knees and with spears dangling from its huge body, did manage to pursue its tormentors, snatching away the tribesmen's shields and tossing them into the air. The crowd, thinking this was a planned trick, cheered. But not for long. As dying elephants trumpeted their agony, the spectators' mood changed to anger, and they demanded that the remaining animals be spared.

To be sure, the slaughter of animals was the rule rather than the exception. In some contests, un-armed men stunned bears with a blow of the fist or choked lions by jamming an arm into the animal's throat and grasping its tongue with the other hand. In others, the animals were pitted against one another. During the celebration of the opening of Rome's Colosseum in AD 81, nine thousand animals died—five thousand in one day. □

In this detail from a third-century-AD mosaic, hunters drive a procession of captured African beasts up a gangway for shipment to the arenas of Rome, where the animals would be slaughtered for the amusement of spectators.

An Imperial Bird Hunt

Some Roman emperors were content merely to sponsor games. Others—among them Commodus, who reigned in the late second century AD—chose to participate in the events. But Commodus's achievements were considerably less than heroic: On his most notable day, he stood with bow and arrows in his royal box at the Colosseum and slaughtered a hundred hapless ostriches. □

Early Soccer

During China's Han dynasty (207 BC to AD 220) two games were played that strongly resembled today's soccer. In one, players juggled, dribbled, and passed the ball from one to another without holding it in their hands. In the other game, they took turns kicking the ball at a target. □

Manhunting

The Etruscans—who flourished in western Italy during the seventh and sixth centuries BC—anticipated the gore of the Roman games with their own brutal sport of manhunting, seen above in an Etruscan tomb painting. At the end of this hunt, the leashed hound mauls a slave, who has a club but is blinded by a hood. The bearded hunter closes in to administer the *coup de grâce,* perhaps by strangling his quarry with the dog's leash. Such pastimes may have had roots in rituals of human sacrifice. □

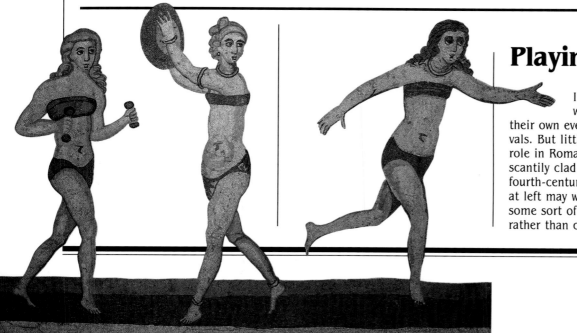

Playing Women

In ancient Greece, women participated in their own events at athletic festivals. But little is known of their role in Roman sport. The trim, scantily clad gymnasts seen in the fourth-century-AD Roman mosaic at left may well be putting on some sort of public performance rather than competing. □

At Sea in Rome

In their constant quest for novelty and spectacle in the games, the emperors of Rome ordered re-enactments of famous battles—including sea fights that were staged with full-size warships. Indeed, until the second century AD, when animal stalls were built beneath its arena floor, the Colosseum itself was sometimes the scene of these mock naval engagements.

Filling and draining the arena was a difficult task, however, and the scope of these watery combats was limited by the size of the Colosseum. So the emperors dug huge basins to accommodate the largest warships and allow ample room for maneuvers. Augustus, for example, ordered construction of a fifty-acre battle pond served by a specially built aqueduct that was nearly twelve miles in length. After one reenactment, in which as many as 3,000 gladiators fought in and over the water, the contents of the pond were used to provide water for the city.

No expense was spared to re-create a battle scene. Once, a fort was built on an island in the center of a basin so that an "Athenian" naval force could prevail over defending "Syracusans." Other re-creations called for bridges on which gladiators could fight to the death for the amusement of spectators lining the shore. □

Clad in the simple clothing of a noble captive, an eighth-century figurine of a Mayan ballplayer stands ready to begin a deadly game. The raised beads on the player's face mark ritual bloodletting.

A Deadly Ball Game

In the early sixteenth century, Hernán Cortés took his band of Spanish adventurers to the Aztec capital of Tenochitlan, site of today's Mexico City, in search of mountains of gold. What he found were heaps of human skulls displayed near the walled court in which was played a dangerous game of ball indeed: The losers often lost their heads. Variations of this grisly game, laden with religious symbolism, were played throughout pre-Columbian Mesoamerica, and some historians trace its origins back to the early Olmec Indians in about 2000 BC. It is thought that the contest symbolized the never-ending war between the forces of light and darkness, a kind of athletic morality play—in which, however, the forces of evil could occasionally triumph over those of good.

Details are sketchy, but it appears that in one version, as played by the Maya in southern Mexico, the game took place on a large flight of stairs. It is thought that the losers were bound tightly into a ball, then rolled down the stairs to death at the hands of a headsman.

More commonly, the game was played in a walled court. Opposing teams of up to seven players each sought to score points by shooting the grapefruit-size hard rubber ball through stone rings that were set high on the wall. Only the players' hips, feet, and elbows could contact the ball, which was not supposed to touch the ground.

The goal rings were so small and high that getting the ball ◊

through them was nearly impossible; the team that managed to do so was declared the winner immediately. Points were normally accumulated by hitting the rings or maneuvering the ball into other specified areas of the court. Sometimes the games were rigged by forcing captives—deliberately weakened by poor diet and perhaps torture—to play on the foreordained losing team.

If the ball game could be fatal to losers, it had its dangers for the victors too: A hard-hit ball could kill a player if it struck him solidly in the head or stomach. To protect themselves, the players wore heavy padding, most notably a horseshoe-shaped yoke of wood, wicker, or reeds wrapped around the waist. The midsection was protected by a flat stone fitted into the yoke, and the uniforms were completed by stone knee guards *(above)* and belts from which were hung effigies of opponents' heads.

Elaborately carved stone replicas of the yokes were worn in post-game ceremonies and were sometimes interred with the remains of sacrificial victims.

The games were often occasions for the frenzied gambling that seemed to be a passion among the Aztecs *(page 101)*. Once, two Aztec rulers bet their respective domains on the outcome of a single ball game. But the loser, rather than paying up, decided to have the winner assassinated.

Although Spanish missionaries did their best to eradicate the old Mesoamerican ball game, some remnants persist to this day in isolated Mexican villages. The modern version is called *ulama*, a less complicated approximation of the Aztec name, *ullamaliztli*. Today's game is less complicated in one other respect as well: The losing players live to play again. □

Pioneer Cardplayers

The Chinese were the first people to develop playing cards, sometime before the ninth century AD. As entertainment, they considered the games that were played with these slender slips of cardboard superior to many other diversions.

In the somewhat enigmatic words of one early enthusiast, cards could be "played by a group of four without annoying conversation, and without the difficulties which accompanied playing chess or meditation." □

VOYAGERS

The course of cultural evolution down through history and across the world has long fascinated scholars, who tend to explain advances in two distinct ways. One holds that societies have matured independently, evolving from nomadic tribes into settled communities—and sometimes great civilizations—in relative isolation. Cultures geographically close no doubt exchanged certain traits, this theory goes, but not until the great voyages of discovery in the fifteenth and sixteenth centuries was there cross-cultural exchange on a global scale. Before then, if widely separated peoples happened to grow along similar lines, it was a coincidence, most scholars think—and not a surprising one. The human mind, after all, does not vary biologically, regardless of divergent surroundings. Faced with similar challenges, therefore, a native of the Arctic tundra might well come up with much the same solutions as a native of the American desert or the Asian steppes.

The second view of cultural development is more speculative and relies on bits of evidence scattered throughout the world—customs shared by tribal peoples separated by thousands of miles, plants growing far from their native soil, artifacts bearing inscriptions alien to the lands where they are found. Such clues suggest that cultural characteristics have been transmitted by transoceanic visitations all but lost in the mists of history.

It is known today, of course, that Norsemen preceded Columbus to America. But there are those who suggest that, hundreds of years before the Norse, Buddhist monks from Asia visited a new world they called Fu Sang and left their mark on its native cultures. They were followed soon after, some say, by an Irish saint named Brendan who crossed the Atlantic in an ox-hide boat, as the illumination from a medieval German manuscript (above) depicts.

Those who believe in such early travels challenge the view that cross-cultural pollination began with the great Renaissance voyages of Columbus, Balboa, and Magellan. Rather, these theorists say, societies in many parts of the world matured by learning from each other—a process spawned by numerous, if unrecorded, voyages of the distant past.

8

A Norse Incursion?

On a 200-pound chunk of gray sandstone supposedly unearthed from Minnesota farmland, a strange tale is inscribed. In 1362, the story goes, a band of Scandinavians—eight Swedes and twenty-two Norwegians—sailed the Atlantic to explore North America. They landed safely and then pushed their way westward into what is now Minnesota, where tragedy struck. One day when twenty of the explorers were off fishing, the ten who stayed behind were massacred by Indians. When the fishing party returned, it found the slaughtered comrades and fled in terror.

The yarn is chilling, but is it history or hoax? Either way, it first came to light one November morning in 1898 when a Swedish immigrant named Olof Ohman and his ten-year-old son Edward were clearing a grove of trees on their farm near Kensington, Minnesota. While uprooting an aspen, the pair saw tangled in the tree's roots a stone some thirty inches long, sixteen inches wide, and five and one-half inches thick. The bottom and one side were covered with a curious inscription.

When news of the discovery reached the public, its reception was about as friendly as that supposedly accorded the Norse explorers by the local Indians. Scholars called in to inspect the Kensington stone, as it came to be known, scoffed at the idea that it might be a genuine fourteenth-century relic inscribed by visiting Norsemen in the ancient runic writing of their people. Had it been authentic, it might have made the case that Scandinavians not only preceded Christopher Columbus to America by a good many years but managed to explore hundreds of miles inland. But the investigators—including academicians from both American and Scandinavian universities—pronounced the stone a crude hoax. Linguists scoffed, noting that the inscription had many grammatical inconsistencies.

Olof Ohman quickly came under fire from skeptics who asserted that he had carved the stone himself. Upset over the accusations, the quiet Swede retrieved his stone and unceremoniously used it as a doorstep for his granary. There it

stood in 1907, when a Norwegian-born writer and lecturer by the name of Hjalmar Rued Holand paid Ohman a visit. Defying the academicians, Holand championed the Kensington stone's authenticity. For more than half a century, until his death in 1963, he tirelessly tried to convince the world that the stone was genuine.

Despite his many critics, Holand did manage to have the Smithsonian Institution exhibit the stone in 1948 and 1949. One of the museum's directors called it "probably the most important archaeological object yet found in North America." But his opinion was by no means universal. Among other arguments, critics noted that the stone's inscription was remarkably unweathered for its purported great age.

Still, the favorable notice was enough to resurrect interest in the stone, and opinions pro and con have led to a plethora of books and articles about it by scientists and laypeople. In a 1982 book, *The Kensington Rune-Stone Is Genuine,* for example, Robert Hall, a professor emeritus of linguistics at Cornell University, asserts the stone's authenticity. Another defender, amateur Danish linguist Richard Neilsen, has published a series of painstakingly documented articles in scholarly journals, claiming that new linguistic evidence proves all the runes on the Kensington stone are authentic fourteenth-century forms.

While the controversy continues, the Kensington stone lies in a modest museum in Alexandria, Minnesota. Watched over by the local Chamber of Commerce, it silently guards its secret. □

Goodbye Columbus

Called by some individuals "the most exciting cartographic discovery of the century" and by others an ingenious forgery, a crude parchment map may hold the key to the question of who really discovered America.

The worn document, known as the Vinland map, is thought by some experts to have been painted by a Swiss monk around 1440. Its name comes from a Latin inscription in its top left corner claiming that the legendary Viking Leif Eriksson "discovered a new land, extremely fertile and even having vines, the which island they named Vinland." Roughly but surely, the map of the world shows this island—labeled Vinilanda Insula—to be North America. If the map is genuine, it is the only known one to

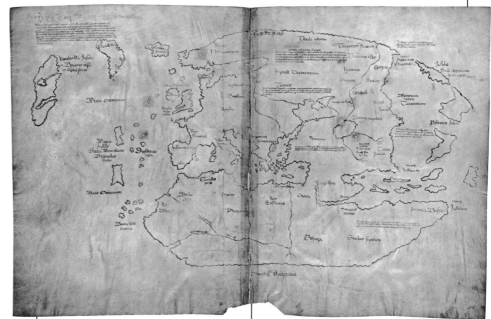

pinpoint the location of America prior to Columbus's 1492 voyage.

In 1957, rare-book dealer Laurence Witten of New Haven, Connecticut, bought the map from a European dealer for $3,500. It came bound with a manuscript called *The Tartar Relation*, a thirteenth-century narrative of a Central Asian journey. Witten later received a fragment of a medieval encyclopedia that seemed to ◊

have been written by the same person who penned *The Tartar Relation*. When he placed the three documents on top of one another, he was amazed to find that wormholes in all three matched, indicating they came from a single bound document. If the map had been compiled with works some two centuries older, Witten reasoned, it must also be very old—and almost surely genuine.

Witten's find went largely unnoticed until 1965, when Yale University put its considerable academic prestige behind the map's authenticity. An anonymous buyer had purchased the chart and its two related documents from Witten and donated them to the school, whose scholars subsequently declared that the Vinland map had indeed been drawn in the fifteenth century. They wrote a book called *The Vinland Map and Tartar Relation*, which concluded that the map was "the oldest surviving map of American lands."

The book made headlines around the world. While several Norse sagas tell of a land called Vinland—and many experts were already convinced that the Vikings had preceded Columbus there by many years—the parchment map was apparently the earliest graphic evidence of such a place. "Somehow a map cannot lie," one expert wrote; "an account can. To the man in the street the description of Vinland in the sagas is so many words; the description of Vinland by a line drawing is a revelation."

But was it? After the Yale findings, a team of independent investigators examined the map and found that its ink contained traces of anatase, a form of titanium dioxide that had not been developed before the 1920s. Thus, adjudged this research team, the Vinland map was a forgery.

But the controversy surrounding the map was not over. In 1985, scientists from respected Crocker Nuclear Laboratory at the University of California at Davis subjected the map to two days of stringent testing, including 159 particle-induced x-ray emission analyses. From its study, this group concluded that the 1974 tests were faulty and that "the prior interpretation that the map has been shown to be a twentieth-century forgery must be reevaluated."

Neither vindicated nor debunked, the Vinland map still lies at Yale, hinting—but not yet offering absolute graphic proof—that the Norse were pre-Columbian voyagers to the New World. □

Looks Are Not Everything

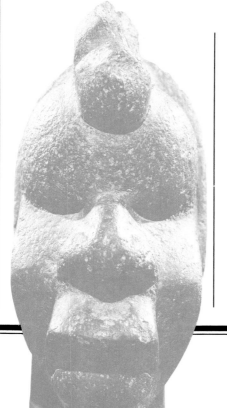

The strong features of the six-inch marble head shown at left look distinctly African. But the head, dating from about AD 600, is the work of a Mexican artist.

Many such pre-Columbian artworks have either an African or an Oriental cast, and some researchers see this fact as evidence that Africans and Asians long ago traveled to the shores of the Gulf of Mexico and influenced the native cultures there. In the absence of other compelling evidence, however, most archaeologists consider such conclusions to be unwarranted. The people of any given culture, they point out, can have a wide variety of physical characteristics, some of which might seem at first glance to be peculiar to a different, distant race. And in any case, artists throughout the ages have frequently been guided by personal vision and individual whim, and they have not necessarily painted or sculpted exactly what they have seen. □

The Riddle of the Well-Traveled Maize

The familiar maize plant—better known to Americans as corn—has generated a spirited scholarly debate that centers on the possibility of ancient, unrecorded sea travel. Botanists know that maize cannot propagate itself; its occurrence must therefore be the result of human agency. They also know that the plant originated in the New World. And yet, some researchers have found evidence that it appeared elsewhere well before the known voyages of discovery linked Old World and New.

That anomalous evidence includes reports that maize preceded the arrival of Europeans in East Africa in the late fifteenth century. Just how it got there, the natives could not say at the time, for they had cultivated it for many generations. Similarly, West Africans could only point north and east when asked about the origin of their maize—and the trail in that direction dwindled in the sands of the Sahara.

Even more intriguing is evidence that maize was well established in Asia long before Columbus's voyages. Eleventh-century temples in southern India, where maize was supposedly unknown at the time, house many stone figures that, according to some cultural geographers, are offering ears of maize to the gods *(right)*. Other experts dispute this interpretation of the Indian art, claiming that the objects are pomegranates or beaded ornaments. Perhaps the debate will someday be resolved, but for now the path that maize followed across the world remains a blurred and dim one. □

Meaningful Gestures

Although found half a world apart, a sixth-century Chinese Buddha *(below, left)* and an eighth-century Mayan maize god *(below, right)* exhibit mirror-image gestures.

Used ritually, such hand gestures are called mudras in the Orient. Throughout the Buddhist and Hindu worlds, there are dozens of gestures and body positions with symbolic meaning, and the ancient mudras persist today. Friends often greet each other with a praying-hands gesture, a mudra of reverence and respect.

The mudras of religious icons signal their benefit to worshipers. This Buddha's outstretched left hand says he is bestowing a gift; his upraised right hand signifies the gift is courage. Although the hand positions of the Mayan statue are reversed, the similarity is thought by some scholars to be too great to be coincidence. Indeed, the hand postures are among several similarities between Asian and New World icons that some researchers see as evidence that pre-Columbian cultures of the Americas may have been influenced by Asian visitors. Parallels have been found in costumes, headdresses, ornaments, physiques, and body positions of religious statues on both sides of the Pacific. □

The Ancient Hebrews of Tennessee

Throughout the river valleys of the southeastern United States lie hundreds of man-made earthen mounds in which American Indians laid their dead to rest. But in one such mound, according to some researchers, there are non-Indian remains as well—the bones of Jewish refugees who may have fled the brutal Roman occupation of Palestine in the first century AD.

This tomb first came to light in 1889, when a team from the Smithsonian Institution excavated three burial mounds along Bat Creek in Loudon County, Tennessee. Nine skeletons were found in one mound, two of them set apart from the other seven. Beneath one of these two skeletons lay several unusual artifacts, among them a stone tablet bearing nine carved letters.

The director of the mound excavation project, a man by the name of Cyrus Thomas, decided that the inscription contained letters of the Cherokee alphabet, which had been devised around 1820 by the Cherokee scholar Sequoya. The bones and the tablet were sent to the Smithsonian for later consideration; Thomas published his report in 1894, and there the matter seemed to rest.

But in the 1950s, archaeologist Joseph Mahan happened upon a picture of the Bat Creek tablet and reached a conclusion remarkably more exotic than Thomas's. Mahan

knew the Cherokee alphabet and, as he wrote later, could see "no relationship whatever between the symbols on the stone and those developed by Sequoya." What Mahan did see, upon turning the picture of the stone upside down, was a striking similarity between several of the letters and ancient Canaanite writing.

No expert in Semitic languages, Mahan sent a photograph to Semitic language scholar Cyrus Gordon, who confirmed Mahan's observation. The characters, said Gordon, were from a Hebrew dialect dating to about the first century AD. They translated as "A Comet for the Jews." He speculated that one of the skeletons was that of a leader—the "comet" memorialized by the tablet.

Others who have compared the inscription with Cherokee, Paleo-

Hebrew, and English characters take the position that, on the basis of their shapes, the carvings are as similar to English letters as to Cherokee characters—but are even more like Hebrew, as Gordon said. Support for Gordon's assessment also comes from carbon-14 dating of wood fibers found with the skeletons. These tests reveal that the bodies were buried sometime in the first two centuries AD.

To be sure, there are many reasons to question the scenario suggested by Gordon's translation of the inscription. For example, the other artifacts recovered at the Bat Creek grave site are clearly American Indian rather than Hebraic. And there is, of course, no hint in voluminous Hebrew lore of how any ancient Hebrews might have come to be among the Indians of Tennessee 1,900 years ago. □

Modern seafaring indicates that ancient peoples could have crossed oceans despite the smallness of their boats. In recent years, the Atlantic has been traversed by, among other things, two rafts, two dugout canoes, two dories propelled only by oars, several dories with sails, and a conventional sailboat less than six feet long.

The Fabled Voyage of Brendan

A monument to the storytelling art of the Irish people, the chronicle of Saint Brendan tells of an abbot and seventeen monks who journeyed to the "promised land of the saints" during a seven-year sojourn in a leather boat. "The Voyage of the Holy Abbot Brendan" was written in Latin during the ninth or tenth century, some 300 to 400 years after the death of Brendan. Most scholars consider the story merely an outstanding example of religious allegory. Some historians, however, suggest that the allegory contains seeds of truth—evidence that Brendan was in the vanguard of Irish sailors who explored the New World long before other Europeans.

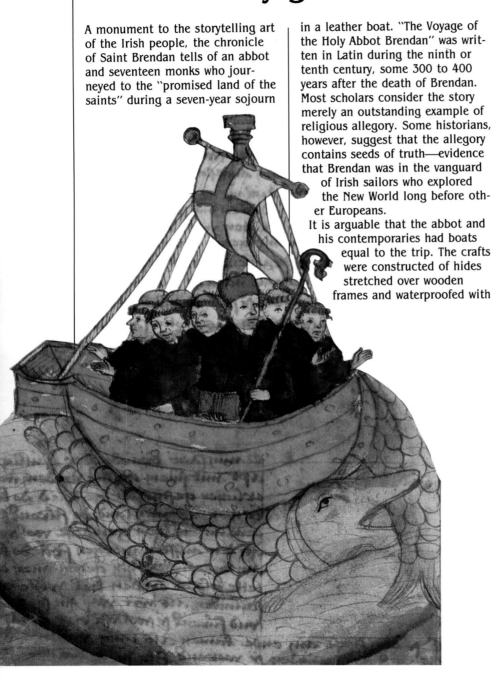

It is arguable that the abbot and his contemporaries had boats equal to the trip. The crafts were constructed of hides stretched over wooden frames and waterproofed with animal fat. They must have been quite durable, since Irish sailors of Brendan's day are known to have traveled the rough waters surrounding the British Isles, venturing at least as far as Iceland. There is speculation that Brendan himself might have been one of these doughty voyagers.

That the boats were capable of sailing across the Atlantic was demonstrated in 1977 by British sailor Timothy Severin, who made the 2,600-mile journey from Ireland to Newfoundland in a thirty-six-foot ox-hide craft *(right)*. Dubbed the *Brendan*, the boat was built to medieval specifications.

Brendan's own voyage, described in the fanciful Latin account, was a nonstop adventure. Each Easter for at least five years, the holy man and his crew supposedly conducted their celebrations while aground on the back of a whale. They visited an island packed with snow-white sheep, and on another island, throngs of birds chanted prayers with them. The monks spent twenty days becalmed on a "coagulated sea" and sailed eight days on waters so clear that they could see to the sandy bottom, where fish lay curled like cats, heads touching their tails.

The crew encountered wild beasts, a pillar of crystal, and an island of fire. Almost always in imminent danger, it seemed, they were invariably rescued from disaster by Brendan's prayers. Eventually, the company made it to the promised land, where they spent forty days and nights gathering wonderful fruits and precious stones before returning home.

Modern researchers find in Brendan's story tantalizing hints that the saint indeed visited exotic lands. The clear sea, they say, could have been the sparkling waters of the Bahamas. The fiery island could describe volcanic Iceland—where Irish monks are known to have settled. The pillar of crystal may have been an iceberg, and the coagulated sea could have been the algae-choked Sargasso, so dreaded by later seafarers.

These speculations find support in certain documents and traditions dating from shortly before the time of Columbus. Maps of the day often placed Brendan's promised land at a spot slightly west of the Canary Islands. The Spanish and Portuguese both sent expeditions to find Brendan's Isle as late as the sixteenth century.

The Renaissance mariners' conclusion—seconded by some modern authors—is that the monks' expedition reached the shores of the St. Johns River at St. Augustine, Florida, where the Spaniard Juan Ponce de León would later search for the fountain of youth. Nevertheless, skeptics maintain that Saint Brendan's voyage was simply a well-told tale, no less a fable than Ponce de León's forever elusive fountain. □

A Mystery of Monks and Megaliths

Scattered on a rocky rise of ground near North Salem, New Hampshire, is one of the more intriguing of America's archaeological oddities—a grouping of cavelike structures that have suggested to some people that venturesome Europeans settled in the New World long before Columbus.

Appropriately known later as Mystery Hill, the place had no name when a farmer, Jonathan Pattee, moved there in 1826. It was still nameless when Pattee died in 1848, but the rumors were starting. Locals speculated about what use Pattee might have made of the apparent caves on the hill. Some said he sheltered runaway slaves there; others guessed that the caves were where the farmer hid his moonshine whiskey. Both stories missed the real puzzle of the hill: questions not about what the so-called caves sheltered but about what they actually were and who had built them.

In fact, they were not caves at all but arrangements of huge rocks. They looked like megalithic ruins—twenty-two structures sprawling across one acre, with outlying stones covering another twelve acres. In the central area, boulders weighing at least five tons lay atop vertical stone slabs, and smaller stones made up arched rooms that were covered over with earth. Amid scattered rocks lay a tablelike slab *(above)* that looked, some said, like a sacrificial altar.

In Britain and elsewhere in Europe, megalithic monuments are not uncommon, but only a few such structures have been found in the New World. Small wonder, then, that the stones on Pattee's old homestead continued to arouse curiosity over the years, finally igniting a near-frenzy of enthusiasm in an amateur archaeologist by the name of William B. Goodwin when he visited the site in 1933. A wealthy retired insurance executive from Hartford, Connecticut, Goodwin took one look and announced that Pattee's caves were, in fact, the remains of a tenth-century monastery established by Irish monks who had fled the Viking invasions of their homeland. This conclusion caused something of a stir in academic circles, as well as in the press.

Goodwin soon bought the place and began cleaning it up and "restoring" it to what he felt must have been its original condition. Much debris was discarded—possibly including artifacts that might have helped determine with certainty the stones' true origins. Massive stones were lifted atop others and rooms were rebuilt. So clumsy and extensive was the work that Goodwin, who had brought the site to the world's attention, also effectively obliterated any chance of finding out the truth about its origins.

Thus a mystery it remained, officially becoming Mystery Hill in name as well as fact in 1957 when Robert E. Stone, another antiquarian, bought the property after Goodwin's death.

Later digs, far more careful than Goodwin's, have yielded no ancient artifacts, and attempts to date the site have been inconclusive. Carbon-14 dating, which cannot be used on stone, was applied to pieces of charcoal found in the area. One bit of charcoal, found beneath a stone wall, was found to date from 1500 BC. However, the piece could just as easily have been the by-product of an ancient forest fire as the leavings of a prehistoric campfire. Eight similar tests were made. Two yielded prehistoric dates, but the other six were from much more recent history—the eighteenth and nineteenth centuries.

Barry Fell, a retired professor of biology at Harvard University, has devoted considerable time to the riddle of Mystery Hill, focusing most of his energies on obscure carvings and inscriptions that he discerns on some of the stones. Fell theorizes that the markings represent an ancient Celtic language called Ogam, indicating to Fell that Mystery Hill's beginnings may date anywhere from 800 BC to the third century AD, considerably earlier than Goodwin's tenth-century Irish monks.

Most archaeologists, though, refuse to accept such findings. They conclude more prosaically that the structures were built by New Hampshire farmers—perhaps in the colonial period or perhaps later by Pattee himself—in order to store roots and vegetables and to shelter cattle. □

Pytheas in Britain and Beyond

In his own time, the Greek navigator Pytheas was a target of scientific scorn. Today, he is revered as one of the ancient world's most acute observers.

By the beginning of the third century BC, this native of Marseilles had circumnavigated Britain, measured it, met its people, noted the farming and tin-mining techniques, and made astronomical observations that would aid navigators for centuries to come.

Pytheas correctly located the North Star, identified the relationship between the moon and the tides, and calculated the latitude of Marseilles.

Even so, for generations Pytheas's findings were roundly dismissed by other scholars. In fact, Greek and Roman sages of the next three centuries—Strabo, Polybius, and Pliny, among them—flatly declared him a liar.

Perhaps the problem was that Pytheas was too good a scientist, reporting everything he saw and heard, no matter how unusual. He saw ice floating in the sea; this sounded preposterous to Mediterranean people. He reported hearing about islands farther north than Britain, where summer nights lasted only two or three hours; that was deemed absurd.

Despite Pytheas's pathfinding voyage, nearly two centuries passed before the next Mediterranean sailors ventured north to Britain. But when they did, they relied on Pytheas's reports to lead them. □

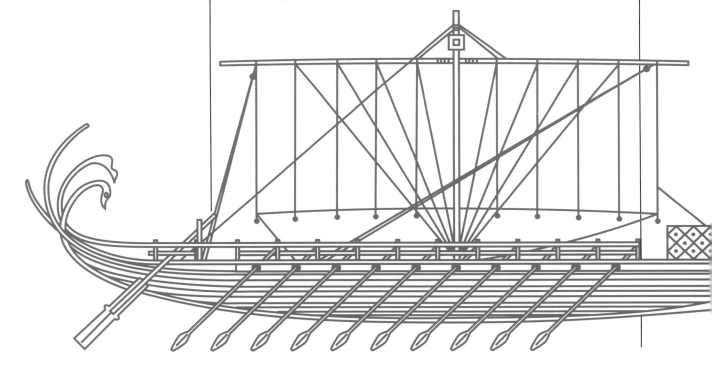

Phoenicians in America?

"We are sons of Canaan from Sidon," begins the manuscript. It is written in a Phoenician language used some 500 years before the birth of Christ. In only eight lines, it tells a story of a voyage around Africa, of storm, human sacrifice, and salvation on the shores of what is now Brazil.

If it was indeed left by a Phoenician sailor, the text memorializes an ancient visit to the New World long suspected by some scholars. If not, the Paraíba Inscription, as it is called, is among history's more intriguing hoaxes.

In 1872, Ladislau Neto, the director of Brazil's National Museum of Rio de Janiero, received from a colleague a copy of a letter. Its author, who was never found, described a stone tablet unearthed by workers on a plantation in Paraíba—now called João Pessoa—at Brazil's easternmost tip. Neto, putting aside his initial doubts about the inscription, published the text in 1874, after unsuccessfully seeking the original tablet and the letter writer.

The inscription was promptly branded a fraud by experts in Phoenician languages, and a long-simmering public debate ensued. Finally Neto himself, after ten years of professional and personal agony, recanted his belief in the text's authenticity.

Until the late 1960s, the case seemed settled and was virtually forgotten. Then, Cyrus Gordon, an American scholar of Semitic languages, studied the text and declared it authentic—ironically, for some of the same reasons that it was adjudged fraudulent nearly a century before.

So-called inaccuracies of vocabulary and grammar cited by critics in 1874 had become, by 1968, mere idiosyncracies of dialect. Similarities between the inscription and ancient Hebrew, once considered evidence of deceit, had since been documented as normal among Phoenicians, a people who mixed readily with a number of other cultures.

Moreover, Gordon's analysis seemed to reveal no fewer than three cryptograms buried in the tale. One, typical of ancient scripts, includes numbers that, when added, confirm the date given by the writer. The other codes, according to Gordon, tell the story once again from the point of view of both a Canaanite pagan and a Jewish crewman. The cryptograms, he claimed, were evidence of authenticity, since few counterfeiters were likely to have taken such pains with their work.

To be sure, Gordon's detailed interpretation has not settled the controversy over the Paraíba Inscription, and the debate is likely to continue until—if ever—the original stone inscription can be found and judged. □

The Venturesome Polynesians

When Europeans began exploring the Polynesian Pacific in the eighteenth century, they found that they were not the first ones to call on the islands. Even on tiny, isolated coral atolls and volcanic rocks where no one lived to greet them, the sailors of England, Spain, and Portugal found the abandoned dwellings and temples of early colonists.

The Polynesian islands are scattered across a vast triangle whose corners are Hawaii, Easter Island, and New Zealand. Most are isolated from one another, sometimes separated by a thousand miles of ocean. Yet, by the time the first European visitors arrived, Polynesians had evidently been traveling among the islands for centuries.

Impressed, the Europeans praised the islanders' sailing skill and told tales of epic voyages. But later generations were skeptical. To achieve the feats attributed to them, it was pointed out, the Polynesians would have required supreme navigational skills—talents that seemed questionable, since the Polynesians knew nothing of charts, compasses, sextants, and the other staples of the sailor's art. Moreover, to travel eastward from what is now believed to have been their original home on the Asian mainland, they must somehow have known how to sail against trade winds and prevailing currents, which flow westward.

In 1968 and 1969, New Zealand yachtsman David Lewis set out to prove that the ancient islanders had indeed been supersailors. For nine months, Lewis and two Polynesian guides sailed back and forth across the Polynesian Pacific without compass or other instruments. Other, later voyages have also tended to establish the exceptional skills of the islanders.

Using seafaring lore passed down for countless generations, the native navigators are extraordinarily adept at using stars to fix their location and guide their way. They mark their position and progress by the rising and setting of certain stars, having memorized the positions of hundreds of them. Their charts are in their heads, and they recall the most minute details of islands, shoals, currents, and reefs. Their knowledge allows the Polynesians to navigate difficult channels and to land on islands that sit alone amid vast stretches of empty ocean.

They are also guided by the pattern of ocean swells that are shaped by islands many miles away, by the look of clouds, and by the flight of seabirds.

As for sailing against currents and trade winds, the island navigators rely on a sophisticated knowledge of ocean weather. Polynesians have apparently known for centuries that the weather systems that sweep across the Pacific cause the winds to reverse for as long as a week at a time. The reversal provides the patient sailor with a favorable wind.

Although the issue is far from settled, enough is known of the voyaging skills of the Polynesians to conclude that they could have ventured well beyond their island realm, sailing to the New World and back sometime in the unrecorded past. □

Against a threatening sky, a replica of an ancient Polynesian sailing canoe voyages through Pacific waters, navigated only by the pattern of ocean swells.

Roman Coins in America

Hundreds, perhaps thousands, of ancient Roman coins have turned up at various sites in the United States, among them a garden in Oshkosh, Wisconsin; a streambed near Black Mountain, North Carolina; and a field just outside Phenix City, Alabama.

Some researchers maintain that such finds are proof of European visits to the New World in antiquity. Skeptics counter that the coins have never been found with other artifacts that might support these claims. They also note that the reports seem 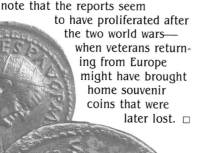 to have proliferated after the two world wars— when veterans returning from Europe might have brought home souvenir coins that were later lost. □

Death-Dealing Clue to Pacific Voyages

The blowgun—accurate, silent, and deadly—is found in many parts of the world. But in tropical Asia and South America, the designs are so alike that some anthropologists propose that the weapon must have been carried to the New World by its Asian inventors, perhaps as many as 6,000 years ago.

The chief proponent of this theory is Stephen C. Jett, a geographer at the University of California at Davis. In a study lasting more than thirty years, Jett has examined hundreds of blowgun reports from explorers and anthropologists. And although some scholars remain skeptical of the geographer's conclusions, none has refuted his specific findings.

A rudimentary blowgun can be made by simply rolling a leaf to form a tube, but the weapon is usually considerably more complex. Jett discovered that blowguns in regular use by ancient peoples in Asia and South America were elaborate and multiform—and, in all their variations, remarkably similar from culture to culture.

The guns could be as short as eighteen inches, Jett found, or as long as twenty-three feet. The most complex ones were made of nested tubes, whose inner barrels were composed of one or two carefully fitted bamboo stems that provided a smooth passage for the projectile. The inner barrels were set inside outer barrels of rigid bamboo or of palm stem. Other guns were made of palm stems that were split, hollowed out, and then rejoined with glue and wrapped with bark.

In all, Jett was able to compare fifty-nine characteristics of the construction and use of blowguns, finding in the process that virtually all types of the weapon had been used on both sides of the Pacific, and used in similar ways for similar purposes.

Both Asian and American blowguns featured sights to help aim them, and the largest often had curved bores to compensate for the inevitable sag in their long barrels. Carved, painted, or inlaid decorations occasionally adorned blowguns of both hemispheres. And, wherever the weapons were found, mouthpieces of various kinds helped make them more efficient. In both Asia and America, a variety of projectiles were used, including darts dipped in poison derived from tree sap.

To Jett, the similarities are telling: Eighty-six percent of the traits of American blowguns are found in Asia. Either American technology developed along a remarkably parallel path or—more likely, says Jett—South American Indians learned much from Asian mentors who somehow made their way across the vast Pacific Ocean. □

The Rabbit in the Moon

From earliest times, people have gazed up at the moon and seen images in its shadowed landscape. In fact, no fewer than thirty creatures and artifacts are associated by various cultures with the patterns formed by the lunar mountains and valleys.

To modern Western eyes, few lunar images might seem less likely than the lowly rabbit. And yet, ancient cultures on opposite sides of the world saw that very animal—a fact that some believe helps prove long-ago contact between peoples of Asia and those of Mesoamerica.

In the years between the birth of Jesus of Nazareth and the arrival of the Spanish in the sixteenth century, the rabbit-in-the-moon motif was ubiquitous in the art of the Mixtec, Maya, Aztec, and other indigenous cultures of Central America. The same theme was common in China during the Han dynasty, which ruled from 207 BC to AD 220, and the Chinese apparently inherited the image from early cultures of India.

To be sure, a symbol's appearance in several cultures is not, in itself, persuasive evidence of trans-oceanic contact. But the sundry rabbits in the moon had several things in common in all the societies where the image appeared, and this intrigues anthropologists exploring the possibility of ancient voyages across the Pacific.

On both sides of the world, there are striking similarities in the myths surrounding the motif: In China, the rabbit was placed on the moon by Buddha as a reward for sacrificing itself so the Holy One could eat. The Aztec legend also involved a rabbit being sent skyward by a god, in this case a disgruntled deity who was trying to dim the light of a second sun. The rabbit accomplished the desired effect, in the process transforming the extra sun into the moon.

Moreover, in the tradition of both Old World and New, the rabbit is associated with intoxication and drugs. Banners and stone carvings in China show hares grinding the mushrooms used for ceremonial drugs. In India, the moon god, Soma, was a patron of liquor and drugs. Similarly, the Aztec moon goddess, Mayauel, held sway over revelry and drunkenness.

Some scholars believe that these correspondences must be more than coincidental. The rabbit in the moon, they contend, is part of a complex of evidence indicating that by the first century AD, Asian mariners had exported certain customs and beliefs to Mesoamerica. □

A number of ancient peoples may have had the ability to plot a course across the seas. Stars were used as navigational aids in a number of seafaring societies as early as the sixth century BC.

Ancient artists' renderings from China (above) and Mesoamerica (top) show the rabbit in the moon. To some researchers, the similar motifs suggest an early contact between the cultures.

A Paper Trail from Asia to the Americas

Wherever in the world humans have lived near tropical forests, it seems, they have sooner or later learned to use trees to make cloth and paper. The basic processes of stripping, softening, drying, and finishing the bark are simple enough, but they can have scores of intricate variations.

A few decades ago, the widespread but differing nature of this technology caught the imagination of the anthropologist Paul Tolstoy. He undertook to learn everything there is to know about how ancient tropics dwellers made cloth and paper. After studying the relics of cultures all over the world, he decided that, in all likelihood, long-ago seafarers from Southeast Asia brought the art of papermaking to the middle Americas.

In reaching this intriguing conclusion, Tolstoy charted the 119 possible features of bark paper manufacturing and correlated them with the practices of fifty-nine ancient societies. He tallied similarities and differences and found varying degrees of both. Finally, he pinpointed a papermaking connection between certain communities of central Mexico and villages of Celebes, now called Sulawesi, an Indonesian island east of Borneo.

Tolstoy's statistics were striking: Of the 119 manufacturing characteristics, 92 were shared by the cultures of central Mexico and Celebes. Moreover, two-thirds of the common characteristics had rarely occurred in the other areas of the world.

In both Celebes and central Mexico, for example, papermakers boiled their bark in an alkaline mixture of water and wood ashes. The boiling process itself is fairly rare among other bark-using peoples, and the use of identical mixtures in this manufacturing step seems beyond mere happenstance. For the subsequent beating, both cultures used grooved stone racquets with flexible handles. In addition, both of them joined pieces of bark by felting them, or beating their edges together so that fibers intertwined.

To the layperson, these similarities alone might seem to lie well outside the possibility of mere coincidence. But Tolstoy, a careful scientist, reasoned otherwise. Since types of beaters and methods of softening and joining were major influences on the finished product, the anthropologist conjectured, it was possible—however unlikely—that two widely separated societies might devise identical tools and strategies, given identical challenges.

So thinking, he sought to pinpoint trivial or arbitrary factors—equipment that could be used or procedures that could be done in almost any fashion, or eliminated entirely, without affecting the quality of the product or ease of processing. But even in this more stringent test, the commonalities held: The two societies seemed to have identical routines for the most arbitrary tasks. For example, both used a special board rather than a log or other surface on which to beat the bark.

Along with method, timing seems to support Tolstoy's argument that the art of bark processing made the journey

Although one is missing a handle, bark beaters from Celebes *(right)* and Mexico *(left)* exhibit similar design. Both are rectangular with grooves on top and bottom, and both took a handle. The implements were used in nearly identical bark paper-making processes on opposite sides of the globe.

from Southeast Asia to central Mexico. Surviving tools and samples of Asian bark cloth and paper date to between 2000 and 1000 BC. The first evidence of bark processing in Mexico is dated a thousand years later.

Paul Tolstoy's diligent scholarship and his stature as professor of anthropology at the University of Montreal have helped muster support for his theory from many of his colleagues in the field. Even so, although he himself is certain of his findings, Tolstoy makes no outsize claims for the theory built on his painstaking research. "I would not consider it proven," he comments. "In our field, I don't think there is too much that can be proven." □

Romans in Brazil

Relics of the days of colonial rule, the remains of more than 100 English, French, and Portuguese ships lie buried in the mud of Rio de Janiero's harbor. Among the wrecks, though, is one anomalous ruin that could challenge the accepted history of South American discovery. It is, some believe, the carcass of a Roman trading ship from the third century AD.

In 1976, a Brazilian diver working in Guanabara Bay, about fifteen miles from Rio, came to the surface with two large amphorae—tall stoneware jars used by ancient Mediterranean seafarers to store such things as water and oil. The government confiscated the jars, whereupon the diver refused to disclose where he had found them.

In 1982, however, he led an American underwater archaeologist, Robert Marx, to the find. Marx retrieved thousands of pottery fragments and more than 200 necks of amphorae from the silt. Working from photographs, Elizabeth Will, a professor of classical studies at the University of Massachusetts at Amherst and an expert on amphorae, dated the jars to the third century AD and pinpointed their origin to the old Roman city of Kouass on

the Moroccan coast.

Marx also probed the harbor floor with sonar and located the remains of a wooden ship—presumably the Roman trader—buried beneath a sixteenth-century wreck.

But before more conclusive exploration could be done, the Brazilian government ordered a halt. Local historians with sentimental ties to Brazil's mother country, Portugal, were outraged at the potential assault on their history. The Portuguese assert that the first European to land on Brazilian soil was Pedro Álvars Cabral. The story is disputed by the Spanish, who say their own Vicente Yáñez Pinzón was first. Both landed sometime in 1500.

In any event, Spain and Portugal became involved in the case, accusing Marx of being an agent of the Italian government—which was, supposedly, bent on establishing claim to an early Roman discovery of the New World. And Brazilian archaeologists, who had once identified the amphorae as Greek or Phoenician, began branding Robert Marx a sensation-seeking fortune hunter.

Other archaeologists are more

open-minded about the wreck's origin. They point to the fact that Roman wrecks have been found as far west as the Azores and that in more recent times hundreds of ships have been forced across the Atlantic by storms and currents. It would not be surprising, they say, if the same had happened to some Roman ships during their voyages along Africa's coast. □

The Shards of Controversy

In 1956, Emilio Estrada, a young Ecuadorian businessman with an interest in the ancient history of his country, began excavating a garbage dump left by the prehistoric residents of the fishing village of Valdivia. Out of the excavation came 36,000 pottery shards, along with numerous artifacts of bone, shell, and stone—and an enduring debate over the meaning of the find.

Estrada himself addressed the problem of origins slowly and carefully. Over a period of several years, he cataloged Valdivia's yield and had the wood and bone fragments carbon-dated. His results showed that the pottery shards were 4,000 to 4,500 years old—at the time, the oldest known pottery in South America. More startling still were the pottery designs. He noted that they were remarkably similar to a style of pottery known as Jomon, which was made during the same ancient period half a world away in Japan.

Estrada concluded that Japanese mariners had sailed to the New World, bringing with them not only their own pots but also pot-making knowledge that was new to the natives. Perhaps the travelers were a band of fishermen, he speculated, blown off course by a Pacific gale. Less likely, they might have been adventurers who set out deliberately to colonize new lands.

No matter how—or if—the Jomon influence arrived, a comparison of Valdivian and Jomon artifacts revealed a remarkable correlation. Experts at the Smithsonian Institution confirmed that twenty-four of the twenty-eight major characteristics of the Valdivian pots were found in Jomon pottery. Their decorative elements and the construction of their spouts were among the most striking of the similarities.

Such resemblances did not, however, settle the matter. Some critics have questioned the accuracy of carbon-dating. Moreover, later excavation in nearby Colombia unearthed pottery that was a thousand years older than the Valdivia finds, casting some doubt on the notion that the Japanese had introduced pottery to Ecuador. Nevertheless, proponents of the Jomon connection cling to their theory and hope that the long-ago garbage dump at Valdivia will one day yield the evidence that will prove them to be right. □

Incised striations on pottery shards from Japan *(far left)* resemble those on shards from Ecuador *(near left)*. Some anthropologists believe the similarity results from transpacific contact between the two cultures in ancient times.

PRE-ANCIENTS

Although it defies the studied findings of historians and archaeologists, the concept is simple enough: Somewhere in the distant past existed civilizations more advanced than those of ancient China, Egypt, Greece, or Rome—and perhaps more advanced even than our own. There are no verifiable chronicles or ruins from those pre-ancient times, the enthusiasts explain, because the wondrous worlds that flourished then were utterly destroyed in a titanic cataclysm. But a handful of lucky survivors escaped the destruction and helped found some of the early civilizations that are known to modern scholarship.

At the heart of this view is the notion that these early civilizations were too brilliant to have leaped into being without guidance and inspiration from the deeper past. Just what the sources of the guidance might have been is not always clear, although some of the more extravagant advocates—such as writer Erich von Däniken—propose that the seeds of pre-ancient earthly civilization were planted by beings from another planet.

Not surprisingly, expert opinion dismisses such beliefs, and proponents are hard put to produce any proofs for their theories. Some point to legends of the lost continent of Atlantis, others to the old and well-nigh universal myths of a pre-ancient existence washed away by a global flood. Still other believers proffer a random array of peculiar signs and curious artifacts—among them a wood-handled metal hammer and a supposed spark plug found encased in apparently solid stone.

Reports of such evidence are fascinating. But without more tangible signs of a pre-ancient world, it is well to acknowledge the fact—almost as marvelous—that the human race as we know it is solely responsible for the climb from primitivism to high civilization.

Map of the Ancient Sea Kings?

In 1929, workers cleaning the Topkapi Palace harem of the last of the Turkish sultans chanced upon a torn and dusty map. It seemed to be a rendering of the coasts of Africa, Spain, and South America. But closer inspection would show it to be more than that. Indeed, it would lead some researchers to claim that ancient seafarers from an unknown civilization discovered Antarctica—and accurately mapped it— thousands of years ago.

Painted on gazelle skin, the map was made in 1513 by a Turkish admiral and one-time pirate named Piri Re'is. No one knows how it disappeared for more than four centuries, but its discovery caused a sensation. What first startled cartographers and historians was an inscription on the map explaining that it was partly based on a chart drawn by Christopher Columbus: "It is reported thus; that a Genoese infidel, his name was Colombo, he it was who discovered these places." There was speculation that the Piri Re'is map might be a link to the fabled Lost Map of Columbus, a chart that the Italian navigator supposedly drew of the West Indies. So thinking, the governments of the United States and Turkey

The Piri Re'is map *(above)* shows part of Africa's west coast and South America's east coast. Some theorists think the southernmost extension of South America at the bottom of the map corresponds to the northwest coast of Antarctica, shown at the bottom of the modern map at left.

began a search for maps related to the sixteenth-century parchment.

They came up empty-handed, and enthusiasm over the map waned, despite important lingering mysteries associated with it. How, for instance, had the map placed Africa and South America at nearly correct longitudes some two centuries before the invention of the chronometer, a precision timepiece modern navigators consider essential for determining longitude? In any case, little was heard of the map for the next twenty-five years or so. Then, in 1956, Arlington Mallery, an archaeologist, engineer, and old-map expert known for propounding the theory that the Vikings reached America before Columbus, studied a copy of it and reached a surprising conclusion.

Mallery claimed that what at first seems to be the extreme southern portion of South America—an area the map depicts as an archipelago stretching southeastward beneath Africa—is actually the bays and islands of Antarctica's northern coast. It has generally been thought that Antarctica's existence was unknown to the world until the 1820s. But if Mallery was right, then someone knew the continent's northern lineaments in the sixteenth century and perhaps—depending on the sources Piri Re'is used to make his map—far earlier.

A hint of just how early the original sources may have been lies in another intriguing feature of the Piri Re'is chart. Geologists believe Antarctica has been buried under ice for two million years. Yet the map appears to include altitudes of mountains now under glaciers. The map's features also correspond dramatically to a 1949 topographical profile of the area, made with seismological equipment. These factors seem to indicate that, somehow, an ancient cartographer mapped at least part of the continent when it was free of ice.

Obviously, no one believes that seafarers visited Antarctica two million years ago. But there is speculation that a much more recent global warming temporarily loosed parts of northern Antarctica from the ice, possibly making it accessible to ancient sailors.

John G. Weihaupt, a University of Colorado specialist in seismology and gravity and planetary geology, is among those holding to this theory. Weihaupt has conducted studies at several antarctic research stations. Along with a number of other geologists, he contends that between 6,000 and 9,000 years ago, the earth was warmer and the glaciers encasing the southernmost continent may have receded for about a thousand years. According to Weihaupt, the melting would have been most likely along Antarctica's western archipelago—the part allegedly shown on the Piri Re'is map.

After reading opinions pro and con about the Piri Re'is map, the scientist questions its authenticity. But he believes certain similarly old maps are authentic and suggest Antarctica may have been known to some seafarers before 1500. Although the original sources used for these Renaissance maps are unknown, Weihaupt says, it is not unthinkable that ancient voyagers trading along the coast of Africa during the global warming thousands of years ago could have gone as far south as Antarctica.

What Weihaupt offers as a tentative theory, another scholar, the late Charles H. Hapgood, asserted as fact. A cartographer and historian at Keene Teachers College in New Hampshire, Hapgood conducted a seven-year investigation of Arlington Mallery's work on the Piri Re'is map. After painstakingly comparing and replotting the topographical features on the Piri Re'is map and other old charts with correspondences on modern maps, the Harvard-trained Hapgood concluded that many geographical features were a close match. In his 1966 book, *Maps of the Ancient Sea Kings: Evidence of Advanced Civilization in the Ice Age*, he wrote that the old maps were "the first hard evidence that advanced peoples preceded all the peoples now known to history." These ancients, Hapgood said, sailed the world pole to pole. "Unbelievable as it may appear," he wrote, "the evidence nevertheless indicates that some ancient people explored the coasts of Antarctica when its coasts were free of ice."

Many experts doubt Mallery's conclusions and deem Hapgood's theory extravagant. Some discount the map's authenticity; others note that even if it is a sixteenth-century chart, Renaissance cartographers often included an "imaginary" southern continent on their maps for symmetry. But if Piri Re'is's Antarctica is a work of the imagination, it seems to be one with an unusual correspondence to reality. Thus controversy about the intriguing parchment continues, and the mystery remains. □

Polar Bearings

Although some scientists doubt the authenticity of the Piri Re'is map *(pages 126-127)*, there is no doubt that another map showing a continent at the South Pole does date from the sixteenth century— some 300 years before the modern discovery of Antarctica. Moreover, this second map *(below)* is more detailed than the Piri Re'is chart, depicting the continent in its entirety and rather closely approximating its correct shape. The map even shows mountain ranges and rivers that, some contend, correspond to those that long ago

vanished beneath glacial ice.

It was devised in 1531 by a Frenchman named Orontius Fineus, a famous cartographer of his day. Fineus carved the world map in the form of a woodcut, and its original prints were bound together in a volume recounting sea voyages. The map's depiction of Antarctica's shape resembles those in modern-day maps, although, when relative scales are adjusted, Fineus's southern continent is much bigger than the real Antarctica, and there are other notable discrepancies. The rotation of the continent in the Fineus map is off by about

twenty degrees, for example, and the long Antarctic Peninsula found on a modern map is absent in the sixteenth-century chart.

Even so, the similarity in shape between Fineus's version and the real Antarctica led historian Charles Hapgood to point to the Fineus map as further proof of his theory that "ancient sea kings," roaming the oceans millennia ago, visited and mapped the polar continent before their civilization mysteriously vanished. Hapgood claimed many corre-

spondences between the old map and modern ones of Antarctica, contending that mountains featured on the Fineus map tally with mountains that have only recently been proved to exist.

His theory has garnered some support. For instance, in 1961, a U.S. Air Force cartographic expert, Captain Lorenzo W. Burroughs, examined the map and vouched for its accuracy. "Beyond a shadow of a doubt," Burroughs said, the Fineus map was "compiled from accurate source maps of Antarctica." By and large, however, the scientific community has discounted Hapgood's assertions. Resemblances between the old map and modern ones, the critics say, are merely coincidences, flukes, the results of lucky guesswork.

According to detractors, Hapgood, though well-intentioned and intellectually honest, was led astray by his enthusiasm for his theory. Cartographic historian David Woodward, a professor of geography at the University of Wisconsin, contends that Hapgood reached his conclusions by vastly overstating similarities between the Fineus map and modern maps and by ignoring discrepancies.

These critics note that the existence of a southern polar continent was widely accepted by sixteenth-century cartographers; indeed, the notion stretched back to antiquity. Many mapmakers of the early Renaissance included a Terra Australis, or "Southern Land," if for no other reason than to give the globe symmetry. In 1520, when the Portuguese navigator Ferdinand Magellan nagivated the strait that now bears his name, most geographers assumed logically—if erroneously—that he had sailed through a

narrow passage separating what is now South America from the long-sought southernmost continent. Thus, at the time Fineus and other cartographers were making their maps, there was fresh support for the polar continent theory.

As to correspondences involving mountains and rivers, critics again contend that Hapgood waxed extravagant in support of his theory. "He didn't realize that unknown coastlines were frequently shown with rivers and headlands," Professor Woodward points out, adding that Hapgood allowed himself considerable geographic license in drawing comparisons between mountains and river channels shown in the Fineus map and actual topographic features that have

been scanned seismologically. And David Jolly, publisher of a handbook for dealers in rare maps, notes that it was common for sixteenth-century cartographers to include in their maps lands more fabled than real and to embellish them not only with rivers and mountains but sometimes even with fictional cities.

Despite these criticisms, Charles Hapgood's theory persists, and the Fineus map continues to intrigue students of cartography. If the likeness between the old woodcut and today's maps is only a coincidence, it is nevertheless a remarkable one. And if Fineus was only guessing when he carved the shape of his polar continent, the guess was uncanny. □

A Rock-Bound Spark Plug

On February 13, 1961, rock hunter Mike Mikesell was working the Coso Mountains near Olancha, California, when he found what he took to be a geode—a hollow stone nodule lined with crystals. But the next day, as he cut the specimen open—ruining a diamond saw blade in the process—he made a singular discovery. His find was not a geode but an ordinary rock—and lodged within it were the apparent remains of a mechanical part, a two-millimeter shaft of porcelain and metal resembling a modern-day spark plug. Mikesell's saw had sliced cleanly through this object.

The Coso artifact, as it soon was called, sparked a continuing controversy. Although the specimen has never been examined closely by independent investigators, the out-

er layer of geological material—sometimes referred to as hardened clay rather than rock—reportedly is peppered with fossil shells and fragments dating to at least 500,000 years ago. This crust is also said to contain two objects resembling a nail and a washer.

Enthusiasts persist in upholding the tantalizing notion that the Coso artifact is a technological remnant of some unknown, long-lost civilization. Critics, noting the numerous abandoned mineshafts in the Coso Mountain area, speculate that the artifact is indeed a spark plug but that it came from an engine used in mining operations. Over the years, they say, the plug became concreted with local mud and fossil debris that took on the appearance of rock. □

A Texas Hammer

During an outing near London, Texas, in June 1934, Emma Hahn and her family came across a rock with a most unusual feature: A fragment of wood was protruding from its surface. Later, after breaking open the rock, the Hahns were surprised to find that the wood was in fact the splintered handle of a hammer—whose well-worn iron head remained intact.

Rock formations in the area where the hammer was found have been reliably dated to the Ordovician geological epoch of nearly a half-billion years ago. The rock encasing the hammer has similar characteristics, leading some enthusiasts to maintain that the tool itself must therefore be an artifact surviving from that distant time.

No part of the implement has been subjected to rigorous testing or dating procedures, however. And most scientists who have considered the case of the rock-bound hammer conclude that it is a result of a natural process of accretion. This occurs when mineral-rich water evaporates, leaving behind deposits that build up until an object becomes completely encased. The process can take place quite quickly: In the Pacific, for example, artifacts from World War II have been found enclosed in rock. The most likely origin of the Texas hammer, it seems, is that it was lost or discarded by a nineteenth-century miner and then encased in material washed from nearby Ordovician rock. □

Atlantean Avenue

For centuries, believers in a great pre-ancient civilization have sought remnants of the lost continent of Atlantis. First described in the fourth century BC by the Greek philosopher Plato—who wrote that his account was based on earlier Egyptian sources—Atlantis is said to have been a huge landmass located somewhere in the Atlantic Ocean. Its inhabitants developed a highly advanced culture and sought to impose their rule on the whole world. Then, some 9,000 years before Plato's time, the entire continent was destroyed by volcanic eruptions and floods.

Many critics, starting with Aristotle, have declared Atlantis a myth concocted by Plato to demonstrate his own political theories. But modern believers have countered that the city of Troy was also deemed a myth until Heinrich Schliemann's discovery in 1873 of a Bronze Age citadel near the Turkish town of Hissarlik. Subsequent excavations have convinced mainstream archaeologists that this was indeed the site of the city-state that inspired the Greek poet Homer's epic work.

Similarly, remnants of Minoan culture on the island of Crete, first excavated in 1900, indicate that this great maritime power was destroyed by a series of cataclysmic volcanic events. This and other parallels have convinced many scholars that garbled tales of the vanished Minoan empire must have been the source of Plato's story about the island of Atlantis.

Opponents of this view agree

that an eruption probably ended Minoan civilization in about 1500 BC but point out that Plato said Atlantis vanished thousands of years before then. Experts explain that this time discrepancy could be the result of a simple error in translation from earlier Egyptian texts; others, though, insist that Plato's chronology is correct and that in any case traces of Atlantis are to be found beyond the Mediterranean—just as Plato declared.

Bolstering this notion are the prognostications of American psychic healer and prophet Edgar Cayce, who died in 1945. Claiming to be in contact with the souls of departed Atlanteans, Cayce predicted that in the late 1960s portions of the lost continent would begin to rise off the coast of the Bahamas. Indeed, in 1968, divers exploring half a mile off the western end of the island of North Bimini discovered a series of intriguing stone slabs lying on the seabed in twenty feet of water. Varying in weight between about one ton and ten tons each, the slabs were arranged in rows, the longest one running along for some 1,600 feet and terminating in a 90 degree bend.

The fitted appearance of the blocks prompted certain enthusiasts to see them as the remains of an ancient wall or road, a view that attracted a number of supporters, among them a Miami zoologist and amateur archaeologist by the name of J. Manson Valentine, who concluded that the arrangement was man-made. Geologists, however, stated that the stones were simply a natural formation of weathered beach rock.

Under the right conditions, they explained, tidal washes of calcium-carbonate-rich seawater can cement together individual grains of sand to form layers of rock in a relatively brief time; temperature extremes and the erosion of sand beneath the formation can then cause regular blocklike fractures. Such formations are not uncommon elsewhere on Bimini and indeed in other parts of the world where there are similar environmental conditions.

Proponents of an arisen Atlantis argued that although the stones may be beach rock, this was merely a convenient local source of building material for the ancients. Moreover, they pointed to the existence of fluted marble columns nearby. But examination of the seabed beneath the columns revealed the remains of a packing crate, along with other debris that indicated a modern-era shipwreck or grounding, a familiar occurrence in those waters. As for the blocks, a series of core samples taken to reveal the characteristics of the stone's internal layers showed that the rocks had not been moved since their natural formation. If there ever was a lost Atlantis, then, it was not located off the shores of Bimini. □

Footprints of the Pre-Ancients

A curious paleontologist from the American Museum of Natural History gave an unwitting boost to the notion of civilizations long predating the scope of modern archaeologists and historians. At the end of a fossil hunting season in the Southwest in 1938, Roland T. Bird was checking a last lead before returning to New York. At a curio shop in Gallup, New Mexico, he examined two thick, flat rocks, each bearing the imprint of a fifteen-inch humanlike foot. The prints were obviously carved fakes (such as the one above), but the store clerk told Bird that some dinosaur tracks, taken from the same locale as the supposed giant human prints, were on display at the owner's other shop in Lupton, Arizona. The reptilian tracks, too, had been recently carved, but they were so anatomically correct that the scientist set out to find the originals from which they had been copied.

His search took him to Glen Rose, Texas. There, firmly imprinted in 100,000,000-year-old rock, he found an abundance of dinosaur tracks. Locals then led him to a ◊

These ancient footprints in a Texas riverbed were once touted as "man tracks," but paleontologists have confirmed that the track makers were dinosaurs, not giant humans.

less distinct print along the Paluxy River. This, they said, was a "man track." Bird at once realized that it was made by a dinosaur. But the print was indistinct and could look human to the untrained eye.

As news of Bird's investigations spread, a garbled version gained currency. It was said that he had found unmistakably human footprints alongside those of a dinosaur. The garbled report was seized upon by numerous enthusiasts, some of whom trekked to Glen Rose and uncovered more of the supposed man tracks—proving, they claimed, that a race of humans walked the earth eons ago. These were the people, said the believers, who raised the advanced civilizations that were destroyed by the cataclysms described in the legends of so many cultures.

Many of the most ardent supporters have long since reexamined and renounced the Glen Rose "man tracks." Others, though, maintain that the area may yet provide proof for their theories. And there are some who buttress their case by citing similar discoveries elsewhere. For example, in 1884, quarry workers near Lake Managua, Nicaragua, found numerous unmistakably human prints in sandstone buried under twelve feet of seemingly ancient strata. At about the same time, humanlike prints were found in a shale stratum at the State Penitentiary in Carson City, Nevada. And, in 1938, prints discovered in 250-million-year-old rock near Berea, Kentucky, looked so human that a local geology professor, Wilbur Burroughs, ascribed them to a creature he dubbed *Phenanthropus mirabilis* (looks human, remarkable).

The scientific community has dismissed such evidence with various explanations. The Nicaraguan footprints, for example, were in a volcanically active area where periodic eruptions, followed by rapid revegetation, could have occurred many times. Hence, the extensive deposition does not necessarily indicate an age greater than the 20,000 years humans are thought to have been in the Americas. The Carson City prints are explained by the fossilized sloth remains found at the same location; sloth prints resemble the human version. And the Berea, Kentucky, footprints were no surprise to anthropologists who had long known of a local Indian tribe that customarily carved such prints along with other figures used in their religion. Still other human-footprint-like features have been ascribed to ancient animal and insect burrows and the random effects of erosion on different forms of rock. □

Some Curious Finds

The belief that advanced human civilizations flourished during prehistoric times stretches back at least to the nineteenth century. So, too, does a record of singular archaeological finds that are often cited to support the possibility. However, it is impossible to examine any of the physical evidence: None of the alleged artifacts or remains has survived to the present time.

Similarly, although many of the reports appear to have been gathered by earnest and dependable witnesses, even accounts by scientific authorities are suspect. Geology and paleontology were young sciences at the time, still lacking a comprehensive body of theory to explain rock formation and develop reliable dating techniques. And the possibility of fraud or hoax cannot be ruled out. Whatever the underlying truth may be, the volume and the variety of these reports make for an intriguing catalog of antiquarian lore:

- In his *Fossils of the South Downs,* published in 1822, British surgeon and amateur geologist Gideon Mantell chronicled a number of anomalous finds, including references to other works. For example, he noted the 1791 account of an M. Leisky of Hamburg, Germany, who fractured a piece of flint and discovered an "ancient brass pin" in the center. Mantell also mentioned the discovery of 126 silver coins enclosed in flints at Grinoe, Denmark.

- In 1831, *The American Journal of Science and Arts* reported a curious find in a marble quarry some twelve miles northwest of Philadelphia. While cutting a thirty-cubic-foot slab, workers found a 1½ by ⅝ inch indentation in the stone. In the center of this were two raised symbols resembling the letters *NI.*

- On Christmas Eve, 1851, the *Times* of London reported the case of a miner who was returning from the California gold fields with a large block of gold-bearing quartz. After accidentally dropping and breaking his sample, the man discovered an iron nail embedded near its center.

- In June 1852, *Scientific American* appealed to its readership for help in solving a puzzling discovery near Dorchester, Massachusetts, the year before. After blasting a formation of pudding stone, workers found two halves of a bell-shaped vessel. Described as 4½ inches high by 6½ inches at the base and 2½ inches at the top, the object, adorned with silver inlaid flowers, baffled local antiquarians. One speculation was that the article was the bowl of an East Indian water pipe lost in the soil near the blast by one of the sea captains known to have lived in the neighborhood.

- In 1853, the Cusick's Mill quarry, near Zanesville, Ohio, yielded the bones of a woman completely entombed in sandstone that also retained the full impression of her once fleshly form. The Zanesville *Courier* also reported an adjacent cavity that had been molded from a pair of human hands.

- James Parsons and his two sons were mining coal at a strip mine in Hammondsville, Ohio, in the autumn of 1868 when a barrier of coal collapsed, revealing a smooth slate wall said to contain twenty-five hieroglyphic characters carved in bold relief. Scholars could not identify the meaning or origin of the symbols.

- During the winter of 1869, the Miner's Saloon in Treasure City, Nevada, exhibited a piece of feldspar containing a two-inch screw, a specimen lately unearthed from the local Abbey Mine.

- In 1877, crowds in Eureka, Nevada, thrilled to a discovery made in the adjacent hills. There, prospectors had found the bones of a supposedly human leg partly embedded in quartzite. Measuring thirty-nine inches from just above the knees to the tip of the toe, the remains indicated a person of extraordinary stature.

- J. Q. Adams, writing in the May 1883 issue of *American Antiquarian,* reported the discovery of a thimble trapped in a lump of lignite mined from the Marshal Coal Bed in Colorado.

- In June 1891, Mrs. S. W. Culp of Morrisonville, Illinois, was surprised to find a ten-inch gold chain embedded in a lump of coal she was breaking apart for her stove. The local newspaper described the event as "a study for the students of archaeology who love to puzzle their brains over the geological construction of the earth from whose ancient depths the curious is always cropping out." □

ACKNOWLEDGMENTS

The editors wish to thank these individuals and institutions for their valuable assistance in the preparation of this volume:

Jan Amnehäl, Göteborgs Stad Etnografiska Museet, Gothenburg, Sweden; Ferdinand Anton, Munich; François Avril, Conservateur au Départment des Manuscrits, Bibliothèque Nationale, Paris; Brigitte Baumbusch, Scala, Florence, Italy; Robert S. Bianchi, The Brooklyn Museum, New York; Allan G. Bromley, University of Sydney, Australia; D. R. Brothwell, Institute of Archaeology, London; Onno Brouwer, University of Wisconsin, Madison; Edmund Buchner, Kommission für Alte Geschichte und Epigraphik, Munich; Carol R. Butler, Smithsonian Institution, Washington, D.C.; Ron Calais, Lafayette, La.; Jeff Chester, National Air and Space Museum, Washington, D.C.; Cathy Crandal, Washington University, St. Louis, Mo.; Edward M. Croom, Jr., University of Mississippi, University; Simmi Dhanda, New Delhi, India; Anna Maria Donadoni, Museo delle Antichità Egizie, Turin, Italy; James A. Duke, Department of Agriculture, Beltsville, Md.; Arne Eggebrecht, Roemer und Pelizaeus Museum, Hildesheim, West Germany; Clark L. Erickson, University of Pennsylvania, Philadelphia; Judith Fields, The Science Museum, London; Ben R. Finney, University of Hawaii, Honolulu; Christian Fischer, Silkeborg Museum, Denmark; Kenneth Franklin, Port Angeles, Washington; Tim Fraser, London; diya' Abou Ghazi, The Egyptian Antiquities Organization, Cairo; William H. Gotwald, Jr., Utica College, New York; Klaus Grewe, Volker Dünnhaupt, Rheinisches Landesmuseum, Bonn; Joel Grossman, Grossman and Associates, New York; Mark Hall, University of California, Berkeley; Ann Harmon, Laytonsville, Md.; James A. Harrell, University of Toledo, Ohio; Michael R. Harris, Smithsonian Institution, Washington, D.C.; Lothar Haselberger, Kommission für Alte Geschichte und Epigraphik, Munich; Barbara Hicks, London; Whitney Hodges, Washington University, St. Louis, Mo.; H. T. Huang, The Needham Research Institute, Cambridge, England; Lynn H. Hutto, Biopharm U.S.A., Charleston, S.C.; Istituto Archeologico Germanico, Rome; Peter L. Jakab, National Air and Space Museum, Washington, D.C.; Michael Jansen, Forschungsprojekt Mohenjo-Daro, Aachen, West Germany; Boma Johnson, U.S. Department of the Interior, Yuma, Ariz.; Charalambos Karakalos, Hellenic Atomic Energy Committee, Athens; Ivan Katic, The Royal Danish Veterinary and Agricultural Library, Copenhagen; Kay Kavanagh, Brussels; David H. Kelley, Calgary, Alberta; Bob Kiener, Washington, D.C.; Mette Korsholm, The National Museum of Denmark, Copenhagen; Glen J. Kuban, North Royalton, Ohio; Georgia Lee, UCLA Archaeology Department, Los Osos, Calif.; Walter H. Lewis, Washington University, St. Louis, Mo.; Liang Lien-Chu, The Needham Research Institute, Cambridge, England; Michael H. Logan, University of Tennessee, Knoxville; Sue Lundene, Runestone Museum, Alexandria, Minn.; Ewan Mackie, The Hunterian Museum, Glasgow, Scotland; Adel Mahmoud, The Egyptian Museum, Cairo; Michael Marshall, Corales, N.Mex.; Khalil Messiha, Cairo University; Mohammad Mohsen, The Egyptian Museum, Cairo; Robert Montgomery, National Museum of Health and Medicine, Washington, D.C.; William Morgan, Jacksonville, Fla.; Musée Gaumais, Virton, Luxembourg; Joseph Needham, The Needham Research Institute, Cambridge, England; Dr. Larry S. Nichter, Children's Hospital of Los Angeles, Calif.; Charles Ortloff, FMC Corporation, Santa Clara, Calif.; Emmerich Pasztory, Hoechst AG., Frankfurt; Gena F. Paulk, Rock Eagle 4-H Center, Eastonton, Ga.; Margaret Ponting, Callanish, Scotland; Dories Reents-Budet, Duke University, Durham, N.C.; Luisa Ricciarini, Milan; Ed E. Richardson, Dumbarton Oaks, Washington, D.C.; Rudy Rosenburg, Leeches U.S.A., Westbury, N.Y.; Colette Roubet, Directeur du Museum d'Histoire Naturelle, Paris; Jean-Loup Rousselot, Museum für Völkerkunde, Munich; Roy T. Sawyer, Biopharm (U.K.) Ltd., Hendy, South Wales; Denise Schmandt-Besserat, University of Texas, Austin; William A. Shear, Hampton-Sydney College, Va.; Nathan Sivin, University of Pennsylvania, Philadelphia; Duncan Spencer, Washington, D.C.; Warren E. Steiner, Smithsonian Institution, Washington, D.C.; Sayyed Tawfig, The Egyptian Antiquities Organization, Cairo; Allen Thrasher, Library of Congress, Washington, D.C.; Paul Tolstoy, University of Montreal, Canada; Lindley Vann, University of Maryland, College Park; John W. Verano, Smithsonian Institution, Washington, D.C.; Jay Von Werlhof, Imperial Valley College Museum, Centro, Calif.; Jeffrey Wadsworth, Lockheed Missiles and Space Company, Palo Alto, Calif.; John G. Weihaupt, University of Colorado, Denver; Wilfried Werner, Universitätsbibliothek, Handschriftenabteilung, Heidelberg, West Germany; Stephen Williams, Harvard University, Cambridge, Mass.; Bonnie Winslow, Bloomfield, N.Mex.; David Woodward, University of Wisconsin, Madison.

BIBLIOGRAPHY

Books

Ackerknecht, Erwin H., M.D. *A Short History of Medicine*. Baltimore: Johns Hopkins University Press, 1982.

Aikman, Lonnelle. *Nature's Healing Arts: From Folk Medicine to Modern Drugs*. Washington, D.C.: National Geographic Society, 1977.

Alcina Franch, José. *Pre-Columbian Art*. Translated by I. Mark Paris. New York: Harry N. Abrams, 1983.

Ascher, Marcia, and Robert Ascher. *Code of the Quipu*. Ann Arbor: University of Michigan Press, 1981.

Ashe, Geoffrey, et al. *The Quest for America*. New York: Praeger Publishers, 1971.

Asimov, Isaac. *Asimov's Biographical Encyclopedia of Science and Technology*. Garden City, N.Y.: Doubleday, 1964.

Auguet, Roland. *The Roman Games*. St. Albans, Hertfordshire, England: Panther Books, 1975.

Aveni, Anthony F. *Skywatchers of Ancient Mexico*. Austin: University of Texas Press, 1980.

Baines, John and Jaromír Málek. *Atlas of Ancient Egypt*. New York: Facts on File Publications, 1980.

Benét, William Rose. *The Reader's Encyclopedia* (2nd ed.). New York: Thomas Y. Crowell, 1965.

Berkow, Robert, M.D. (Ed.). *The Merck Manual of Diagnosis and Therapy*, (14th ed.). Rahway, N.J.: Merck Sharp & Dohme Research Laboratories, 1982.

Berlitz, Charles. *Mysteries from Forgotten Worlds*. Garden City, N.Y.: Doubleday, 1972.

Blunden, Caroline, and Mark Elvin. *Cultural Atlas of China*. Oxford: Phaidon Press, 1983.

Bord, Janet. *Mazes and Labyrinths of the World*. New York: E. P. Dutton, 1976.

Bord, Janet, and Colin Bord:
Ancient Mysteries of Britain. Manchester, N.H.: Salem House, 1986.
Mysterious Britain. New York: Granada Publishing, 1974.

Brecher, Kenneth, and Michael Feirtag (Eds.).

Astronomy of the Ancients. Cambridge, Mass.: MIT Press, 1979.

Brennan, Martin. The Stars and the Stones: Ancient Art and Astronomy in Ireland. London: Thames & Hudson, 1983.

Brooksmith, Peter (Ed.). The Unexplained: Mysteries of Mind, Space and Time (Vol. 7). New York: Marshall Cavendish, 1986.

Builders of the Ancient World: Marvels of Engineering. Washington, D.C.: Special Publications Division, National Geographic Society, 1986.

Burton, David M. The History of Mathematics: An Introduction. Newton, Mass.: Allyn & Bacon, 1985.

Calder, Nigel. Timescale. New York: Viking Press, 1983.

Canby, Courtlandt. The Past Displayed: A Journey through the Ancient World. Oxford: Phaidon Press, 1980.

Carcopino, Jérôme. Daily Life in Ancient Rome. Edited by Henry T. Rowell, translated by E. O. Lorimer. New Haven: Yale University Press, 1940.

Casson, Lionel, et al. Mysteries of the Past. Edited by Joseph J. Thorndike, Jr. New York: American Heritage, 1977.

Castleden, Rodney. The Wilmington Giant: The Quest for a Lost Myth. Wellingborough, Northamptonshire, England: Turnstone Press, 1983.

Cavendish, Richard:
Mysteries of the Universe. New York: Galahad Books, 1981.
Prehistoric England. New York: British Heritage Press, 1983.

Cazeau, Charles J., and Stuart D. Scott, Jr. Exploring the Unknown: Great Mysteries Reexamined. New York: Plenum Press, 1979.

Charroux, Robert. Forgotten Worlds. Translated by Lowell Bair. New York: Walker, 1973.

Childress, David Hatcher. Lost Cities of Ancient Lemuria & the Pacific. Stelle, Ill.: Adventures Unlimited Press, 1988.

Chippindale, Christopher. Stonehenge Complete. New York: Thames & Hudson, 1983.

Closs, Michael P. (Ed.). Native American Mathematics. Austin: University of Texas Press, 1986.

Coe, Michael, Dean Snow, and Elizabeth Benson. Atlas of Ancient America. New York: Facts on File Publications, 1986.

Cohen, Daniel. The Encyclopedia of the Strange. New York: Dodd, Mead & Co., 1985.

Corliss, William R. (Comp.). Ancient Man: A Handbook of Puzzling Artifacts. Glen Arm, Md.: Sourcebook Project, 1978.

Cornell, Tim, and John Matthews. Atlas of the Roman World. Oxford: Phaidon Press, 1982.

De Camp, L. Sprague, and Catherine C. De Camp.

Ancient Ruins and Archaeology. Garden City, N.Y.: Doubleday, 1964.

Durán, Fray Diego. Book of the Gods and Rites and the Ancient Calendar. Edited and translated by Fernando Horcasitas and Doris Heyden. Norman: University of Oklahoma Press, 1971.

Empires Ascendant (TimeFrame series). Alexandria, Va.: Time-Life Books, 1987.

Facts & Fallacies. Pleasantville, N.Y.: Reader's Digest Association, 1988.

Fischer, Steven Roger. Evidence for Hellenic Dialect in the Phaistos Disk. Berne, Switzerland: Peter Lang, 1988.

Fisher, Douglas Alan. The Epic of Steel. New York: Harper & Row, 1963.

Forbes, R. J. Man the Maker. New York: Abelard-Schuman, 1958.

Fraser, Peter Marshall. Ptolemaic Alexandria. London: Oxford University Press, 1972.

Fu Tianchou. Wonders from the Earth: The First Emperor's Underground Army. San Francisco: China Books and Periodicals, 1989.

Garvin, Richard M. The Crystal Skull. Garden City, N.Y.: Doubleday, 1973.

Gibbs-Smith, Charles H. A History of Flying. London: B. T. Batsford, 1953.

Gordon, Cyrus H. Riddles in History. New York: Crown Publishers, 1974.

Grant, Michael. The Etruscans. New York: Charles Scribner's Sons, 1980.

Gray, Randal, Susan Hill, and Robin L. K. Wood (Eds.). Lost Worlds: Alastair Service. London: Collins, 1981.

Hadingham, Evan. Early Man and the Cosmos. New York: Walker Publishing Co., 1984.

Haining, Peter. Ancient Mysteries. New York: Taplinger Publishing Co., 1977.

Hall, Robert A., Jr. The Kensington Rune-Stone Is Genuine: Linguistic, Practical, Methodological Considerations. Columbia, S.C.: Hornbeam Press, 1982.

Hapgood, Charles H. Maps of the Ancient Sea Kings: Evidence of Advanced Civilization in the Ice Age. New York: Chilton Books, 1966.

Harris, Harold A. Sport in Greece and Rome. London: Thames & Hudson, 1972.

Hart, Olive:
The Dream of Flight. New York: Winchester Press, 1972.
The Prehistory of Flight. Berkeley: University of California Press, 1985.

Hawkins, Gerald S., with John B. White. Stonehenge Decoded. Garden City, N.Y.: Doubleday, 1965.

Hellemans, Alexander, and Bryan Bunch. The Timetables of Science. New York: Simon & Schuster, 1988.

Hitching, Francis. The Mysterious World: An

Atlas of the Unexplained. New York.: Holt, Reinhart & Winston, 1979.

Hyde, Walter Woodburn. Ancient Greek Mariners. New York: Oxford University Press, 1947.

Ifrah, Georges. From One to Zero: A Universal History of Numbers. Translated by Lowell Bair. New York: Viking Penguin, 1985.

Jackson, Ralph. Doctors and Diseases in the Roman Empire. Norman: University of Oklahoma Press, 1988.

Jones, Henry Stuart. Companion to Roman History. Oxford: Clarendon Press, 1912.

Katz, Friedrich. The Ancient American Civilizations. Translated by K. M. Lois Simpson. New York: Praeger Publishers, 1972.

Keuneman, Herbert. Sri Lanka. Edited by John Gottberg Anderson. Hong Kong: APA Productions, 1984.

Kincaid, Chris (Ed.). Chaco Roads Project Phase 1. Albuquerque, N.Mex.: Department of the Interior, Bureau of Land Management, 1983.

Kramer, Samuel Noah. History Begins at Sumer: Thirty-Nine Firsts in Man's Recorded History. Philadelphia: University of Pennsylvania Press, 1981.

Kreig, Margaret B. Green Medicine: The Search for Plants that Heal . . . . Chicago: Rand McNally, 1964.

Krupp, E. C. (Ed.):
Echoes of the Ancient Skies. New York: Harper & Row, 1983.
In Search of Ancient Astronomies. New York: McGraw-Hill, 1978.

Kumar Das, Sri Surendra. Ramayana. Orissa, India: Panchali Publications, 1977.

Laufer, Berthold. The Prehistory of Aviation (Studies in Culture History series). Chicago: Chicago Natural History Museum, 1928.

Leonard, Jonathan Norton, and the Editors of Time-Life Books. Ancient America (Great Ages of Man series). New York: Time Incorporated, 1967.

Lewis, David. We, the Navigators. Canberra: Australian National University Press, 1972.

Leyenaar, Ted J. J., and Lee A. Parsons. Ulama: The Ballgame of the Mayas and Aztecs. Leiden, The Netherlands: Spruyt, Van Mantgem & De Does, 1988.

Lisowski, F. P. "Prehistoric and Early Historic Trepanation." In Diseases in Antiquity, edited and compiled by Don Brothwell and A. T. Sandison. Springfield, Ill.: Charles C Thomas, 1967.

Lyons, Albert S., M.D., and R. Joseph Petrucelli II, M.D. Medicine: An Illustrated History. New York: Harry N. Abrams, 1978.

Lyttle, Richard B. The Games They Played: Sports in History. New York: Atheneum, 1982.

McKern, Sharon S. *Exploring the Unknown: Mysteries in American Archaeology.* New York: Praeger Publishers, 1972.

McMann, Jean. *Riddles of the Stone Age: Rock Carvings of Ancient Europe.* London: Thames & Hudson, 1980.

Magic and Medicine of Plants. Pleasantville, N.Y.: Reader's Digest Association, 1986.

Majno, Guido. *The Healing Hand: Man and Wound in the Ancient World.* Cambridge, Mass.: Harvard University Press, 1975.

Margetts, Edward L. "Trepanation of the Skull by the Medicine-Men of Primitive Cultures." In *Diseases in Antiquity,* edited and compiled by Don Brothwell and A. T. Sandison. Springfield, Ill.: Charles C Thomas, 1967.

Marshack, Alexander. *The Roots of Civilization: The Cognitive Beginnings of Man's First Art, Symbol and Notation.* New York: McGraw-Hill, 1972.

Matthews, William Henry. *Mazes and Labyrinths.* Detroit: Singing Tree Press, Book Tower, 1969 (original publication, 1922).

Mayr, Otto (Ed.). *Philosophers and Machines.* New York: Science History Publications, 1976.

Menninger, Karl. *Number Words and Number Symbols: A Cultural History of Numbers.* Translated by Paul Broneer. Cambridge, Mass.: MIT Press, 1969.

Michell, John. *Megalithomania.* Ithaca, New York: Cornell University Press, 1982.

Michell, John, and Robert J. M. Rickard. *Phenomena: A Book of Wonders.* London: Thames & Hudson, 1977.

Moffatt, Michael. *The Origins* (Vol. 1 of *The Ages of Mathematics).* Garden City, N.Y.: Doubleday, 1977.

Morley, Sylvanus Griswold, and George W. Brainerd. *The Ancient Maya* (4th ed.). Revised by Robert J. Sharer. Stanford: Stanford University Press, 1983.

Morley, Sylvanus Griswold, and J. Eric S. Thompson. *An Introduction to the Study of the Maya Hieroglyphs.* New York: Dover Publications, 1975.

Moscati, Sabatino. *The Phoenicians.* New York: Abbeville Press, 1988.

Mysteries of the Ancient Americas. Pleasantville, N.Y.: Reader's Digest Association, 1986.

Mystic Places (Mysteries of the Unknown series). Alexandria, Va.: Time-Life Books, 1987.

Needham, Joseph:

Clerks and Craftsmen in China and the West. Cambridge, England: Cambridge University Press, 1970.

Science and Civilisation in China (Vols. 3 & 4). Cambridge, England: Cambridge University Press, 1959.

Trans-Pacific Echoes and Resonances; Listening Once Again. Philadelphia: World Scientific Publishing Co., 1985.

Neugebauer, O. *The Exact Sciences in Antiquity.* Providence, R.I.: Brown University Press, 1957.

Nickell, Joe, with John F. Fischer. *Secrets of the Supernatural: Investigating the World's Occult Mysteries.* Buffalo, N.Y.: Prometheus Books, 1988.

Noorbergen, René. *Secrets of the Lost Races.* New York: The Bobbs-Merrill Co., 1977.

Nordenskiöld, Erland. *Modifications in Indian Culture through Inventions and Loans.* Gothenburg, Sweden: Elanders Boktryckeri Aktiebolag, 1930.

O'Kelly, Michael J. *Newgrange: Archaeology, Art and Legend.* London: Thames & Hudson, 1982.

Palmer, Martin (Ed.). *T'ung Shu: The Ancient Chinese Almanac.* Translated by Martin Palmer with Mak Hin Chung, Kwok Man Ho, and Angela Smith. Boston: Shambhala, 1986.

Parsons, Edward Alexander. *The Alexandrian Library: Glory of the Hellenic World.* New York: Elsevier Press, 1952.

Piggott, Stuart. *The Earliest Wheeled Transport: From the Atlantic Coast to the Caspian Sea.* London: Thames & Hudson, 1983.

Pomerance, Leon. *The Phaistos Disc: An Interpretation of Astronomical Symbols.* Gothenburg, Sweden: Paul Åströms Förlag, 1976.

Ponting, Gerald, and Margaret Ponting. *New Light on the Stones of Callanish.* Callanish, Isle of Lewis: G & M Ponting, 1984.

Prideaux, Tom, and the Editors of Time-Life Books. *Cro-Magnon Man* (The Emergence of Man series). Alexandria, Va.: Time-Life Books, 1973.

Quest for the Past. Pleasantville, N.Y.: Reader's Digest Association, 1984.

Ragette, Friedrich. *Baalbek.* Park Ridge, N.J.: Noyes Press, 1980.

Raschke, Wendy J. (Ed.). *The Archaeology of the Olympics: The Olympics and Other Festivals in Antiquity.* Madison, Wis.: University of Wisconsin Press, 1988.

Renfrew, Colin. *Before Civilization: The Radiocarbon Revolution and Prehistoric Europe.* New York: Alfred A. Knopf, 1973.

Riley, Carroll L., et al. (Eds.). *Man across the Sea: Problems of Pre-Columbian Contacts.* Austin: University of Texas Press, 1971.

Robinson, David M. *Baalbek Palmyra.* New York: J. J. Augustin Publishers, 1946.

Ronan, Colin A. *Lost Discoveries.* New York: McGraw-Hill, 1973.

Sagan, Carl. *Cosmos.* New York: Random House, 1980.

Sanderson, Ivan T. *Investigating the Unexplained: A Compendium of Disquieting Mysteries of the Natural World.* Englewood Cliffs, N.J.: Prentice-Hall, 1972.

Saunders, E. Dale. *Mudra: A Study of Symbolic Gestures in Japanese Buddhist Sculpture.* New York: Pantheon Books, 1960.

Schele, Linda, and Mary Ellen Miller. *The Blood of Kings: Dynasty and Ritual in Maya Art.* Fort Worth, Tex.: Kimbell Art Museum, 1986.

Service, Alastair. *Lost Worlds.* London: Collins, 1981.

Shao, Paul. *Asiatic Influences in Pre-Columbian American Art.* Ames: Iowa State University Press, 1976.

Shirley, Rodney W. *The Mapping of the World: Early Printed World Maps, 1472-1700.* London: Holland Press, 1984.

Singer, Charles, et al. (Eds.). *The Mediterranean Civilizations and the Middle Ages, c. 700 B.C. to c. A.D. 1500* (Vol. 2 of *A History of Technology).* London: Oxford University Press, 1956.

Smith, J. Russell. *The Story of Iron and Steel.* New York: D. Appleton and Co., 1908.

Smith, William, William Wayte, and G. E. Marindin (Eds.). *A Dictionary of Greek and Roman Antiquities* (Vol. I). London: John Murray, 1914.

Stefansson, Vilhjalmur. *Beyond the Pillars of Heracles: The Classical World Seen through the Eyes of Its Discoverers.* Edited by Evelyn Stefansson Nef. New York: Delacorte Press, 1966.

Strange Stories, Amazing Facts. Pleasantville, N.Y.: Reader's Digest Association, 1981.

Sullivan, John W. W. *The Story of Metals.* Cleveland, Ohio: American Society for Metals; Ames: Iowa State College Press, 1951.

Swaddling, Judith. *The Ancient Olympic Games.* London: British Museum Publication, 1980.

Taton, René (Ed.). *Ancient and Medieval Science* (Vol. 1 of History of Science). Translated by A. J. Pomerans. New York: Basic Books, 1963.

Temple, Robert K. G. *China: Land of Discovery.* Wellingborough, Northamptonshire, England: Patrick Stephens, 1986.

Thorndike, Joseph J., Jr. (Ed.). *Discovery of Lost Worlds.* New York: American Heritage Publishing Co., 1979.

Thorwald, Jürgen. *Science and Secrets of Early Medicine.* Translated by Richard Winston and Clara Winston. New York: Harcourt, Brace & World, 1963.

Throckmorton, Peter (Ed.). *The Sea Remembers: Shipwrecks and Archaeology.* New York: Weidenfeld & Nicolson, 1987.

Tomas, Andrew. *We Are Not the First: Riddles of*

Ancient Science. London: Souvenir Press, 1971.

Veer, M. H. J. Th. van der, and P. Moerman. *Hidden Worlds: Fresh Clues to the Past*. London: Souvenir Press, 1974.

Von Hagen, Victor W. *The Desert Kingdoms of Peru*. Greenwich, Conn.: New York Graphic Society Publishers, 1965.

Welfare, Simon and John Fairley. *Arthur C Clarke's Mysterious World*. New York: A & W Publishers, 1980.

Wernick, Robert, and the Editors of Time-Life Books. *The Monument Builders* (The Emergence of Man series). New York: Time-Life Books, 1973.

White, K. D. *Greek and Roman Technology*. London: Thames & Hudson, 1984.

White, Randall. *Dark Caves, Bright Visions: Life in Ice Age Europe*. New York: American Museum of Natural History, in association with W. W. Norton & Co., 1986.

Williamson, Ray A. (Ed.). *Archaeoastronomy in the Americas*. Los Altos, Calif.: Ballena Press, 1981.

Woolf, Harry (Ed.). *The Analytic Spirit*. Ithaca, New York: Cornell University Press, 1981.

The World Almanac Book of the Strange. New York: New American Library, 1977.

The World's Last Mysteries. Pleasantville, N.Y.: Reader's Digest Association, 1977.

Zaslavsky, Claudia. *Africa Counts*. Boston: Prindle, Weber & Schmidt, 1973.

Zhongmin, Han, and Hubert Delahaye. *A Journey through Ancient China*. New York: Gallery Books, 1985.

PERIODICALS

Abercrombie, Thomas J. "Young-Old Lebanon Lives by Trade." *National Geographic*, April 1958.

"African Presence in Early America." *Journal of African Civilizations* (New Brunswick, N.J.), 1987.

Agogino, George A. "The Crystal Skull: Fine Fake or Authentic Artifact?" *Pursuit*, 1982, Vol. 15, no. 3.

Aikman, Lonnelle. "Nature's Gifts to Medicine." *National Geographic*, September 1974.

Aufderheide, Arthur C., M.D. "The Enigma of Ancient Cranial Trepanation." *Minnesota Medicine*, February 1985.

Bergman, Arieh, et al. "Acceleration of Wound Healing by Topical Application of Honey: An Animal Model." *American Journal of Surgery*, March 1983.

Bird, Roland T. "Thunder in His Footsteps." *Natural History*, May 1939.

Bliquez, Lawrence J. "Classical Prosthetics." *Archaeology*, September/October 1983.

"Bloodsuckers from France." *Time*, December 14, 1981.

Browman, David L. "New Light on Andean Tiwanaku." *American Scientist*, 1981, Vol. 69, pp. 408-419.

Brown, Raymond Lamont. "Medicine and Magic in Ancient Eqypt." *History of Medicine*, Autumn 1972.

Cahill, T. A. "The Vinland Map, Revisited: New Compositional Evidence on Its Inks and Parchment." *Analytical Chemistry*, March 15, 1987.

Carlson, John B. "Pre-Columbian Voyages to the New World: An Overiew." *Early Man*, Spring 1980.

Carter, George F. "Fu-Sang: China Discovers America." *Oceans*, May 1978.

Civil, Miguel. "The Invention of Writing." *Humanities*, October 1986.

Colimore, Edward. "In Peru, Unearthing Ancient Farm Methods." *Philadelphia Inquirer*, March 31, 1989.

Conniff, Richard. "The Little Suckers Have Made a Comeback." *Discover*, August 1987.

Cooper, Chris. "Ancient Technology: A Catalogue of Curious Finds." *The Unexplained: Mysteries of Mind, Space & Time* (London), Orbis, 1981.

Cross, Frank Moore, Jr. "The Pheonician Inscription from Brazil: A Nineteenth-Century Forgery." *Orientacia*, 1968, Vol. 37, no. 4.

Dam, Laura van. "Old Lore, New Cure." *Technology Review*, October 1986.

Daniel, Glyn. "The Minnesota Petroglyph." *Antiquity*, 1958.

D'Errico, Francesco. "Palaeolithic Lunar Calendars: A Case of Wishful Thinking?" *Current Anthropology*, 1989, Vol. 30, no. 1.

DeWitt, David A. "The Water-Powered Pyramid." *Pursuit*, 1984, Vol. 17, no. 1.

Efem, S. E. E. "Clinical Observations on the Wound Healing Properties of Honey." *British Journal of Surgery*, July 1988.

Eisner, T., and H. E. Eisner. "Mystery of a Millipede." *Natural History*, March 1965.

Epstein, Jeremiah F. "Pre-Columbian Old World Coins in America: An Examination of the Evidence." *Current Anthropology*, February 1980.

Erickson, Clark L. "Raised Field Agriculture in the Lake Titicaca Basin." *Expedition* (The University Museum), 1989, Vol. 30, no. 3.

"From Reckoning to Writing." *Scientific American*, August 1975.

Godfrey, Laurie R., and John R. Cole. "Blunder in Their Footsteps." *Natural History*, August 1986.

Gray, Willard F. M. "A Shocking Discovery." *Journal of the Electrochemical Society*, September 1963.

Greenwood, Stuart W. "Golden Models of An-

cient Spacecraft?" *Info Journal*, January 1977.

Habeck, Reinhard. "Electricity in Ancient Times." Translated by Ulrich Magin. *Pursuit*, 1985, Vol. 18, no. 1.

Hamblin, Dora Jane. "Unlocking the Secrets of the Giza Plateau." *Smithsonian*, April 1986.

Hathaway, Bruce. "The Ancient Canal That Turned Uphill." *Science 82*, October 1982.

Hencken, Hugh O'Neill. "What Are Pattee's Caves?" *Scientific American*, 1940, Vol. 163, pp. 258-259.

Hitching, Francis. "Sirius B.: Memories of a Distant Star?" *The Unexplained: Mysteries of Mind, Space & Time*, (London), Orbis, 1980.

Hood, M. S. F. "The Tartaria Tablets." *Antiquity*, 1967, Vol. 41, pp. 99-113.

Jett, Stephen C. "The Development and Distribution of the Blowgun." *Annals of the Association of American Geographers*, December 1970.

Jolly, David C. "Was Antarctica Mapped by the Ancients?" *Skeptical Inquirer*, Fall 1986.

Kolata, Alan L. "Tiwanaku and Its Hinterland." *Archaeology*, January/February 1987.

Lechtman, Heather. "Pre-Columbian Surface Metallurgy." *Scientific American*, June 1984.

Lieberman, Stephen J. "Of Clay Pebbles, Hollow Clay Balls, and Writing: A Sumerian View." *American Journal of Archaeology*, July 1980.

Lothrop, Eleanor. "Mystery of the Prehistoric Stone Balls." *Natural History*, September 1955.

McCulloch, J. Huston. "The Bat Creek Inscription: Cherokee Or Hebrew?" *Tennessee Anthropologist*, Fall 1988.

McEwan, Gordon F., and D. Bruce Dickson. "Valdivia, Jomon Fishermen, and the Nature of the North Pacific . . . . ." *American Antiquity*, 1978, Vol. 43, pp. 362-371.

Mahan, Joseph B., Jr. "The Bat Creek Stone." *Tennessee Archaeologist*, February 1973.

Mapes, Glynn. "In Swansea, Wales, There's a Sucker Born Every Minute." *The Wall Street Journal*, September 21, 1989.

Marshack, Alexander:

"Exploring the Mind of Ice Age Man." *National Geographic*, January 1975.

"An Ice Age Ancestor?" *National Geographic*, October 1988.

"Ice Age Art." *Symbols*, Winter 1981.

Maryon, Herbert. "A Note on Magic Mirrors." *Archives of the Chinese Art Society of America*, 1963, Vol. 17.

Meggers, Betty J. "Did Japanese Fishermen Really Reach Ecuador 5,000 Years Ago?" *Early Man*, 1980, Vol. 2, pp. 15-19.

Mendelssohn, Kurt. "A Scientist Looks at the Pyramids."*American Scientist,* 1971, Vol. 59, pp. 210-220.

Mullen, William. "An Empire to Rival Rome, Part II." *Fate,* August 1988.

Murray, Julia K., and Suzanne E. Cahill. "Recent Advances in Understanding the Mystery of Ancient Chinese 'Magic Mirrors.'" *Chinese Science,* 1987, Vol. 8.

Neustupny, Evzen. "The Tartaria Tablets: A Chronological Issue." *Antiquity,* 1968, Vol. 42, pp. 32-35.

Nichter, Larry S., Raymond F. Morgan, and Mark A. Nichter, "The Impact of Indian Methods for Total Nasal Reconstruction." *Clinics in Plastic Surgery,* October 1983.

"A $1 Million Forgery?" *Time,* February 4, 1974.

Ortloff, Charles R. "Canal Builders of Pre-Inca Peru." *Scientific American,* December 1988.

Park, Chris C. "Water Resources and Irrigation Agriculture in Pre-Hispanic Peru." *Geographical Journal,* 1983, Vol. 149, p. 153.

Peterson, I. "Ancient Technology: Pouring A Pyramid." *Science News,* 1984, Vol. 125, p. 327.

Price, Derek de Solla. "Gears from the Greeks." *Transactions of the American Philosophical Society,* (Philadelphia), November 1974.

Protzen, Jean-Pierre. "Inca Stonemasonry." *Scientific American,* February 1986.

"Pyramids Are Not Made of Polymers, Say Experts." *Pursuit,* 1984, Vol. 17, p. 92.

Randi, James. "Atlantean Road: The Bimini Beach-Rock." *The Skeptical Inquirer,* Spring 1981.

Reinhard, Johan. "Sacred Mountains: An Ethno-Archaeological Study of High Andean Ruins." *Mountain Research and Development,* 1985, Vol. 5, no. 4.

Richards, Douglas G. "Archaeological Anomalies in the Bahamas." *Journal of Scientific Exploration,* 1988, Vol. 2, no. 2.

Safer, John. "Las Bolas Grandes: An Archaeological Enigma." *Oceans,* July/August 1975.

Salwi, Dilip. "The Enigmatic Pillar of Delhi." *New Scientist,* January 3, 1985.

Schmandt-Besserat, Denise:
"An Archaic Recording System in the Uruk-Jemdet Nasr Period." *American Journal of Archaeology,* 1979, Vol. 83, pp. 19-48.
"The Earliest Precursor of Writing." *Scientific American,* June 1978.
"The Precursor to Numeral and Writing." *Archeology,* November/December 1986.

Sheckley, Robert. "Romans in Rio?" *Omni,* June 1983.

Sherby, O. D., and J. Wadsworth. "Damascus Steels." *Scientific American,* February 1985.

Shinn, E. A. "Atlantis: Bimini Hoax." *Sea Frontiers,* 1978, Vol. 23, pp. 130-141.

Stepston, Harold. "Baalbek the Mysterious." *Scientific American,* 1913, Vol. 109, pp. 456-457.

Stock, Chester. "Origin of the Supposed Human Footprints of Carson City, Nevada." *Science,* 1920, Vol. 51, p. 514.

Sullivan, Walter:
"Artifacts in Rio Bay May Be Roman." *New York Times,* October 10, 1982.
"16th Century Charts Seen as Hinting Ancient Explorers Mapped Antarctica." *New York Times,* September 26, 1984.

Tolstoy, Paul. "Cultural Parallels between Southeast Asia and Mesoamerica in the Manufacture of Bark Cloth." *Transactions of the New York Academy of Sciences,* April 1963.

Topping, Audrey. "China's Incredible Find." *National Geographic,* April 1978.

Wadsworth, J., and O. D. Sherby. "On the Bulat-Damascus Steels Revisited." *Progress in Materials Science,* 1980, Vol. 25, pp. 35-68.

Wesley, W. H. "Footprints of Prehistoric Man." *Knowledge,* 1888, Vol. 12, pp. 28-30.

Other Sources

Barnard, Noel (Ed.). "Oceania and the Americas" (Vol. 3 of *Early Chinese Art and Its Possible Influence in the Pacific Basin).* Symposium. New York: Intercultural Arts Press, 1972.

Capon, Edmund. "Qin Shihuang: Terracotta Warriors and Horses" (3rd ed.). Exhibition catalog. International Cultural Corporation of Australia Limited, 1982.

Carlson, John B., and James Judge (Eds.). *Astronomy and Ceremony in the Prehistoric South.* Papers of the Maxwell Museum of Anthropology, No. 2. Albuquerque: University of New Mexico, 1987.

Erickson, Clark L. "Applied Archaeology and Rural Development: Archaeology's Potential Contribution to the Future." Paper presented at the Circum-Pacific Prehistory Conference, Seattle, Wash., August 2-6, 1989.

Jett, Stephen C. "Further Information on the Geography of the Blowgun, and Its Implications for Early Transoceanic Contacts." Draft paper. Department of Geography, University of California at Davis, no date.

Kendall, Timothy. *Patolli: A Game of Ancient Mexico.* Belmont, Mass.: Kirk Game Co., 1980.

Kjellson, Henry. "Letter to the Editor." *Pursuit,* Third Quarter 1985, Vol. 18, no. 3.

Rowe, John H. "What Kind of Settlement Was Inca Cuzco?" *Ñawpa Pacha.* International series for Andean archaeology. Berkeley, Calif.: Institute of Andean Studies, 1967.

PICTURE CREDITS

morial Collection, bequest of Nelson A. Rockefeller—Platin Gilde International Frankfurt, courtesy Museum für Völkerkunde, Staatliche Museen Preussischer Kulturbesitz, West Berlin. **23:** MacQuitty International Photographic Collection, London. **24, 25:** The Metropolitan Museum of Art, bequest of George Cameron Stone, 1936 (36.25.1294a) (2)—cat. no. 311244, photo H. S. Rice, courtesy Department Library Services, American Museum of Natural History, New York. **26, 27:** Jean Vertut—Barry Iverson, courtesy Egyptian Museum, Cairo. **28, 29:** Cloud art by Fred Holz; Barry Iverson, courtesy Egyptian Museum, Cairo; Smithsonian Institution, photo no. 75-6669, Washington, D.C.—line art by Time-Life Books; Larry Sherer, from *Ramayana*, in Ordisi Pata Painting, by Sri Surendra Kumar Das, Panchali Publications, Orissa, India, 1977. **30:** Smithsonian Institution, Department of Anthropology, photo no. 148148, Washington, D.C.—Biblioteca Nacional, Madrid. **31:** MacQuitty International Photographic Collection, London—Scala, Florence. **32:** Musée Gaumais, Virton, Luxembourg—MacQuitty International Photographic Collection, London. **33:** Carmelo Guadagno, courtesy Museum of the American Indian, Heye Foundation, New York (2); cat. no. 326744, courtesy Department Library Services, American Museum of Natural History, New York—Justin Kerr. **34:** The National Museum, Copenhagen, Department of Near Eastern and Classical Antiquities, inventory no. ABb 96. **35:** Craig Aurness/West Light, inset, Massimo Listri/FMR, Milan. **36:** Courtesy San Diego Museum of Man. **38, 39:** From *Seaweeds: A Color-Coded, Illustrated Guide to Common Marine Plants of the East Coast of the United States*, by Charles James Hillson, The Pennsylvania State University, 1977; Massimo Listri/FMR, Milan. **40, 41:** From *The Healing Hand: Man and Wound in the Ancient World*, by Guido Majno, Harvard University Press, 1975—The New York Botanical Garden, photographs and hand coloring by James McInnis. **42:** Courtesy William A. Shear. **43:** Courtesy Biopharm, Ltd.—courtesy Dr. William H. Gotwald, Jr. **44:** The Wellcome Collection, Science Museum, London; Riccardo Villarosa/Overseas s.r.l., Milan, from *Gli Etruschi e il Fegato di Piacenza*, by Viviano Domenici, Camillo Corvi S.P.A., Piacenza, Italy. **45:** Louis Michel Gohel, courtesy Musée de Bar Le-Duc, France. **47:** FPG International, inset, Urs F. Kluyver/Focus, Hamburg, West Germany. **48:** Damm, Düsseldorf/Zefa. **49:** Artwork by Fred Holz. **50:** From *Mazes and Labyrinths: A General Account of Their History and Developments*, by W. H. Matthews, Longmans, Green & Co., London, 1922. **51:** Sonia Halliday, Buckinghamshire, England. **52:** Adam Woolfitt/Woodfin Camp; Nikos Kontos, Athens. **53:**

Hoffman-Buchardi, Düsseldorf/Zefa; Adam Woolfitt/Susan Griggs Agency, London. **54:** Courtesy Thomas and Shelia Pozorski—Urs F. Kluyver/Focus, Hamburg, West Germany. **55:** Robert Frerck/Panoramic Stock Images. **56:** Mark Sherman/Bruce Coleman. **57:** Artwork by Fred Holz—Loren McIntyre (2). **58, 59:** Artwork by Fred Holz. **61:** C. M. Dixon, Kent, England. **62:** Anthony Marshal/Woodfin Camp. **63:** Courtesy Lindley Vann. **64:** Forschungsprojekt Mohenjo-Daro, Aachen Foto Helmes. **65:** Melville Bell Grosvenor, © 1958 National Geographic Society. **66:** Newton Morgan, courtesy William Morgan Architects. **67:** Georg Gerster/Comstock. **68:** Georg Gerster/The John Hillelson Agency, London. **69:** David Brill. **70:** From *The Complete Encylcopedia of Illustration*, by Johann G. Heck, Crown Publishers, New York, 1979. **71:** M. Angelo/West Light, inset, © 1988 Lawrence Migdale/Photo Researchers. **72, 73:** Jean Vertut. **74:** Anna Mitchell-Hedges, F.R.G.S. **75:** Dr. Jevan Berrange/South American Pictures, Suffolk, England. **76:** Courtesy the Trustees of the British Museum, London (2)—Janet and Colin Bord, Wales. **77:** Courtesy Harry Casey. **78, 79:** Courtesy Harry Casey; Malcolm Aird/Robert Estall, Colchester, England; courtesy Marilyn Bridges—courtesy Johan Reinhard; Georg Gerster/Comstock, background Allan Zarling, National Park Service, negative no. 2039. **80:** Courtesy Dr. Suzanne E. Cahill. **81:** Work in Progress/Luisa Ricciarini, Milan—© 1988 Lawrence Migdale/Photo Researchers. **82:** Lino Pellegrini, Milan. **83:** Courtesy Johan Reinhard. **84:** Adam Woolfitt/Susan Griggs Agency, London. **85:** Dennis de Cicco/Sky and Telescope—The Royal Observatory, Edinburgh—Scala, Florence. **86:** Adam Woolfitt/Susan Griggs Agency, London. **87:** Artwork by Fred Holz. **88, 89:** Artwork by Fred Holz, copied by Larry Sherer—artwork by Time-Life Books. **90, 91:** Irving W. Lindelblad, courtesy U.S. Naval Observatory; Bryan and Cherry Alexander, Sturminster, Newton, Dorset, England, from *Masked Dancers of West Africa: The Dogon* (Peoples of the Wild series), © 1982 Time-Life Books; Scala, Florence. **92:** Photograph of disc and details, Scala, Florence—artwork by Fred Holz. **94:** Charalambos Karakalos, Hellenic Atomic Energy Committee, Athens; The National Archaeological Museum, Athens—Cambridge University Library. **95:** John Carlson, Center for Archaeoastronomy, College Park, Maryland—Von Del Chamberlain, Hansen Planetarium, Salt Lake City, Utah. **96:** From *The Complete Encyclopedia of Illustration*, by Johann G. Heck, Crown Publishers, New York, 1979. **97:** Robert Landau/West Light, insets, Landesinstitut für Pädagogik und Medien, Dudweiler, West Germany (2). **98:** Scala, Florence. **99, 100:**

Courtesy the Trustees of the British Museum, London. **101:** Donato Pineider, courtesy Biblioteca Nazionale Centrale, Florence. **102:** Landesinstitut für Pädagogik und Medien, Dudweiler, West Germany. **103:** Erich Lessing, Culture and Fine Arts Archives, Vienna. **104:** Takashi Okamura, Rome—Erich Lessing, Culture and Fine Arts Archives, Vienna. **105:** New Orleans Museum of Art, Women's Volunteer Committee Fund. **106:** Museum of the American Indian, Heye Foundation, New York. **107:** Guy Motil/West Light, inset, Universitätsbibliothek Hiedelberg, West Germany, "Codex Palatinus Germanicus," 60. **108:** Minnesota Historical Society. **109:** From *The Vinland Map and the Tartar Relation*, by R. A. Skelton, T. E. Marston, and G. D. Painter, Yale University Press, 1965. **110:** Dumbarton Oaks Research Library and Collections, Washington, D.C. **111:** Courtesy Carl L. Johannessen. **112:** Courtesy of the Freer Gallery of Art, Smithsonian Institution, Washington, D.C., detail of 14.36 Chinese Stone Sculpture: Eastern Wei (534-550) Buddhist tablet: seated figure of the Buddist Sakymauni in high relief. H: 132.4 x 73.8 cm x depth 38.4 cm; courtesy the Trustees of the British Museum, London. **113:** James H. Pickerell. **114:** Universitätsbibliothek Heidelberg, West Germany, "Codex Palatinus Germanicus," 60. **115:** Nathan Benn/Tim Severin, Brighton, England. **116:** © Janny Kowynia 1989. **117:** Artwork by Time-Life Books. **118, 119:** Artwork by Time-Life Books; Frank Wandell, © 1976 National Geographic Society. **120:** Smithsonian Institution/National Numismatic Collection Photos, Washington, D.C. **121:** Akademische Druck und Verlagsanstalt, Graz, Austria—Larry Sherer, from *Jinshisuo: Illustrated Index to Ancient Bronze and Stone Tablets*, compiled by Yunpeng Feng and Yunyuan Feng, 1820. **122:** Öystein Brochs, courtesy Göteborgs Stad Ethnografiska Museet, Gothenburg, Sweden—Larry Sherer, Smithsonian Natural History Museum, Department of Anthropology, Washington, D.C. **123:** Courtesy Robert F. Marx. **124:** Renee Comet, from *Early Formative Period of Coastal Ecuador: The Valdivia and Machalilla Phases*, by Betty J. Meggers, Clifford Evans, and Emilio Estrada, Smithsonian Institution, Washington, D.C., 1965. **125:** Ken Rogers/West Light, inset, courtesy Ron Calais. **126, 127:** Photo by Ara Güler, Istanbul, courtesy Topkapi Palace Museum, Istanbul, except lower left, map by Fred Holz. **128:** Library of Congress. **130:** Courtesy Ron Calais. **131:** From *The Complete Encyclopedia of Illustration*, by Johann G. Heck, Crown Publishers, New York, 1979; courtesy Glen J. Kuban. **132:** Courtesy Glen J. Kuban. **133:** From *The Complete Encyclopedia of Illustration*, by Johann G. Heck, Crown Publishers, New York, 1979.

INDEX

LIBRARY OF CURIOUS AND UNUSUAL FACTS

This edition published in 2004
by the Caxton Publishing Group
20 Bloomsbury Street, London WC1B 3JH
Under license from Time-Life Books BV.

SERIES Director: Russell B. Adams, Jr.
Series Administrator: Elise Ritter Gibson
Designer: Susan K. White
Associate Editors: Sally Collins
Blaine Marshall (pictures)
Cover Design: Open Door Limited, Rutland UK

Editorial Staff for *Feats and Wisdom of the Ancients*
Text Editors: Laura Foreman (principal), Carl A. Posey
Researchers: Susan Stuck (principal), Sydney J. Baily, Roxie
France-Nuriddin, Charlotte Fullerton, M. Tucker Jones,
Robert H. Wooldridge, Jr.
Assistant Designer: Alan Pitts
Copy Coordinators: Jarelle S. Stein (principal),
Darcie Conner Johnston
Picture Coordinator: Kate Griffin
Editorial Assistant: Terry Ann Paredes

Special Contributors: Lesley Coleman, Christine Hinze (London
research); William Barnhill, Sarah Brash, Dan Darvishian,
Donal Gordon, Sandra Salmans, John Sullivan, Ricardo
Villaneuva, Roger Witherspoon (text); Bill Battaile, Jr.,
Kathryn Pfeifer (research); Victoria Agee (index)

Correspondents: Elisabeth Kraemer-Singh (Bonn); Christine
Lieberman (New York); Maria Vincenza Aloisi (Paris); Ann
Natanson (Rome). Valuable assistance was also provided by
Wibo Van de Linde (Amsterdam); Mirka Gondicas (Athens);
Brigid Grauman (Brussels); Nihal Tamraz (Cairo); Barbara
Gevene Hertz (Copenhagen); Ara Güler (Istanbul); Elizabeth
Brown (New York); Dag Christensen (Oslo); Ann Wise (Rome);
Mary Johnson (Stockholm); Dick Berry, Mieko Ikeda (Tokyo);
Traudl Lessing (Vienna).

Title: **Feats and Wisdom of the Ancients**
ISBN: 1 84447 027 X

The Consultants:

William R. Corliss, the general consultant for the series,
is a physicist-turned-writer who has spent the last twenty-five
years compiling collections of anomalies in the fields of
geophysics, geology, archaeology, astronomy, biology, and
psychology. He has written about science and technology
for NASA, the National Science Foundation, and the Energy
Research and Development Administration (among others).
Mr. Corliss is also the author of more than thirty books on
scientific mysteries, including *Mysterious Universe, The
Unfathomed Mind, and Handbook of Unusual Natural Phenomena.*

John B. Carlson helped develop a new interdisciplinary
speciality, the study of astronomy in ancient cultures.
He is founder and director of the centre for
Archaeoastronomy, in College Park, Maryland.

Kenneth L. Feder, associate professor in anthropology
at Central Connecticut State University, is a consulting
editor for *The Skeptical Inquirer.*

Bob Rickard is the founder and editor of *The Fortean
Times* in London and coauthor of *Phenomena: A Book of
Wonders.* To preserve rare data and documentation he has
also founded the Fortean archives and picture library.

John Scarborough is professor of the history of pharmacy
and medicine at the University of Wisconsin. He has published
extensively on Greek, Roman, and Byzantine pharmacy, zoology
and botany.

Marcello Truzzi, a professor of sociology at Eastern Michigan
University, is director of the Center for Scientific Anomalies
Research (CSAR) and editor of its journal, *Zetetic Scholar.*

Stephen Williams is Peabody Professor of American
archaeology and ethnology at Harvard University and also
serves as curator of North American archaeology at the
Peabody Museum.

IRELAND AND THE FIRST WORLD WAR

IRELAND AND THE
AND THE
FIRST WORLD WAR

A Photographic History

Cormac Ó Comhraí

MERCIER PRESS
IRISH PUBLISHER – IRISH STORY

MERCIER PRESS

Cork

www.mercierpress.ie

© Cormac Ó Comhraí, 2014

ISBN: 978 1 78117 248 3

10 9 8 7 6 5 4 3 2 1

A CIP record for this title is available from the British Library

Printed and bound in Dubai.

CONTENTS

INTRODUCTION

'Every culture needs to be wary of such concepts as heroism, patriotism, and national glory ... however, I now know that all cultures need pride and courage in order to survive and to adapt.'[1]

Philip Orr

Every year, all over the world, those who have fallen in battle are commemorated for their heroism and sacrifice. However, the commemoration of the Irishmen who fought and died as part of the British Army in the First World War has often been a subject for debate because of events in Ireland during and after the war. Recently there has been much discussion about how to best mark the centenary of the war and to honour the Irishmen who gave their lives in it, particularly those who died in British uniforms, and the Irish state has been making increasing efforts to engage with the memory and legacy of those who fought during the First World War. One example of this is the construction of the round tower in the The Island of Ireland Peace Park (*right*) in Messines, Belgium.

Every July the Republic of Ireland holds a day of commemoration, to remember all those who have fallen in war. However, this doesn't attract the same attention as Britain's Remembrance Sunday, partly because for several weeks before that November Sunday the poppy is an inescapable sight on British television. There is a regular, if limited, debate in the British media about what the wearing of the poppy means. Some identify it with the First World War,

---

1   Orr, P., *The Road to the Somme: Men of the Ulster Division Tell Their Story* (Belfast, 2008 edition), p. 302.

some with both world wars and others with all conflicts that Britain has been involved with since. Some see wearing it as a symbol of remembrance and grieving, some as a charitable act, but others see wearing it as a justification of imperialism and a cynical effort to mobilise the dead for contemporary advantage. For a minority in the Republic, who have strong opinions for or against the poppy, the occasion is a charged one, yet the debate largely passes the general public by. Nowhere on either island, however, is the symbolism of the poppy more controversial than in Northern Ireland. There, the poppy is identified with heroism and sacrifice by the unionist community, but its association with the British military, regarded by many in the nationalist community as an enemy occupying force, will remain problematic as long as there is conflict. Many nationalists draw little distinction between the activities of the British state and pro-British paramilitaries, a view clearly shared by those who drew the loyalist murals pictured above.

Culturally the First World War has failed to have the impact upon Ireland that a war of its size and scale should have had.[2] One yardstick of the opposition to Irishmen serving in the British Army can be found in folk music, a tradition which is still strong in Ireland. For hundreds of years the idea of Irishmen serving in that army has attracted criticism. Anti-recruitment songs, a number of them still commonly sung, warned of the negative consequences of military service. Connemara folk singer Seosamh Ó hÉanaí (Joe Heaney, *right*), grew up knowing First World War veterans and derived much of his material from local oral traditions. One of the songs most closely identified with him is the anti-recruitment song 'Condae Mhaigh Eo'. While Republicans such as Kevin Barry, Terence MacSwiney and James Connolly, and events such as the Kilmichael Ambush, are all commemorated in songs that glorify them, there are only two songs about the First World War which really entered Irish consciousness, both written years later by a Scot and both anti-war songs. In this lack of representation of the First World War, Ireland is not unique among English-speaking countries, of course, but the reasons for this are very different. For example, the more recent, and in the latter case more controversial, conflicts of the Second World War and Vietnam dominate any list of war films made in the United States, but what makes Ireland unique in the English-speaking world is that the First World War was followed by large-scale revolutionary upheaval.

Many of the Irish who fought in the war were from ordinary Catholic families, like the Shines of Waterford, who buried three sons, including Second Lieutenant Hugh Shine and Second Lieutenant John Denys Shine (*pictured overleaf*). Not every family was this unlucky. Colm Ó Cluanáin (*right*) from Baile na Cille, Lettermullen, Co. Galway, was one of four brothers who served in the navy.

2 The same can be argued about many other major traumas and events in Ireland, including the influenza pandemic of 1918–19 or the US Civil War, for example.

Second Lieutenant John Denys Shine.

(*Courtesy of Waterford County Museum, UK 1197*)

Second Lieutenant Hugh Shine.

(*Courtesy of Waterford County Museum, UK 1198*)

All four Ó Cluanáin brothers survived the war.

The lack of interest in men like the Shines and Ó Cluanáins has been both a nationalist and a unionist phenomenon. For instance, the Ulster Tower in Thiepval (*right*) commemorates soldiers from the unionist tradition, rather than both traditions.

There are a number of reasons why the war has proved less enduring in the public consciousness than other events. Firstly the narrative of the war changed from one 'for civilisation' to one of an appalling waste that resolved little. Ramsay MacDonald, an anti-war Labour MP, hooted and stoned for his opposition to the war throughout its duration, was British prime minister by 1924.[3] As empires and imperialism became less popular over the course of the decades, the war has often come to be viewed as merely a natural continuation of imperial rivalries. Controversy remains about the propaganda used to gain recruits for the army and to harden hearts against the Germans. Many of the wartime leaders, products of the Victorian age, have not proved sympathetic in a vastly changed society. Moreover, many of those who died in the war did so childless, obscuring their memory. Finally there was a reluctance among some veterans to talk about the conflict to relatives. London-Irishman Edward Casey wrote in his old age:

> When my young son many years ago asked, 'Daddy, what did you do in the Great War?' 'Nothing,' I growled, 'You just go on and polish those medals.'[4]

However, the extent that the First World War has dropped out of the public memory in Ireland is due to additional uniquely Irish factors. Many were alienated from British symbols by the manner in which the crown forces responded to the increasingly radical demands of Irish nationalists, though this should not be exaggerated, as hundreds of thousands of poppies were sold in Dublin in 1924.[5] There was a question mark over the 'Irishness' of ex-soldiers, whose descendants were sometimes proud to serve in the British armed forces in subsequent conflicts. These conflicts included not just the Second World War but

3   Hochschild, A., *To End All Wars: A Story of Protest and Patriotism in the First World War* (London, 2012), p. 353.

4   Bourke, J. (ed.), *The Misfit Soldier: Edward Casey's War Story 1914–1918* (Cork, 1999), p. 71.

5   Hanley, B., *The IRA 1926–1936* (Dublin, 2002), p. 71.

also campaigns against Asian and African nationalists whose struggles reflected the Irish struggle for independence. Added to this was the fact that, over time, partition allowed a dilution of the connection with British culture as the Irish educational system focused on those who struggled against British rule in Ireland rather than representing the complexity of the Irish relationship with Britain.

Many, though far from all, Republicans were dismissive of Irishmen who served in the British Army. At the beginning of the war Kerry Republicans Tadhg Kennedy and Austin Stack were asked about their attitude towards men joining the army. Kennedy recalled:

> I replied that if I was satisfied that he was acting conscientiously in joining up I would accompany him to the gate of the barracks and wish him luck; whereupon Stack said that he would do his best to prevent him joining and if he failed he would cut his throat as he was going in the gate.[6]

Not all Republicans came from radical families, and there are many cases of brothers who served in opposing forces at the same time. One such family was Ernie O'Malley's. A Republican guerrilla and later literary figure, O'Malley (*left*) wrote about the attitude of the men in his Dublin Irish Volunteer unit to Irishmen in the British Army. Describing two friends who were British officers, O'Malley wrote:

> No longer they believed in what they were fighting for but, in honour felt bound to return to their battalion in France. 'When I come back next time,' one began, but did not finish, as we shook hands. Both were dead within three weeks. When I spoke of these two I did not find sympathy or understanding. Men in the company had relatives and friends at the Front; their creed was simple. They believed either in an uncompromising Ireland – or not at all.[7]

Two of O'Malley's own brothers joined the British Army. Frank (*left*) was wounded during the war and died of disease in Africa in the 1920s. Ernie himself came close to joining the colours before being radicalised by the Easter Rising. His younger brother Charlie (*right*) followed him into the Republican movement and was killed in the Civil War.

6   Tadhg Kennedy, Bureau of Military History (BMH) Witness Statement (WS) 1413, p. 19.
7   O'Malley, E., *On Another Man's Wound* (Dublin, 1979), p. 45.

Republican activism was not restricted to men, of course. Pictured above is the Minihan family, butter merchants and publicans from Corofin, Co. Clare. Helen and Kathleen, the two daughters (*standing*), were members of Cumann na mBan, the Republican women's organisation. Joe (*far left*) was a member of the Royal Irish Regiment during the war. John, the other son, was involved in the Republican Irish Volunteers.

Despite the divisions that have arisen over the participation of Ireland in the First World War, there are still many physical hints around the country commemorating those who took part. There are monuments, church windows and plaques erected by families, local committees and businesses, like the bust in Wexford of William Redmond MP (*right*), who served and died in the uniform of the Royal Irish Fusiliers.

It is also worth remembering that the general attitude of trying to forget what happened was not limited to the First World War. When

13

Richard Mulcahy, leader of the National Army during the Civil War, was approached for assistance to erect a monument to four members of that army killed in Wexford during the Civil War he said: 'I very much dislike the idea of … erecting a monument at the site of an ambush between Irishmen.' Those who died helping to protect the state established in 1922 were left with, in the words of historian Anne Dolan, 'a mean and dreary plot hidden behind the gravedigger's shed'. Dolan contrasts this with 'the relative splendour of Islandbridge', Ireland's most significant monument to those who died during the First World War.[8] Facilitated and supported by the governments of W. T. Cosgrave (*above left*) and Éamon de Valera (*above right*), the National War Memorial Gardens was a massive project that involved the employment of Sir Edward Lutyens, possibly the world's pre-eminent designer of monuments for the dead of the war. However, this did not signal that the sacrifices of ex-British soldiers were being fully embraced, and by the 1960s the remaining ex-soldiers and their families were feeling forgotten. Fianna Fáil minister Todd Andrews was approached to build a bridge across the Liffey connecting the Phoenix Park with the Memorial Gardens in recognition of the sacrifices of men who served with the British. Andrews wrote: 'I thought it was a highly imaginative and generous idea. I broached it with Seán Lemass. He was not prepared to go along with it, feeling that it was too late to do anything. I regretted that Dev [de Valera] was no longer Taoiseach.'[9]

Over the past two decades Irish writers and historians have begun to seriously examine the First

8   Dolan, A., *Commemorating the Irish Civil War: History and Memory, 1923–2000* (Cambridge, 2003), pp. 122, 129–30.
9   Andrews, C. S., *Dublin Made Me* (Dublin, 1979), p. 79.

World War. Local studies and studies of particular individuals are becoming increasingly common. One of those individuals was William Redmond, and his lonely grave (*above*) was the subject of a 1995 book by Terence Denman.

A desire to know more has driven descendants of First World War soldiers to travel to places where the Irish fought and died, including Flanders, the Somme and Gallipoli. One of these was historian James Colin Cousins (*right*), who has visited the grave of his great-uncle James (*pictured overleaf*). James was killed in action at the Battle of the Marne when the war itself was only a few weeks old. One reason for this increase in family pilgrimages is the

Pte J Cousins 2nd Royal Inniskilling Fusiliers

Left: James Cousins. (© *Colin Cousins*)

Above: 'The Death Penny' of William Bentley. (*Courtesy of Pádraig Óg Ó Ruairc*)

Below: The Mass card for William Bentley. (*Courtesy of the family of William Bentley*)

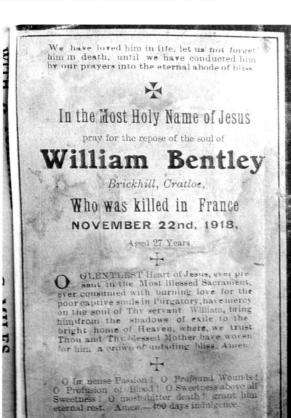

We have loved him in life, let us not forget him in death, until we have conducted him by our prayers into the eternal abode of bliss.

✠

In the Most Holy Name of Jesus

pray for the repose of the soul of

William Bentley

Brickhill, Cratloe,

Who was killed in France
NOVEMBER 22nd, 1918,

Aged 27 Years

✠

O GENTLEST Heart of Jesus, ever present in the Most Blessed Sacrament, ever consumed with burning love for the poor captive souls in Purgatory, have mercy on the soul of Thy servant William, bring him from the shadows of exile to the bright home of Heaven, where, we trust Thou and Thy blessed Mother have woven for him a crown of unfading bliss. Amen.

✠

O Immense Passion! O Profound Wounds! O Profusion of Blood! O Sweetness above all Sweetness! O most bitter death! grant him eternal rest. Amen.—100 days indulgence.

All I ask of you is that wherever you may be you will remember me at Holy Communion and at the foot of the Altar of the Lord.

✠

O SWEET JESUS, for the sake of Thy bitter Passion, and the sorrows of Thine Immaculate Mother, have mercy on the soul of Thy servant William, and let the perpetual light of Thy countenance shine upon him.

✠

Jesus, meek and humble of heart, make my heart like unto Thine.—300 days each time.

Sweet Heart of Jesus, be thou my love.—300 days indulgence.

Sweet Heart of Mary, be thou my salvation.—300 days indulgence.

rapid expansion of information available on the Internet, which has facilitated an investigation of documents and photographs. This research tool has allowed passionate amateurs, effectively self-taught experts, to expedite a process of familial discovery along which they themselves have travelled.

Many Irish homes possess 'The Death Penny', a medal awarded to the families of those who lost their lives in the service of the British. Pictured opposite is one such medal, that of William Bentley from Cratloe, Co. Clare, who lost his life in a booby trap explosion after the war's end, when he picked up an accordion.

A thousand photographs scattered across a thousand attics also survive from this period, providing a pictorial record of those who fought. Many were taken immediately before people left for war or, in the case of Mickey and Monie Mahony from Waterford (*above*), when Mickey was at home on leave from Salon, India, and Monie from Flanders, Belgium. While it has been possible to give the faces in this photograph a certain amount of their identity back, this is not the case in all examples.

Researching family history is a frustrating addiction. The picture on the right shows an unidentified Royal Irish Regiment soldier. An approximate date can be assigned to the photograph through the style of his uniform, but beyond that we don't know anything about him.

Photographs from before and after the war also carry the story of the conflict. The image of the two cherubic little boys above shows Michael (*left*) and Maccon McNamara. They were the sons of a Co. Clare doctor. Maccon was killed in the war in March 1918.

Another photograph, which holds a personal significance for the author, shows the Corry family from Clondrinagh, Cranny, also in Co. Clare, probably in the 1920s. The men in the back row (*left to right*) are Stephen, Marty and Jack, in the front (*left to right*) Tom and Peter Snr. Even in their isolated hamlet, where they were afforded a degree of independence from both the church and state, they were affected by the war and its attendant troubles. The stories of the six male members of the family reflect the impact of the war years. Tom and Jack attempted to emigrate to America during the war and were turned back at Liverpool. Jack's passport, the photograph from which is reproduced here (*right*), was stamped with the word refused. Marty joined the local company of the Irish Volunteers, becoming a lieutenant while still only in his mid-teens. He once swung a sledgehammer at a policeman who suggested he enlist. Stephen, my paternal grandfather, born in 1905, was refused permission to go to an Irish college in Carrigaholt, Co. Clare in the aftermath of the Easter Rising. His father, Peter, a native speaker, worried about the potential long-term consequences of being associated with radical nationalism. Pikes had been kept in the house in preparation for the Easter Rising. Eighty years later in one of our last conversations, as he drifted between the present and the past while on his deathbed, Stephen warned me that the pikes were going to have to be moved out of the house, that there was a raid coming. Finally, the sixth male member of the family is missing from the picture. Peter Junior, the pet of the family, died along with perhaps 20,000 other Irish people in the largely forgotten influenza epidemic of 1918–19. His death haunted his parents.

The sheer scale of the mobilisation that occurred in 1914 makes the Irish-born British or American serviceman anonymous in a way that the Republican revolutionary is not. To some degree we've lost the ability to assign motivations and emotions, positive and negative, to people like Con Tobin, for example. Tobin (*right*) was a member of the British Army from Glandore. Being from the Cork coast Tobin, his family and his friends must have been aware of the damage that the German submarines were inflicting along the Irish coast, but we have no way of knowing how this made them feel.

It is all too easy to allow stereotypes to dictate the manner in which these soldiers are portrayed. They weren't all pro-British or proud Irishmen, mercenaries or heroes, tortured by what they had seen or turned into maniacs, unemployable misfits or upstanding citizens. It is hoped that this book goes

some way towards showing what they were, as well as showing how the war affected not only the men who were involved, but also the people left at home, and how the events of 1914–18 would dominate the future of Ireland. As the photograph below of Edward Kenny (a member of the Royal Navy from Courtown, Wexford, who was killed in action in 1915) appeals to us, it is hoped that we will forget them not.

Image acknowledgements: round tower in The Island of Ireland Peace Park © Richard Grayson; murals in the Shankill, Belfast © Richard Grayson; Seosamh Ó hÉanaí © Warren Fahey; Colm Ó Cluanáin courtesy of John Bhaba Jeaic Ó Conghaile and Ionad Oidhreachta Leitir Mealláin; Ulster Tower, Thiepval © Richard Grayson; Ernie, Frank and Charlie O'Malley courtesy of Cormac O'Malley; Minihan family courtesy of Clare County Museum; bust of William Redmond MP © Niall Ó Síocháin; Cosgrave and de Valera courtesy of Mercier Archive; grave of William Redmond © Niall Ó Síocháin; James Colin Cousins © Colin Cousins; Mickey and Monie Mahony courtesy of Waterford County Museum, UK 487; unidentified soldier courtesy of Waterford County Museum, UK 1246; Michael and Maccon McNamara courtesy of Clare County Library; images of the Corry family and Jack Corry courtesy of Martin Cleary and John Corry; Con Tobin courtesy of Waterford County Museum UK 3612; Edward Kenny courtesy of Mary Kenny and Colin Stone.

1. IRELAND BEFORE THE WAR

'Englishmen do not understand Irishmen'[1]

British officer and RIC/RUC officer John M. Regan

1 Augusteijn, J., *The Memoirs of John M. Regan: A Catholic Officer in the RIC and RUC 1909–1948* (Dublin, 2007), p. 99.

RIGHT

At the beginning of the twentieth century the vast majority of Irish people were nationalists and favoured the establishment of a parliament in Dublin. Although Sinn Féin was founded in 1905, up to the war most nationalists still supported the Irish Parliamentary Party (IPP) led by John Redmond (*right*), which was working towards having a bill introducing Home Rule passed through the British parliament. (*Courtesy of Mercier Archive*)

BELOW

Home Rule did not mean full independence, a breaking of the link with the monarchy or the Empire, or even full control over Irish affairs. Many nationalists were comfortable within the Empire and loyal to the royal family, whose visits were greeted with great enthusiasm in Ireland. Pictured below is the proclamation of George V as king at Dungarvan Court House, Waterford, in 1910. (*Courtesy of Waterford County Museum, EK 143*)

ABOVE

Amongst the major allies of the IPP was a Catholic fraternal organisation, the Ancient Order of Hibernians (AOH), the members of which saw themselves as protecting the interests of their community as well as being a social organisation. This organisation was resented by Republicans, with one from Belfast describing it as being 'more intent on adopting the tactics of Masonic Orangism than on following a line of real national advancement'.[1] Members of the AOH physically intimidated nationalist opponents of the IPP, as well as groups (such as socialists and suffragettes) which were hostile to individual IPP leaders.

The AOH was also despised by unionists, with one Cork unionist commenting in 1917 that: 'One thing he admired about the Sinn Feiners is their determination to wipe out that pestilent body, the A.O.H.'[2]

Pictured is a group of Hibernians from Athlone. (*Courtesy of Athlone Library*)

1 Seamus Dobbyn, BMH WS 279, p. 3.
2 Hart, P., *The IRA and Its Enemies* (Oxford, 1998), p. 140.

ABOVE

Another important ally of the IPP was the United Irish League's agrarian agitators, who mobilised communities against landlords and cattle graziers. Their goal was to maximise the number of families that could live comfortably on the land through agitation for land distribution. This brought them into conflict with the Royal Irish Constabulary (RIC), rural Ireland's armed police force. While Republicans and agrarian agitators had legitimate grievances about policing, the vast majority of people respected their local constable. Pictured are members of the RIC in Adare, Co. Limerick, during 1915. (*Courtesy of Aimee Olcese*)

OPPOSITE

Land agitation was public and often involved the mobilisation of large crowds. Confrontation with the police was generally encouraged. United Irish League agitator Dermot O'Brien, a great-grand-uncle of the author, served three months in prison after telling an audience in Kilfenora, Co. Clare, that: 'it was ridiculous to be sneaking and driving cattle at night. They should go and do it in broad daylight.' (*Courtesy of Dominic Cronin*)

LEFT

The most serious opposition to the IPP in the years before the First World War came from Ulster's unionists. These were largely the descendants of English and Scottish Protestants who had acquired land at the expense of the native Gaelic Irish during the seventeenth century. Belfast derived much of its industrial strength from the British market and its impressive industrial performance was a source of great pride. One of its major industries was ship building. The most famous of all ships built there was the Titanic, the propellers of which are pictured here just before the ship was launched. (*Courtesy of the Library of Congress, LC-USZ62-34781*)

BELOW

Unionists who wanted to maintain the British connection in southern Ireland comprised a small minority of the population, the wealthiest members of whom were called Anglo-Irish. Many of the better off attended British schools and universities, represented British parliamentary constituencies, had estates in Britain and served in its military. Field Marshal Sir Henry Wilson, an Anglo-Irishman from Longford, was a key figure in the British Army before and during the First World War. (*Courtesy of Mercier Archive*)

ABOVE

Overwhelmingly unionist in politics, the Protestant communities in many rural areas of the south relied heavily on the landed class, but also on the crown forces for their vitality. Research seems to suggest, however, that these communities weren't particularly fertile recruiting grounds for the army during the war. Similarly, recruitment among rural Protestants in unionist Ulster also seems to have been relatively poor.[1]

Pictured is the Pollard family from Lismore in Waterford. They were members of the Church of Ireland. James Snr was an ex-RIC man. James Jnr (*front right*) served with the Royal Army Medical Corps during the war. Jane (*back right*) married Ebenezer Gibbons, from Cork city, a captain in the Royal Munster Fusiliers. (*Courtesy of Waterford County Museum, UK 2609*)

1   Bowman, T., 'The Ulster Volunteer Force and the Formation of the 36th (Ulster) Division', *Irish Historical Studies*, November 2001, pp. 498–518.

Southern Protestants were disproportionately represented in the professions. Half of the south's engineers, including Waterford County Engineer Captain T. J. Biggs, from Bandon, Co. Cork, were Protestant. During the war Biggs' expertise helped the war effort. He worked in the Royal Engineers office in Dublin Castle. (*Courtesy of Waterford County Museum, UK 14*)

High levels of emigration meant that a large Irish diaspora existed and its members tended to maintain strong links with Ireland. Irish immigrants in America went to great lengths to retain a sense of their own identity and were keen to influence events in Ireland. Their opinion of the British state played a major role in developing attitudes, such as supporting American neutrality during the First World War. Pictured is an Irish translation of the American national anthem 'The Star-Spangled Banner', published by the bilingual Irish-American journal *The Gael*. (*Courtesy of Digital Library @ Villanova University*)

AN BRATAC GEAL-RÉALTAC.

(THE STAR-SPANGLED BANNER.)

THE
STAR SPANGLED
BANNER
IN
IRISH.

TRANSLATED BY REV. EUGENE O'GROWNEY.

The same was true about the Irish in Britain. A particularly prominent example of a London-Irishman is the Gaelic Athletic Association activist William MacCarthy, better known as Liam MacCarthy in GAA circles. He was born in London in 1851 to a father from Cork and a mother from Limerick. (*Courtesy of the MacCarthy family*)

Amongst the diaspora, an interest in Irish culture and affairs was not limited to nationalists. Pictured is an Orange Order march in Newfoundland, Canada, in 1913. (*Courtesy of the Provincial Archive of Newfoundland and Labrador, A 36-155*)

Despite the strength of nationalism in Ireland, the British Army provided an important employment opportunity for many Irishmen. The First World War was not the first conflict they faced in the twentieth century, with many fighting in the Boer War in South Africa (1899–1902). During that war a 'wave of almost hysterical anti-British feeling' swept the country. Nationalist MP John Dillon (*seated left*) told his listeners on one occasion: 'There is a gentleman coming over here looking for recruits for the Irish Guards. If he comes here I hope you will put him out of Kerry.'[1] (*Courtesy of Athlone Library*)

1   Denman, T., 'The Red Livery of Shame: The Campaign against Army Recruitment in Ireland 1899–1914', *Irish Historical Studies*, 1994–95, p. 216.

Some viewed the army as a place that absorbed those who were unable or unwilling to settle down in life. The use of the term ex-soldier to describe people who didn't fit into easy categories of employment during court cases further associated the term with petty crime, alcoholism and mental illness. This cartoon shows a young offender who avoids a jail sentence by enlisting. (*Courtesy of Mercier Archive*)

Catching .
Recruits. .

John Kelly, aged 10, arrested for having "kicked up his feet" and thrown a piece of bread at a woman in the streets of Limerick. He was let out on condition he became a drummer boy in the English Army.

Irish recruits to the British Army at this time were predominately members of the gentry, the urban poor or the sons and grandsons of ex-soldiers. Pictured is a group of Royal Munster Fusiliers *c.* 1900 in South Africa during the Boer War. That conflict was controversial both for the treatment of Boer civilians by the British, whose efforts to break the Boers saw thousands of children die due to conditions in British camps where civilians were interned, and for what was perceived to be the poor performance of the British Army, which led to efforts to improve its efficiency. (*Courtesy of the Library of Congress, LC-USZ62-42613*)

British casualties in the Boer War included significant numbers of Irishmen. The Fusiliers Arch in Dublin (*top*) commemorates Dubliners who died during the course of the conflict. It was nicknamed the Traitors' Arch by Republicans. In their eyes the honour of Ireland was redeemed by the Irish Brigade (*below*), who fought on the side of the Boers. One of its most prominent officers was Major John MacBride, who was later executed for his part in the Easter Rising. He is pictured here with Irish Brigade officers, standing on the extreme right. (*Fusiliers Arch courtesy of the National Library of Ireland, L_ROY_10569; Irish Brigade courtesy of Kilmainham Gaol Museum, 17PO-1A24-10*)

ABOVE

The British Army was a major employer among the urban poor. Dublin had little regular, well-paid employment and was the scene of a violent and bitter protracted dispute between unionised workers led by Jim Larkin on one side and employers, police and strike breakers on the other in 1913. The most infamous moment in this dispute occurred on what has become known as Bloody Sunday, 31 August 1913 (*pictured*), when the Dublin Metropolitan Police broke up a banned public meeting in O'Connell Street, leading to the deaths of two of the protestors and the arrest of Larkin. Not all union men regained their employment following the end of the dispute and later there were shouts of 'Up Larkin' among Dubliners at the Front. (*Courtesy of Mercier Archive*)

OPPOSITE

There was a common belief in Europe that European imperialism was of major benefit to Asia and Africa and that large numbers of casualties inflicted by European armies during conflicts were an acceptable, if regrettable, by-product of the civilising process. There were dissenting voices, however, who linked twentieth-century British behaviour abroad with earlier British campaigns in Ireland, such as in this cartoon in the Irish magazine *Lepracaun*. (*Courtesy of Digital Library @ Villanova University*)

THE OLD, OLD STORY.

"John Bull's Upas Tree."

["The Editor of *Ulatine Journal*, Hind Swarajya, who was condemned on July 2nd to two years' rigorous imprisonment for publishing two seditious articles, but appealed against his sentence, was sentenced to three-and-a-half years' imprisonment, and ordered to pay a fine of 2,000 rupees."—*Daily Papers*.]

Criticism of imperialism was not restricted to criticism of the British. Sir Roger Casement (*opposite inset*) from Co. Antrim, who worked as a British consul in Africa, was a prominent critic of the abuse of people in the Congo Free State, a personal possession of King Leopold II of Belgium (*opposite*), for example. The abuses included enslavement, mass killings and mutilations. The international outcry generated by the work of Casement led to Leopold handing over his possession to the Belgian state. (*Casement courtesy of Mercier Archive; Leopold courtesy of the Library of Congress, ggbain-00748*)

Many saw the army as an extension of sporting life. When Lieutenant George Brooks of the Irish Guards was killed by German shrapnel in France in 1914 his dying words were 'Play the Game'.[1] The most famous example of the crossover between war and sport was at the Battle of Loos (1915) when members of the London Irish Rifles dribbled a football across no man's land while advancing towards the German position. Pictured is a tug of war team made up of members of the Irish Guards. (*Courtesy of Niall Ó Síocháin*)

1 Hochschild, A., *To End All Wars: A Story of Protest and Patriotism in the First World War* (London, 2012), p. 9.

The bayonet fighting team of the 2nd Battalion, Prince of Wales Leinster Regiment. (*Courtesy of Collins Barracks, Cork, the Clarke collection*)

Many Irish also served in the Royal Navy. William Bateman (*seated left*) from Helvick Head near Dungarvan in Waterford joined the navy in 1907. He was a farm labourer before going to sea. During the war he had several postings including, between January 1917 and January 1919, HMS *Dido,* during which time this photograph was taken.[1] (*Courtesy of Waterford County Museum, UK 5298*)

1   William Bateman (The National Archives (TNA): Public Records Office (PRO), ADM 188/510/311772).

Doctor Bill Egan (*pictured*) from Dungarvan, Waterford was a member of the Royal Army Medical Corps (RAMC). It was difficult to break into the world of medicine for those who went to unfashionable Irish and Scottish universities. The army provided an opportunity to develop a career. In the years after the Boer War, the RAMC was improved dramatically by Sir Alfred Keogh, a graduate of University College Galway. Keogh recruited London's top surgeons into the army reserve, knowing that their expertise would be invaluable during a major war, which he suspected was coming.[1] (*Courtesy of Noel Harty*)

1   Shephard, B., *A War of Nerves: Soldiers and Psychiatrists 1914–1994* (London, 2002), pp. 23–24.

ABOVE

In the decades before the outbreak of war, radical nationalists despaired of the increasing anglicisation of Irish society. Many of them felt that the nation was in terminal decline. One Republican, in the aftermath of the Easter Rising, described the rebels as 'the last of the Mohicans – hundreds of years too late'.[1] This sense of decline led to the creation of sporting, cultural and literary organisations dedicated to reviving Irish culture. Though some were obsessed with a glorious Celtic past, others were modernisers who wanted a confident, modern society based on Gaelic culture rather than merely imitative of English culture. Members of all political organisations were involved in these movements, although they increasingly came to be identified with radical nationalists and were a major influence on those who dominated the politics of an independent Ireland. Pictured is a group performing an Irish-language play at the start of the twentieth century. Of the five people in this photograph, two were to become Republican martyrs, two were to become presidents of Ireland and one was to marry a president. Pictured standing (*left to right*): Seán T. O'Kelly (president, 1945–59), Peadar Macken (killed during the Easter Rising), Michael O'Hanrahan (executed after the Rising) and Douglas Hyde (president, 1938–45); and seated: Sinéad Flanagan, who later married Éamon de Valera.[2] (*Courtesy of Kilmainham Gaol Museum, 12PC-1A25-02*)

1   Good, J., *Enchanted by Dreams: The Journal of a Revolutionary* (Kerry, 1996), p. 79.
2   The significance of this photograph was spotted by historian Deirdre Ní Chonghaile.

One manifestation of radical nationalist sentiment was the tiny Sinn Féin party founded by Arthur Griffith, a Dublin journalist. His party sought to establish their own parliament in Dublin through refusing to attend Westminster. Although Griffith sought more independence than that offered by Home Rule, Sinn Féin was not a Republican party. (*Courtesy of Mercier Archive*)

Ultimately, however, it was the Irish Republican Brotherhood (IRB), nicknamed the Fenians, that was to prove the most important of the radical nationalist groups. This small, secret, revolutionary society sought to break all links with the British state, monarchy and Empire, knowing that the British wouldn't concede a republic without armed insurrection. Their plan was to strike when Britain was embroiled in a major conflict. Two key figures in the IRB were Tom Clarke (*above right*) and Seán Mac Diarmada *(right)*. (*Clarke courtesy of Shane Kenna; Mac Diarmada courtesy of Mercier Archive*)

As tensions between Britain and Germany escalated, it became clear to Irish Republicans that contact should be established with the Germans. A key figure in that effort was veteran Kildare Republican John Devoy (*right, in the company of Roger Casement*), who had spent decades involved in Irish Republican politics in the United States. (*Joseph McGarrity collection: courtesy of Digital Library @ Villanova University*)

Joseph McGarrity from Carrickmore, Co. Tyrone, pictured here (*right*) panning for emeralds in the 1920s, was another Irish revolutionary prominent in Irish-American politics. During the First World War McGarrity was one of the most important members of what came to be known as the Hindu-German conspiracy, an attempt by Germany to destabilise British rule in India by smuggling guns from the United States to Indian radicals using Irish-American radicals. (*Joseph McGarrity collection: courtesy of Digital Library @ Villanova University*)

In 1912, no longer protected by the House of Lords' veto, which had previously prevented Home Rule from passing through the British parliament, Ulster's unionists had to face the fact that some measure of Home Rule was going to be enacted by Herbert Asquith's Liberal government by 1914. Led by Sir James Craig, a prominent businessman (*left*), and Dubliner Sir Edward Carson (*right*) they demanded the exclusion of Ulster from the area to be governed by the imminent Irish parliament. (*Courtesy of Mercier Archive*)

The Ulster Volunteer Force (UVF) was established in 1913 to resist Home Rule. There was a great deal of sympathy for Ulster unionism in Britain, with hostility directed towards any change to the structure of the United Kingdom. Part of this hostility arose from a fear of weakening the Empire and mistrust of the intentions of Irish nationalists, but it was also partially rooted in anti-Catholic and anti-Irish prejudice. Pictured is the 2nd Battalion, South Down Regiment, UVF. (*Courtesy of the Deputy Keeper of the Records, Public Records Office, Northern Ireland, D1540/3/119*)

ABOVE

As a response to the creation of the Ulster Volunteer Force, Athlone nationalists formed their own paramilitary group known as the Midland Volunteer Force. In the picture James Gough (*seated front right*) pays his first subscription of a half-crown to these Volunteers. The transaction is being recorded by the secretary Seán O'Mullany (*the tall man standing left*) and watched by (*left to right*) Michael Curley, Patrick Croughan and Alfred Warby. (*Courtesy of Athlone Library*)

The Midland Volunteers were soon incorporated into the Irish Volunteer Force, which was formed in November 1913 and was determined to fight to protect the implementation of Home Rule. Pictured is a group of Volunteers at Tralee, Co. Kerry, in the summer of 1914. (*Courtesy of the Military Archives, P18-02*)

The need to develop the two Volunteer organisations along military lines led to a mobilisation of those with skills and assets already in the community. Particularly useful were ex-British soldiers, such as Colonel Maurice Moore of the Irish Volunteers, who were enlisted to help train the men. (*Courtesy of Mercier Archive*)

Carpenters made dummy rifles, blacksmiths made pikes and even bicycles took on military significance. Pictured is the Dungarvan National Volunteers Cycle Section in Co. Waterford. (*Courtesy of Waterford County Museum, EK 134*)

Dungarvan Corps of National Volunteers, showing Cycle Section. E.K.D.

RIGHT

With the development of two armed forces, both determined to have their own way, the British government was faced with the spectre of a civil war in Ireland that could spread to Great Britain. Conservative leader Andrew Bonar Law (*right*) declared: 'I can imagine no length of resistance to which Ulster can go in which I should not be prepared to support them'.[1] Matters were not helped in March 1914 when a significant number of British officers indicated that they were prepared to lose their jobs rather than coerce Ulster unionists. Though not a mutiny in the strictest sense, it became known as the Curragh Mutiny to nationalists and showed the weakness of the British government. The Liberal government increasingly favoured partition of some kind. Members of the IPP also began to accept that partition of some kind was a probability. The debate moved towards the numbers of counties to be excluded and whether or not it would be permanent. (*Courtesy of the Library of Congress, LC-DIG-ggbain-23420*)

1 Fanning, R., *Fatal Path: British Government and Irish Revolution 1910–1922* (London, 2013), p. 71.

51

Arming themselves became the main priority for both groups of Volunteers and in April 1914 the UVF imported German guns into Larne, Co. Antrim. The Irish Volunteers quickly emulated them. The ship *Gladiator* (*opposite, top*) was used in the early stages of a smuggling operation that culminated at Howth in Dublin on 26 July 1914 (*opposite, bottom*). In Dublin, later that same day, British soldiers of the King's Own Scottish Borderers, frustrated by their inability to seize the smuggled arms and having clashed with members of the Volunteers, struck out at a large, hostile group of civilians. The soldiers opened fire, killing three and wounding dozens. Pictured above is the funeral of one of the victims. Given the heightened tensions, a major confrontation seemed inevitable between Irish nationalists and Ulster unionists. Then war was declared and the issue of Home Rule was overshadowed. (*Gladiator and Howth gun-running images courtesy of Mercier Archive; funeral courtesy of Kilmainham Gaol Museum, 16PO-1A23-09*)

2. THE OUTBREAK OF WAR

'Before the war, scapegoats, those in debt or in trouble over a girl had joined the ranks; now all trades, professions and classes were found there.'[1]

Republican activist Ernie O'Malley

LEFT

The assassination of Franz Ferdinand, heir to the throne of the Austro-Hungarian Empire, in Sarajevo by a Bosnian-Serb on 28 June 1914 was the first of a series of events and decisions that led directly to the outbreak of the First World War. The Serbian state was blamed for his death. When Austria began to make menacing moves towards Serbia, Russia, which regarded itself as a protector of Serbia, was drawn into the conflict. Allied with Austria, Germany now faced a war on two fronts – against Russia and her ally France. This encouraged the Germans to act swiftly and focus on overcoming France quickly so that they could then concentrate their forces on Russia. (*Courtesy of the Library of Congress, LC-B2-1395-4*)

LEFT

Even as Europe moved towards war, the shape that events would ultimately take was not inevitable. The French had been assured of assistance by the British Foreign Secretary, Sir Edward Grey, in the event of a German invasion. However, Grey privately commented that the French had 'nothing in writing'.[1] (*Courtesy of the Library of Congress, LC-H261-4395*)

1 Hastings, M., *Catastrophe: Europe Goes to War 1914* (London, 2013), p. 36.

ABOVE

On 3 August Germany declared war on France. In an attempt to capture Paris quickly, they attacked through Belgium, violating Belgian neutrality and causing outrage amongst the British public. On 4 August Britain declared war on Germany. In Ireland the Catholic population sympathised with Catholic Belgium and was particularly revolted by the sacking of Louvain by German soldiers on 19 August. The Belgian university of Louvain had played an important part in preserving Catholicism and Gaelic culture during Ireland's conquest several centuries earlier. Some unionists had recently praised Germany as the 'greatest Protestant country in the World'.[1] However, the *Portadown News* proved worthy of the challenge of fostering anti-German sentiment, explaining that Germany was fighting in support of Austria, whose royal family was related to Philip II of Spain, a hate figure for European Protestants because of the Spanish Inquisition in the sixteenth century. Pictured are German troops in Antwerp, August 1914. (*Courtesy of the Library of Congress, LC-DIG-ggbain-17976*)

1   Cousins, C., *Armagh and the Great War* (Dublin, 2011), pp. 74–76.

OPPOSITE

There was intense sympathy across the Western world for the civilian victims of the conflict. Bishop Richard A. Sheehan of Waterford and Lismore held a collection in his diocese and raised £750 to aid Belgians displaced by the war.[1] (*Courtesy of Waterford County Museum, UK 1517*)

1   *Irish Independent*, 23 October 1914.

RIGHT

Accompanying the sympathy was xenophobia directed at Ireland's small but noticeable German community. German shops were attacked by mobs. Germans of military age were interned. Among them was Albert Muckley, a jeweller in Midleton in Cork, who was interned in a camp on the Isle of Man for four years. The family had changed their name from Muckle to Muckley before the war. (*Courtesy of Albert Muckley*)

LEFT

Unsurprisingly for an island, the strength of Britain's military had always been concentrated in its navy, and the military was to prove itself relatively unready for the swift creation of a huge army. Regular soldiers like Michael Higgins of the 4th Battalion of the Connaught Rangers, who was from Boyle in Roscommon, as well as reservists, were the first to be impacted by the war. There were 730,000 regular and reservist soldiers across the UK. (*Courtesy of Martin Higgins*)

Company Sergeant Major, later Captain, Tom Corry (*front row, second from right*), 1st Battalion of the Irish Guards, from Labasheeda in Co. Clare, was luckier than many of the men who became known as 'The Old Contemptibles', pre-war soldiers who served during the conflict. Wounded in 1917, he survived and went on to become active in the British Legion, looking after former comrades. (*Author's collection*)

Men like Captain Jervais Biggs from Water-ford, of the 5th Royal Irish Lancers, now had to face life in a vastly different army. Between August 1914 and November 1918 about half of those who joined the British Army were volunteers, the others were conscripts. About six million men served during the war.[1] Many of the pre-war soldiers looked down on the quality of the volunteers and even more so on that of the conscripts. (*Courtesy of Waterford County Museum, UK 19*)

1   Simkins, P., 'The Four Armies 1914–1918' in Chandler, D .G. and Beckett, I. (eds), *The Oxford History of the British Army* (Oxford, 2003), pp. 235–36.

In order to encourage enlistment the British developed 'Pals' Battalions'. These were units where friends and colleagues would serve together. Newcastle in England raised four battalions known as 'The Tyneside Irish' because of the ethnicity of the soldiers and/or their place of birth.[1] Another of these 'Pals' units was the 8th (City of London) Battalion, London Regiment (*pictured*). Dungarvan Post Office workers Willie Duggan and Patrick Duggan both served with this regiment (*back row, third and fourth from left*). (*Courtesy of Waterford County Museum, UK 1524*)

1   Keegan, J., *The First World War* (London, 1999), p. 298.

The driving force behind the rapid expansion of the army was Field Marshal Horatio Herbert Kitchener, who was born into an Anglo-Irish family in Ballylongford, Co. Kerry. Appointed Secretary of State for War, Kitchener forecast a long and costly war, which many others failed to envision. It was felt that conscription would be divisive and so in the first couple of years of war this was avoided. Kitchener, an imperial icon, was responsible for recruiting hundreds of thousands of volunteers.[1] (*Courtesy of Mercier Archive*)

1   Simkins, P., 'The Four Armies 1914–1918' in Chandler, D. G. and Beckett, I. (eds), *The Oxford History of the British Army* (Oxford, 2003), p. 237.

ABOVE

Ulster unionists tended to join the 36th (Ulster) Division, formed in September 1914. It was commanded by Cavan man Major General Sir Oliver Nugent from 1915 to 1918. (*Courtesy of the Deputy Keeper of the Records, Public Records Office Northern Ireland, D3394/3*)

LEFT

The 16th (Irish) Division, under the command of Major General William Bernard Hickie, was identified with Irish nationalism. Hickie, a native of Terryglass, Co. Tipperary, was both a Catholic and a nationalist. Irish troops were generally regarded as being aggressive when on the offensive but poor defensively. Such opinions were influenced by stereotypes that both critics and supporters of the Irish soldiers invoked. Criticism of their battle performance was unduly harsh on occasion, probably accentuated by suspicions about their loyalty after the Easter Rising. Irish soldiers were reputed to be more informal with their officers and discipline had to be administered in a more tactful manner than in other units. Attention was also paid to their consumption of alcohol. One officer of the 6th Connaught Rangers commented that his men got drunk on the slightest pretext but generally behaved well, even when drunk.[1] (*Courtesy of Patrick Lynch*)

1   Denman, T., 'The Catholic Irish Soldier in the First World War: The "Racial Environment"', *Irish Historical Studies*, November 1991, pp. 350–65.

Propaganda encouraging people to enlist was everywhere. Pictured is a decorated recruiting tram in Dublin. (*Courtesy of Kilmainham Gaol Museum, 10PO-1A57-03*)

It has been estimated that 15 per cent of the propaganda used in Ireland focused on atrocities, real and imagined, by German forces in Belgium during the invasion, and the danger of similar atrocities being carried out in Ireland in the event of a German invasion of the country.[1] (*Courtesy of the Library of Congress, LC-USZC4-1097*)

1 Horne, J. and Kramer, A., *German Atrocities 1914: A History of Denial* (New Haven and London, 2001), p. 292.

IS **YOUR** HOME WORTH FIGHTING FOR?

IT WILL BE TOO LATE TO FIGHT WHEN THE ENEMY IS AT YOUR DOOR

SO JOIN TO-DAY

HELY'S LIMITED, LITHO: DUBLIN, P661.

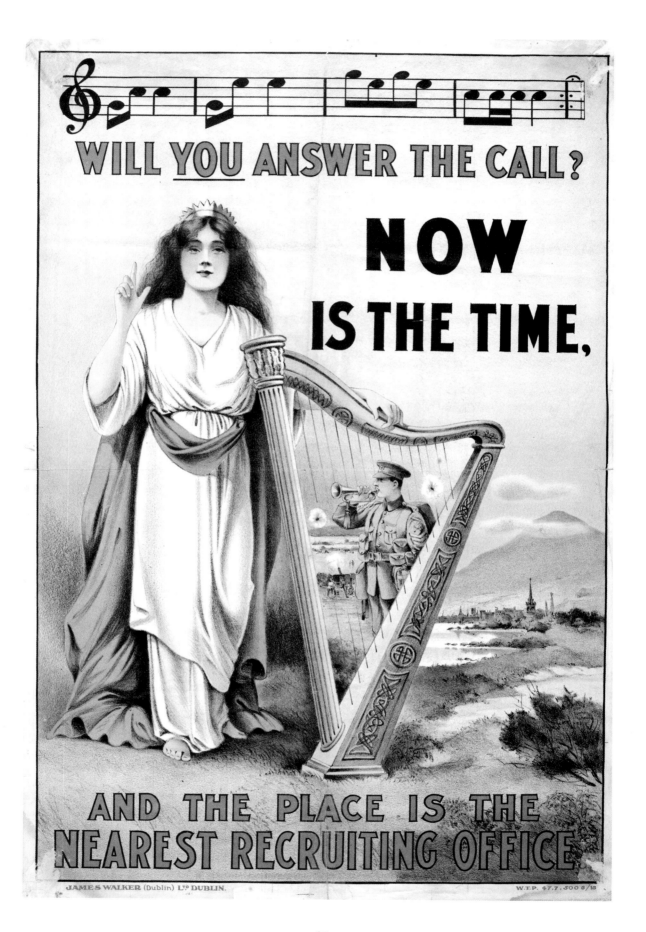

The symbols of Irish nationalism were also mobilised to stimulate recruitment. Rather bizarrely, posters even utilised the anti-British 1798 rebellion and invoked folk memory of the brutality of German Hessian mercenaries employed by the British in order to encourage men to fight against the Germans.[1] (*Courtesy of the National Library of Ireland, EPH 110*)

1   Beiner, G., *Remembering the Year of the French: Irish Folk History and Social Memory* (Madison, 2007), p. 105.

Propaganda also emphasised Ireland's position in the United Kingdom, and that the Scots, the Welsh, the English and the Irish were all part of the same war effort. Pictured is a postcard from the period, which talks of the Irish shamrock and English rose 'side by side'. (*Courtesy of Aribert Elpelt*)

YOUR DEAR OLD DAD WAS IRISH (2).

Take this bunch of shamrock and guard it with pride,
The rose of Old England, keep them side by side;
If anyone asks what their meaning can be,
Just say they're an emblem of sweet liberty.

TOP LEFT

Many thousands of boys who were underage enlisted, often with the connivance of their enlisting officers. Less well remembered are the people who lowered their age in order to join. Pictured is Private George Forrest, a Tyrone man who joined the Australian Army by passing himself off as forty-five. He arrived for service on the Western Front in November 1916 and was killed in action at Messines, Belgium, on 7 June 1917. He was sixty years of age. (*Courtesy of the Australian War Memorial Museum, P08568.001*)

TOP RIGHT

Men of all backgrounds served in the British forces or assisted with recruiting during the war. For example Patrick Kerr from Fanad in Co. Donegal, a prominent Irish language writer, joined as an army chaplain. (*Courtesy of Donegal County Museum collection*)

RIGHT

Professor Edward H. Harper, Head of the Maths Department in University College Cork died in France in 1916. (*Courtesy of University Archives, University College Cork*)

Another branch of the British armed services that had many Irish members was the Royal Navy. Jack Barron (*probably right*) from Cappoquin in Co. Waterford was a chief petty officer. A member of the RIC, he joined the navy in 1915. He was fortunate enough to survive the war. Of 752 RIC men who served with the army during the war, 163 were killed and 182 were wounded.[1] (*Courtesy of Waterford County Museum, UK 3912*)

1 Herlihy, J., *The Royal Irish Constabulary* (Dublin, 1997), p. 100.

LEFT

One reason for enlisting was the presence of so many sporting heroes in the ranks, giving others a chance to serve with their heroes. It is quite likely that high profile casualties amongst these heroes later damaged recruiting efforts, of course. Prominent sporting casualties included P. J. Roche, an Olympic sprinter and British Isles Champion, who died of fever in Iraq.[1] (*Courtesy of University Archives, University College Cork*)

1   Borgonovo, J., *The Dynamics of War and Revolution: Cork City 1916–1918* (Cork, 2013), p. 188.

BELOW

As always, urban poverty remained a major cause of enlistment, regardless of religious background. Pictured is the Claddagh, Galway city, an area that supplied a large number of recruits to the Royal Navy.[1] (*Courtesy of Tom Kenny*)

1   Henry, W., *Galway and the Great War* (Cork, 2006), p. 33.

Men enlisted largely, but not exclusively, in their local regiments. Pictured is Ballymullen Barracks, Tralee, which was the regimental depot of the Royal Munster Fusiliers. Factors that had an impact in determining a volunteer's choice of regiment included the politics or religious makeup of the regiment and family tradition, but sometimes it was merely the result of contact with a particular recruiter. (*Courtesy of Collins Barracks, Cork, Clarke collection*)

It was in Ballymullen that Maurice O'Connell from Ballybunion, Co. Kerry, enlisted. He was killed in action in 1915. (*Courtesy of Kerry County Museum*)

Irishmen did not serve exclusively in regiments raised in Ireland. Matt Moroney (*top left*) from Loughmore, Dungarvan, Co. Waterford, served in the King's Shropshire Light Infantry Regiment. Colin Biggs (*above*) was born in Co. Kildare, but had emigrated and served in the Manitoba Regiment of the Canadian Army. He was killed in 1916.[1] Tom Power (*left*) from Burgery, near Dungarvan, served in the Australian Army. (*Courtesy of Waterford County Museum, UK 3881; UK 18; UK 3424*)

1   Burnell, T., *The Waterford War Dead: A History of the Casualties of the Great War* (Dublin, 2010), p. 23.

As well as barracks, prominent buildings were used as recruiting centres, such as the Royal Hotel in Eyre Square, Galway city. (*Courtesy of Tom Kenny*)

Many British men of Irish extraction joined Irish regiments. Sergeant Edward John Murphy was born on Jersey of Irish descent. He joined the Royal Munster Fusiliers and served as a machine-gun instructor. He was killed in action on 21 March 1918, aged twenty-five. The Irishness of Irish units was diluted, particularly as they shipped casualties. The Royal Irish Rifles 14th Battalion, which was based in the north-east, admitted 2,402 members. Out of these, 1,203 gave Belfast as the address of their next of kin, but 652 identified their next of kin as living in England.[1] The 7th Battalion of the Leinster Regiment had to be supplemented with 600 recruits from Bristol.[2] (*Courtesy of Waterford County Museum, UK 2784*)

1   Bowman, T., 'The Ulster Volunteer Force and the Formation of the 36th (Ulster) Division', *Irish Historical Studies*, November 2001, pp. 498–518.
2   Simkins, P., 'The Four Armies 1914–1918', in Chandler, D. G. and Beckett, I. (eds), *The Oxford History of the British Army* (Oxford, 2003), p. 243.

The British Army also saw many Irish Catholic clergymen becoming chaplains. These included Fr Phelan (*above*) from Dungarvan and Fr Jim Shine (*right*), also from Co. Waterford. (*Courtesy of Waterford County Museum, UK 323 and UK 1530*)

LEFT

Archbishop Patrick Clune, originally of Ruan, Co. Clare, was involved with the Australian Army. Of the 166 British Army chaplains who died as a result of the war, thirty-four were Catholic priests.[1] (*Courtesy of Perth Catholic Diocese*)

1   Snape, M., *God and the British Soldier: Religion and the British Army in the First and the Second World War* (London and New York, 2005), p. 103.

RIGHT

Irish Protestant clergymen of all denominations suffered as well. Pictured is Methodist Chaplain David De Venny Hunter of the Australian Army. A native of Banbridge, Co. Down, he was killed by a shell. He is buried in Belgium. (*Courtesy of the Australian War Memorial Museum, P10427.014*)

Some men took a little time to involve themselves in the war. Pictured above is the Hamiltonsbawn Company of the UVF, Co. Armagh. When the company captain encouraged the men to enlist in the British Army, they initially refused, not knowing what the British government's intentions regarding Ulster were.[1] Their attitude to recruitment improved when Sir Edward Carson received assurances on partition and the formation of an Ulster division. It was quickly decided to shelve Home Rule for the duration of the war. (*Courtesy of Colin Cousins*)

1   Cousins, C., *Armagh and the Great War* (Dublin, 2011), pp. 31–32.

There was a crisis of accommodation for soldiers across the United Kingdom at the start of the war. Barracks accommodation could be provided for only 262,000 men. This led to the housing of men in tents, which was pleasant while the weather was fine, but unsuitable for colder weather. By 31 January 1915, 300 soldiers had died of pneumonia across the UK.[1] Pictured above are Royal Dublin Fusiliers encamped at Bray, Co. Wicklow. (*Courtesy of Collins Barracks, Cork, Clarke collection*)

1   Simkins, P., 'The Four Armies 1914–1918', in Chandler, D. G. and Beckett, I. (eds), *The Oxford History of the British Army* (Oxford, 2003), p. 246.

Regardless of the wishes of nostalgic officers, the age of cavalry charges was coming to an end. Nevertheless armies relied on animals as much as they ever had for the transportation of men and materials, so soldiers skilled in handling animals were essential. Pictured is an unidentified soldier on a horse called 'Fireflight' in Co. Clare. In the first twelve days of the war the British military bought 165,000 horses.[1] (*Courtesy of Clare County Library*)

1   Hastings, M., *Catastrophe: Europe Goes to War 1914* (London, 2013), p. 522.

The horses needed to be maintained and fed. Pictured is a farrier attached to the Royal Irish Regiment. (*Courtesy of Waterford County Museum, UK 3936*)

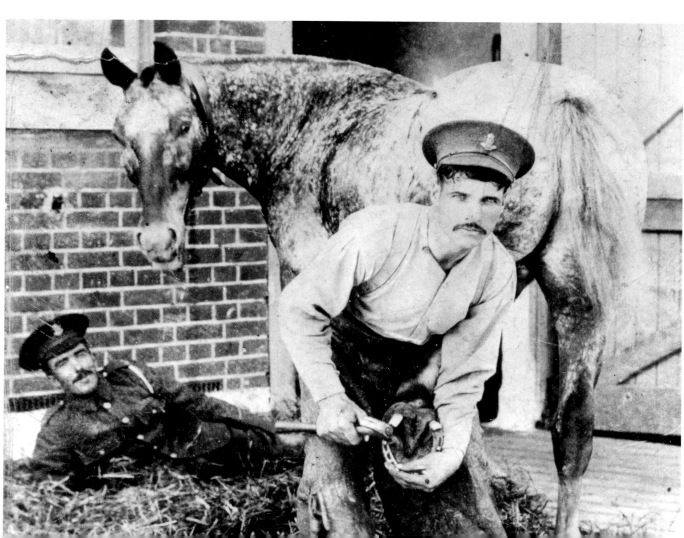

With so many men at war, it fell to the women left behind to fill the jobs they had vacated and the jobs created by the war. Pictured are Nell Keenan and Nellie Byers from Belfast, both munitions workers. Shell production increased from 872,000 rounds in 1914 to 23.7 million rounds in 1915, and the number of women involved in munitions work in the UK grew from 212,000 in 1914 to 520,000 in 1916.[1] (*Courtesy of Dave Donatelli*)

1   Simkins, P., 'The Four Armies 1914–1918', in Chandler, D. G. and Beckett, I. (eds), *The Oxford History of the British Army* (Oxford, 2003), pp. 235–55.

The war also created massive demand for uniforms, which were supplied by workers such as these women in the Galway Woollen Mill. (*Courtesy of Tom Kenny*)

Many other women served as nurses. This group from Ulster accompanied troops to France. (*Courtesy of Getty Images, 83513312*)

Those destined for war needed to be trained. Pictured is Finner Camp in Donegal, a training camp for the 109th Brigade of the 36th (Ulster) Division. The politics of the Division were clear to all and sundry. According to the *Southern Star* of 28 November 1914: 'In Letterkenny ... 200 of the Ulster Division stationed at Finner Camp arrived to the tune of "The Boyne Water" and left to the strains of "Dolly's Brae".' (*Courtesy of Donegal County Museum collection*)

The Royal Dublin Golf Club, Dollymount, was also used as a base for military training, including the clubhouse shown here. (*Courtesy of Peter Finnegan and the Royal Dublin Golf Club*)

There was a race against time to arm units before they sailed to war. This had a major effect on the quality of the training received. One artillery brigade had just three days' training with full equipment before they sailed.[1] Pictured is the Royal Field Artillery operating an 18-pounder gun. (*Courtesy of Waterford County Museum, UK 2430*)

1   Simkins, P., 'The Four Armies 1914–1918', in Chandler, D. G. and Beckett, I. (eds), *The Oxford History of the British Army* (Oxford, 2003), p. 248.

After the start of the war, all parts of society in the Empire who felt that they had been denied their legitimate rights were forced to choose between conciliation or confrontation with their rulers, including Irish and Indian nationalists, and women. Choosing the path of conciliation was a gamble, as each of these groups had radical fringes that could quickly undermine any leader who delivered war support but failed to be adequately compensated for that support. One of the best examples of this is John Redmond. In 1914, with the prospect of Home Rule finally in sight, he was at the peak of his powers. Keen to keep the support of the British government, he called for Irish nationalists, including the Irish Volunteers, to join the British Army, a move that would eventually lead to his downfall. Redmond's decision split the Volunteers. The vast majority agreed with him, in theory at least. They became known as the National Volunteers. Redmond is pictured here on the podium at the blessing of the National Volunteer colours. (*Courtesy of Mercier Archive*)

National Volunteers at Dungarvan, Co. Waterford. (*Courtesy of Waterford County Museum, EK 345*)

Bishop Thomas Gilmartin of Clonfert told his flock: 'It was the right of a sovereign state to make war for just and grave reasons, and once citizens are satisfied of its justness it becomes their sacred duty to place their services at the disposal of the country. A prosperous nation indifferent to the miseries of the poor and ignoring God and despising His laws needed punishment and purification. They might assume that as God has permitted the present war He is using this scourge to punish and chasten His erring children.'[1] (*Courtesy of Tuam Diocesan Archives*)

1   *Irish Independent*, 11 February 1915.

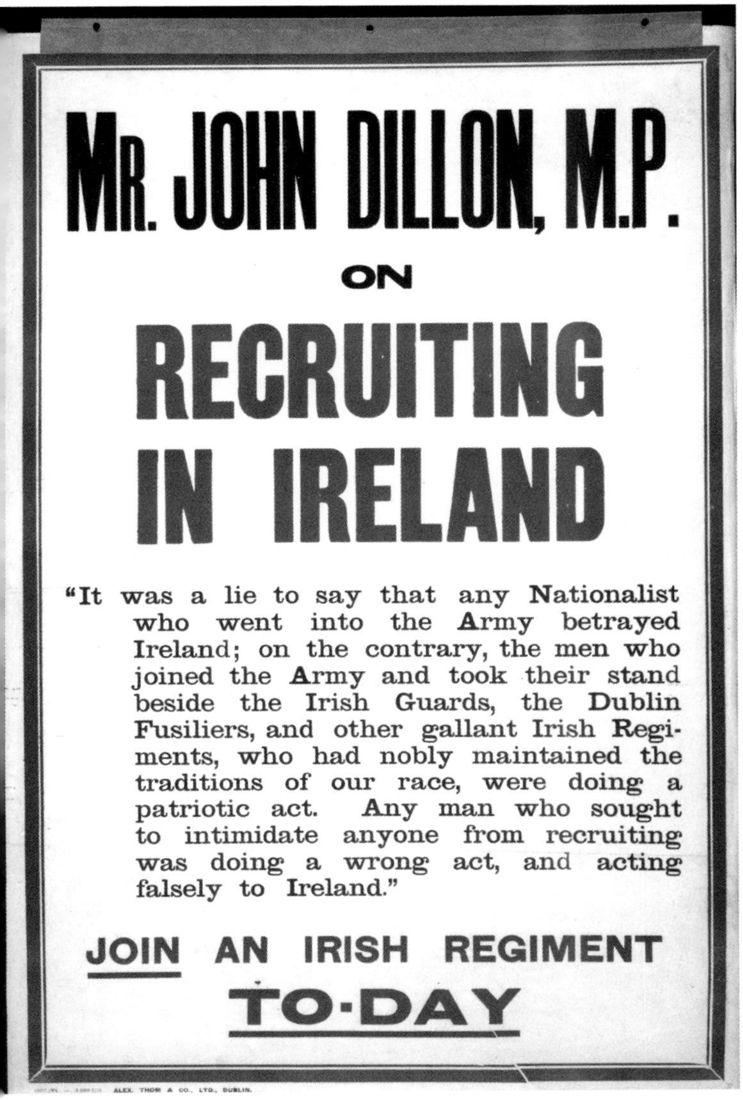
MR. JOHN DILLON, M.P.
ON
RECRUITING IN IRELAND
"It was a lie to say that any Nationalist who went into the Army betrayed Ireland; on the contrary, the men who joined the Army and took their stand beside the Irish Guards, the Dublin Fusiliers, and other gallant Irish Regiments, who had nobly maintained the traditions of our race, were doing a patriotic act. Any man who sought to intimidate anyone from recruiting was doing a wrong act, and acting falsely to Ireland."
JOIN AN IRISH REGIMENT
TO-DAY
ALEX. THOM & CO., LTD., DUBLIN.

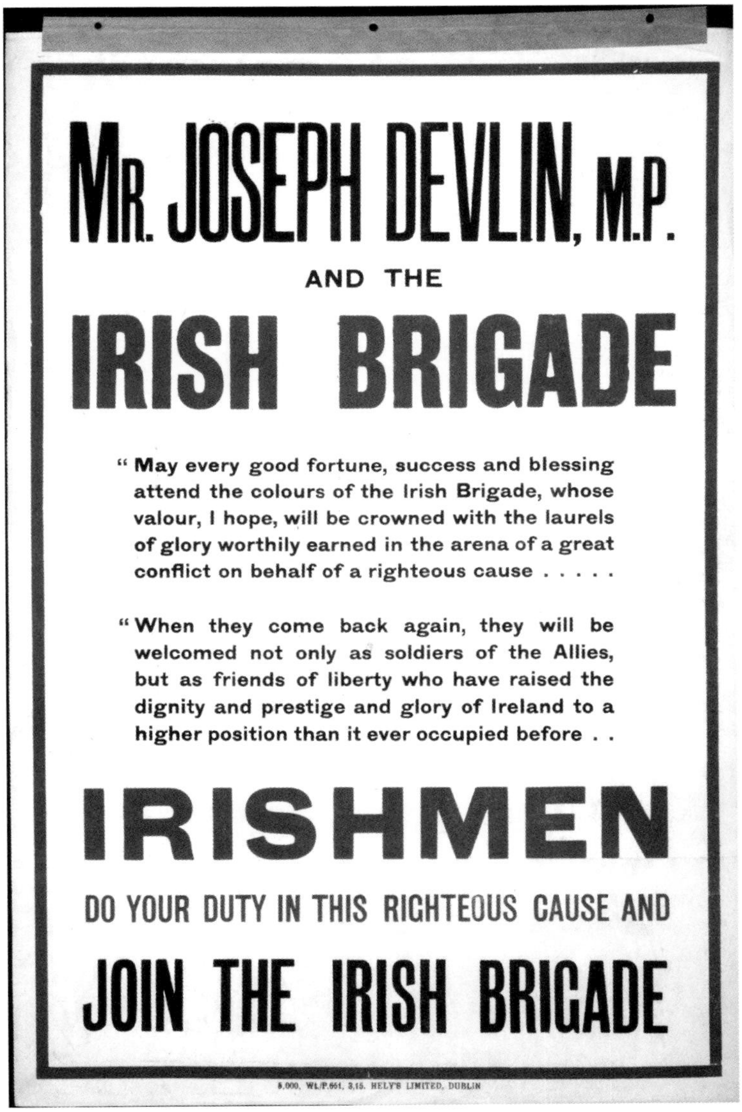
MR. JOSEPH DEVLIN, M.P.
AND THE
IRISH BRIGADE
"May every good fortune, success and blessing attend the colours of the Irish Brigade, whose valour, I hope, will be crowned with the laurels of glory worthily earned in the arena of a great conflict on behalf of a righteous cause . . . . .
"When they come back again, they will be welcomed not only as soldiers of the Allies, but as friends of liberty who have raised the dignity and prestige and glory of Ireland to a higher position than it ever occupied before . .
IRISHMEN
DO YOUR DUTY IN THIS RIGHTEOUS CAUSE AND
JOIN THE IRISH BRIGADE
5,000. WL/P.661, 3,15. HELY'S LIMITED, DUBLIN

Nationalist figures who had previously been critical of service in the British forces now openly advocated recruiting, amongst them John Dillon MP. Belfast nationalist MP Joe Devlin also lent his considerable influence to the recruitment campaign. (*Courtesy of the Library of Congress, LC-USZC4-10990 and LC-USZC4-10991*)

RIGHT

After the split in the organisation, the Irish Volunteers who chose to reject Redmond's call to go to war, began to reorganise themselves, sending organisers to the provinces. They retained the name Irish Volunteers and remained under the leadership of Eoin MacNeill (*right*). These men felt that the only place where Irishmen should fight was at home in Ireland. (*Courtesy of Mercier Archive*)

LEFT

The IRB quickly and secretly gained control of the Irish Volunteers and were active in efforts to revive the organisation which had collapsed in many areas under the moral and physical pressure of supporters of the war effort. Amongst the Irish Volunteer organisers involved in the revival was Robert Monteith, a Protestant from Wicklow and an ex-British soldier, who was sent to Limerick. (*Courtesy of Mercier Archive*)

ABOVE

In Ireland many of the war's opponents were Republican militants, but the war was also opposed by the pacifist Francis Sheehy-Skeffington (*above left*). He was sentenced to six months in prison for a speech, recorded in *The Kerryman* of 12 June 1915, in which he declared: 'Germany never did us any harm; the only Power that has ever done us any harm is England.' He was released after commencing a hunger strike. In Britain opponents of the war included Dublin-born writer George Bernard Shaw (*above right*). Conscientious objectors were despised in Britain, but one group sent to France and then sentenced to death when they refused to serve, found sympathy among the soldiers there. They were brought cake, fruit and chocolate by a sergeant of the Irish Guards. The conscientious objectors were later reprieved but received prison sentences.[1] (*Sheehy-Skeffington courtesy of Mercier Archive; Bernard Shaw courtesy of the Deputy Keeper of the Records, Public Records Office, Northern Ireland, D3084/R/1*)

1   Hochschild, A., *To End All Wars: A Story of Protest and Patriotism in the First World War* (London, 2012), pp. 200–2.

OVERLEAF

A cartoon by labour activist Ernest Kavanagh mocks a number of prominent people and institutions that supported the war effort, including the IPP, the prime minister, British officials in Ireland, the Dublin Metropolitan Police and the AOH. (*Courtesy of the Military Archives, P27-08*)

The Mansion House Recruiting Fiasco from Within.

LEFT

One of the criticisms levelled at many prominent recruiters was that they themselves didn't serve. One Tipperary recruiter joined up after being heckled: 'You ask us to France, why don't you go yourself?'[1] A number of MPs paid a high personal price during the war. The war's major sea battle occurred at Jutland in the North Sea during 1916. One casualty was John, the son of Sir Thomas H. Grattan Esmonde MP (*pictured*), a vice-president of the County Recruiting Committee for Wexford. (*Courtesy of Mercier Archive*)

1   Margaret McKenna (TNA: PRO CO 762/205).

RIGHT

For family members, parting with a loved one leaving for the war and knowing that it might be the last time they would ever see each other was extremely painful. The distress can clearly be seen in this image of Private Patrick Halloran, 1st Battalion, Connaught Rangers, saying his last goodbye to his mother, Mary, and sister, Bridget, at Ennistymon Railway Station, Co. Clare, in 1914 on his way to war. Patrick was mortally wounded and died at 11.13 a.m. on 29 April 1915. (*Courtesy of Gus O'Halloran and Clare County Library*)

Parents and wives asked older brothers, neighbours and officers to look after their loved ones. In Armagh John McAlindon's mother asked a relation, Sergeant Tom McAlindon (*pictured*), to look after her son. On 31 October 1914 Sergeant McAlindon wrote to her shortly after John's death: 'I feel in a way that I'm talking to my own mother and apologising to you both. When I see you opening that telegram I imagine her doing the same, something I dread for her sake, and so my pity for you is great.'[1] (*Reproduced by kind permission of Lilliput Press, from the book McAlindon, T.,* Two Brothers, Two Wars *(Dublin, 2008)*)

1   Cousins, C., *Armagh and the Great War* (Dublin, 2011), p. 165.

Members of the Irish Guards preparing to leave Wellington Barracks, London, 6 August 1914. They were part of what was known as the British Expeditionary Force, the force sent to fight on the Western Front. (*Courtesy of the Imperial War Museum, Q 66157*)

3. A SOLDIER'S LIFE

'D'you hear that? They're doing that to frighten you.'
'If that's what they're after, they might as well stop.
They succeeded with me hours ago.'

*Conversation between Lieutenant Colonel George Morris of
the Irish Guards and an anonymous soldier during a lull in shellfire.*[1]

1   Kipling, R., *The Irish Guards in the Great War: The First Battalion* (Staplehurst, 1997), p. 38.

Despite an initial impressive battle performance, the British Expeditionary Force was quickly left with little choice but to retreat because of the size of German forces and a French retreat. This was known as the retreat from Mons. On 1 September 1914 Lieutenant Colonel George Morris of the Irish Guards (*above*), who was from Spiddal, Co. Galway, was killed. A lecturer on military matters, his son Michael was born just before war was declared, on 31 July. Having known the excitement of the pregnancy, George barely got to know his son before shipping out. Michael went on to become Lord Killanin and was the sixth president of the International Olympic Committee. George Morris was regarded as a popular, competent and brave officer.[1] (*Courtesy of the Morris family*)

1   Kipling, R., *The Irish Guards in the Great War: The First Battalion* (Staplehurst, 1997), p. 38.

Serious doubts about the ability of certain officers to use the men under their command in a non-wasteful manner began almost as soon as the war commenced. Michael Curley (*seated*) from Athlone was an ex-soldier and a reservist. Called up when war broke out, he deliberately killed his superior officer in the Connaught Rangers with a hand grenade, probably on 31 October 1914. As this happened in the confusion of battle, he got away with it. Curley was unhappy with orders to attack a German position with little hope of either success or survival. Shortly after the officer was killed orders were received commanding him to refrain from the attack.[1] (*Courtesy of Athlone County Library*)

1 Richardson, N., *A Coward if I Return, a Hero if I Fall* (Dublin, 2010), pp. 234–47.

Many officers were unprepared for the demands of modern warfare. Some were incompetent, some were physically unable for the strain and for others the training they had received at Staff College had failed to prepare them to act with the independence of mind needed for battle situations, where decisions need to be made quickly and under pressure. Another problem was personality clashes and intrigue in the higher ranks, as men manoeuvred for position and power. In the case of Field Marshal Sir Douglas Haig (*right*), who commanded the British Expeditionary Force, he intimidated those around him and received poor advice as a result, but he was also a poor communicator. Deeply interested in the spiritual world, Haig had communicated with Napoleon during a seance and, thanks to the influence of a Presbyterian chaplain, he was convinced of his own importance to God's plan for the world. (*Courtesy of the Library of Congress, LC-USZ62-103116*)

The reputation of the military leadership also suffered because of their perceived reluctance to put themselves in danger, their tolerance of casualties and their apparent attention to serving their own comforts. Pictured is one of the buildings used by the leadership of the British Expeditionary Force near Saint-Omer, France. Much of the criticism levelled at the leadership, including Haig, has been unfair, however. Men in battle are poorly served by dead generals, the sheer size of battlefields necessitated the avoidance of closeness to one flank or the other, communication between units was poor and slow, and once the fighting started generals were very much in the dark about what was happening.[1] One valid point of criticism, perhaps, was their inability to fully understand the new technology. Even after the war ended Haig would still comment that 'Aeroplanes and tanks ... are only accessories to the man and the horse.'[2] (*Courtesy of the Deputy Keeper of the Records, Public Records Office, Northern Ireland, D1977/10*)

1   Travers, T., 'The Army and the Challenge of War 1914–1918', in Chandler, D. G. and Beckett, I. (eds), *The Oxford History of the British Army* (Oxford, 2003), pp. 222–34; Keegan, J., *The First World War* (London, 1999), pp. 310–11, 337–41.
2   Hochschild, A., *To End All Wars: A Story of Protest and Patriotism in the First World War* (London, 2012), p. 367.

ABOVE

Within months of the start of the war both sides were dug in along the Western Front. The trenches moved little during the course of the conflict. Allied trenches, like this one being used by members of the 5th Royal Irish Fusiliers (10th Irish Division), were very basic. Allied soldiers were shocked when they later saw the relative comfort that the German soldiers lived in. (*Courtesy of the Imperial War Museum, Q 13444*)

During the winter, as snow melted and rain fell, or in areas that had suffered severe bombardment, movement was difficult in the mud. Pictured are a chaplain and officers of the Royal Irish Rifles in February 1918 slogging through the liquid mud that has built up at the bottom of a trench. (*Courtesy of the Imperial War Museum, Q 10681*)

ABOVE

During the war engineers, such as these men from the Royal Engineers, were vital to maintaining infrastructure, trenches, fortifications and weapons. (*Courtesy of Waterford County Museum, UK 2786*)

LEFT

Barbed wire was laid in front of both the British and the German trenches. Thousands died in battle when they were caught up in this barbed wire when attempting to capture opposing trenches. This photograph shows a German barbed wire entanglement at Beaucourt-sur-Ancre in France. (*Courtesy of the Imperial War Museum, Q 4592*)

Snipers were a constant danger to those in the trenches as well. Pictured is a Royal Irish Fusilier at Gallipoli in 1915 attempting to draw the fire of a Turkish sniper. He may have been doing this to get the sniper to reveal his position, or he might simply have been bored. (*Courtesy of the Imperial War Museum, Q 13447*)

There were a number of weapons that defined the First World War, one of them being the machine gun. Pictured are members of the 2nd Battalion, Royal Munster Fusiliers. Sergeant Edward John Murphy, is standing to the right. (*Courtesy of Waterford County Museum, UK 2785*)

Poison gas was a horrific new weapon. Pictured are members of the Irish Guards at respirator drill, September 1916. At precisely the time that the Easter Rising was occurring in Dublin, the German Army carried out a massive gas attack at Loos on the Western Front. Its victims were members of the 16th (Irish) Division who suffered heavy casualties. They received little sympathy from their fellow soldiers, with allegations being made of poor discipline, panic and even men cutting holes in their own masks so that they could smoke. The reality was much more terrifying. The Irishmen had proven up to the challenge, the masks had not – they were unable to cope with the sheer amounts of gas that were used in the attack.[1] (*Courtesy of the Imperial War Museum, Q 4232*)

1   Denman, T., 'The Catholic Irish Soldier in the First World War: The "Racial Environment"', *Irish Historical Studies*, November 1991, pp. 350–65.

As the war progressed, and with no end in sight, casualties began to mount. The unidentified Royal Dublin Fusilier above is wearing the 'hospital blues' that were issued to all patients in military hospitals. (*Courtesy of Waterford County Museum, UK 1690*)

Sir James Craig volunteered his home in Belfast, Craigavon House, for what became known as the UVF hospital. As well as treating regular patients, the institution was used to treat those suffering from what came to be called 'shell-shock'. Pictured are patients at the hospital in November 1918. (*Courtesy of Dave Donatelli*)

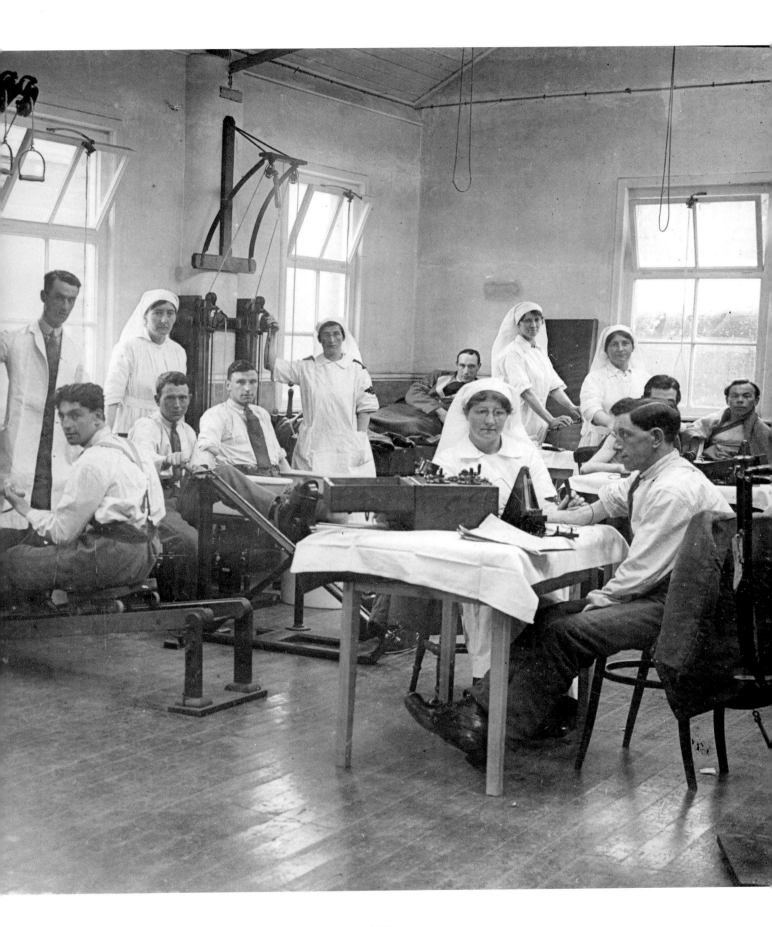

ABOVE

Believed to be caused by the noise and trauma of being under artillery barrage, 'shell-shock' had any number of potential triggers. Sufferers showed a wide range of physical or mental symptoms which rendered them unfit as soldiers. Sir Alfred Keogh (*pictured*), director general of the Army Medical Service until March 1918, tried to provide resources to deal with and encourage research into the condition. Keogh was born in Dublin in 1857, the son of Henry Keogh, a barrister and magistrate. Treatment varied from institution to institution with some using electrical currents, hypnosis and physiotherapy. Ultimately Keogh arranged for a team of academics to try a new approach at an institution near Liverpool, allowing the patient to discuss his problems and memories of the trauma, and this approach was largely successful. In the twelve months up to 30 June 1917, 731 patients were discharged: 160 returned to military duties while about 500 were deemed capable of returning to civilian life. Only 1 per cent were sent to mental hospitals. It was suspected that the staff might have been even more successful at returning men to military duty had the patients not quickly realised that the more talkative they were, the more likely they were to be considered fully cured and fit to return to military duty.[1] (*Courtesy of the Army Medical Services Museum*)

1   Shephard, B., *A War of Nerves: Soldiers and Psychiatrists 1914–1994* (London, 2002), pp. 73–83.

Victoria Barracks, Athlone, was used for soldiers recuperating from their injuries during and after the First World War. It was located on 'the Sick Horse Field' adjacent to the Watergate and was dismantled in the early 1920s shortly after the takeover of the barracks by the National Army. These images show interior and exterior views of the soldiers' home in the barracks. This home was part of the Sandes Soldiers' Homes movement. (*Courtesy of Athlone Library*)

ABOVE

Pictured are members of the Royal Army Medical Corps in the Military Hospital, Dundalk, Co. Louth. (*Courtesy of the Deputy Keeper of the Records, Public Records Office Northern Ireland, D1593/3*)

LEFT

Combat injuries were not the only danger in the trenches. Ignatius Furey, a private in the Royal Newfoundland Regiment, died of tetanus, always a risk in a war where there was frequent contact with barbed wire. (*Courtesy of the Archive of Newfoundland and Labrador, VA 36-18.7*)

LEFT

Vermin caused serious hygiene issues and spread disease. Pictured is a dead soldier covered in flies. Dysentery, was another major problem during the war, caused by contaminated water and poor sanitation and hygiene. Symptoms included severe and sometimes fatal diarrhoea. With typical gallows humour men joked that they were caught 'between the Devil and the W.C.'[1] (*Courtesy of the Imperial War Museum, Q 7914*)

1   Leonard, J., 'Survivors', in Horne, J. (ed.), *Our War: Ireland and the Great War* (Dublin, 2008), pp. 211–23.

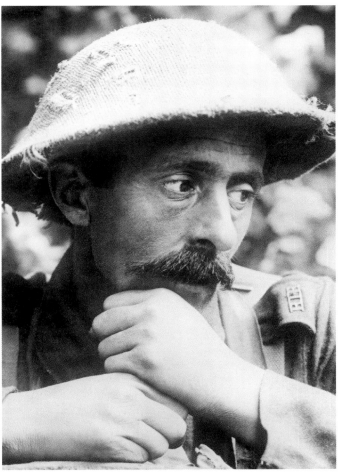

RIGHT

The other main danger was, of course, capture by the enemy. Pictured is a member of the Royal Irish Rifles who was taken prisoner by the Germans. Despite having escaped the trenches, he was not out of danger yet. Soldiers on both sides shot prisoners out of hand. (*Courtesy of the Imperial War Museum, Q 23839*)

Although the higher ranked officers were criticised for staying out of the fight, non-commissioned officers and some of the lower ranked officers on the ground felt the need to lead by example, and they suffered heavy casualties. One such NCO was Lance Corporal Richard Fitzpatrick, Affane, Cappoquin, Co. Waterford, who served in the Royal Irish Regiment of the British Army for four years in India and subsequently in the First World War. He was killed in action on 15 February 1915 and is buried in Elzenwalle Brasserie Cemetery, Voormezeele, Ieper, West-Vlaanderen, Belgium. (*Courtesy of Waterford County Museum, UK 5261*)

Lieutenant Richard Kinkead, the son of a professor at University College Galway, wrote home commenting: 'Even when things burst over one's head, one must not duck or jump – the men would see it.' The letter arrived on the same day as the telegram informing his family of his death.[1] (*Courtesy of NUI Galway*)

1   Henry, W., *Galway and the Great War* (Cork, 2006), pp. 168–69.

For those whose actions were considered above and beyond the call of duty there were a number of awards they could receive. The awarding of these honours was a major occasion and an opportunity to meet royalty. Pictured is Lieutenant Commander Henry Hew Gordon Stoker from Dublin, who served in the campaign in the Dardanelles, where his submarine was holed and he was captured, spending three and a half years as a prisoner of war in Turkey. He is seen here leaving Buckingham Palace after receiving a Distinguished Service Order from King George V. (*Courtesy of Dacre Stoker*)

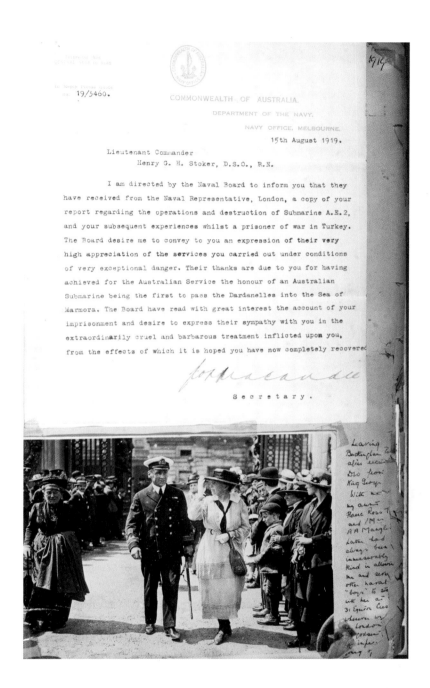

Lieutenant Michael Lavelle, Clifden, Co. Galway, was attached to the 4th Battalion of the Connaught Rangers and then the 9th Battalion of the Royal Inniskilling Fusiliers. He was the only one out of four officers who survived one particular attack. The night before the attack Lavelle and a Lieutenant Kempston from Roscommon had made a pact that if either of them was killed the other would bring his body back from no man's land. Against the advice of his commander, Lavelle crawled back out into no man's land to retrieve the body of the unfortunate Kempston.[1] Lavelle was awarded the Military Cross for his actions during the attack. (*Courtesy of Kathleen Villiers-Tuthill*)

1 Villiers-Tuthill, K., *Beyond the Twelve Bens* (Galway, 1986), p. 190.

The highest award that was given to British forces was the Victoria Cross (VC). Many of these were awarded to men who saved the lives of others, rather than for inflicting casualties. Private James Duffy from Gweedore in Co. Donegal was awarded a VC while acting as a stretcher-bearer. (*Courtesy of Donegal County Museum collection*)

Robert Hanna, originally from Kilkeel, Co. Down, was a member of the Canadian Expeditionary Force. He won the VC for leading the capture of a German machine gun in Lens, France, on 21 August 1917. (*Courtesy of the Canadian Department of National Defence (DND)*)

Medals could also be awarded posthumously. Claude Nunney, who claimed to be from Dublin, a member of the Canadian Expeditionary Force, was one such case. He was awarded the VC for demonstrating conspicuous bravery during an attack against German defensive lines on 1–2 September 1918. Sixteen days later he died of wounds received during this action. (*Courtesy of the Canadian Department of National Defence (DND)*)

War heroes such as Mike O'Leary from Inchigeela in west Cork became instant celebrities and were used extensively in recruiting drives. His father also had a career as a speaker at recruiting meetings, a career that came to a screeching halt after one meeting, when he told his listeners: 'If you don't (enlist) the Germans will come here and will do to you what the English have been doing for the last seven hundred years.'[1] (*Courtesy of the Library of Congress, LC-USZC4-11356*)

1   Hogan, D. (Frank Gallagher), *The Four Glorious Years* (Dublin, 1953), p. 43.

ABOVE

One of the reasons that the Germans behaved so harshly in Belgium was their distrust of the local population. They were not alone in this reaction. All the countries involved in the war became infected with the fear of an internal enemy passing information, both at home and where their armies were serving. Even amongst sympathetic populations close to the Western Front, Allied soldiers carried out legally dubious killings of suspected spies. Private B. W. Page of the London Irish Rifles described one such incident: 'One gunner said there were many spies among the peasants. One officer of theirs found telephone in estaminet with pretty girl who supplied fried spuds and things to the troops. They shot the inhabitants of the house.'[1]

Pictured is a suspected German spy being harassed in Amiens, France. (*Courtesy of the Imperial War Museum, Q 11582*)

1   Sheehan, W., *The Western Front: Irish Voices from the Great War* (Dublin, 2011), p. 45.

One legitimate German spy was Carl Hans Lody, who was arrested at the Great Southern Hotel, Killarney, Co. Kerry, having escaped from Britain in an attempt to avoid arrest. He was executed in the Tower of London on 6 November 1914. (*Courtesy of Bundesarchiv, Bild 134-B2626*)

Not all aspects of the war were unpleasant. Troops were rotated and there was always a chance of a quiet posting, which is what Ireland was, Easter Week apart. This photograph shows members of a Scottish regiment enjoying the sunshine near Doolin, Co. Clare, in 1918. (*Courtesy of Clare County Museum*)

For many, military service was one of their few opportunities to see the world. Pictured (*above*) are Catholic chaplains at the Pyramids at Giza in Egypt. On the right is Fr John Butler OFM Cap., from Sheestown, Co. Kilkenny. On the opposite page are Catholic troops at prayer at Deir el Belah in Palestine (*top*) and British troops at the Vatican (*bottom*). Seated third from left is Fr Ignatius Collins OFM Cap. Born in Cork he entered the Capuchin Order and was ordained in 1910. (*Courtesy of the Irish Capuchin Provincial Archives*)

*Cav. G. Felici
Roma*

OPPOSITE

Pictured above is a soldiers' camp, probably in Alexandria, Egypt, while the photograph below shows a riding school at Colincomps, France. (*Alexandria © Noel Harty; Colincomps courtesy of Clare County Museum*)

ABOVE

Some soldiers even found love. In this image Captain Leslie Craig of the Australian Army and his fiancée, Frances Eileen Boyd, are photographed in the garden of Dr J. C. Boyd in Lifford, Co. Donegal. Craig was wounded at Gallipoli and was sent to London where he was fitted for a prosthetic leg. While convalescing he met Boyd, a voluntary nurse. They were married in Lifford on 17 September 1917, and left for Australia the following month. The couple made their home at Dardanup, Western Australia, and raised four children. (*Courtesy of the Australian War Memorial Museum, P08414.005*)

Undoubtedly, however, the majority of soldiers would have been too caught up in the action to appreciate their exotic surroundings. As casualties mounted British officers increasingly felt the need to stiffen discipline and morale. F. P. Crozier (*pictured*), commander of the 9th Battalion, Royal Irish Rifles, ordered his namesake James, from Belfast, executed for desertion. The execution troubled Crozier, as he had promised James' mother that he would look after him. He attempted to make amends to James by letting him get so drunk that he barely knew what was happening. Crozier himself became a hate figure for supporters of British forces in Ireland during the War of Independence for resigning and publicising the failure of the British government to enforce discipline on its forces. (*Courtesy of Mercier Archive*)

Hatred of the enemy was less prevalent among frontline soldiers who shared the same depredations than it was on the Home Front. Christmas 1914 saw a spontaneous display of solidarity among opposing frontline troops on both the Western and Eastern Fronts which included senior officers. Gifts were exchanged, carols sung and even football played. When Sir John French (*front left*), commander of the British Expeditionary Force, learned of this, he issued orders forbidding similar displays in future.[1] (*Courtesy of Mercier Archive*)

1   Hochschild, A., *To End All Wars: A Story of Protest and Patriotism in the First World War* (London, 2012), p. 131.

Christmas 1914 was not the only instance of solidarity among enemies. Many officers suspected that live and let live arrangements existed between soldiers from opposing sides, where troops would avoid attacking each other, or attack in a deliberately ineffectual way. Officers made an effort, not always successfully, to prevent arrangements of these types. Pictured are men of the Irish Guards attending to the needs of a wounded German soldier at Passchendaele, July 1917. (*Courtesy of the Imperial War Museum, Q 2628*)

Pictured is a member of the London Irish Rifles operating as a sniper during the final months of the war. One example of a failure to seize an opportunity to inflict injury was the order of one officer of the 6th Connaught Rangers not to shoot at a particular German sentry because of his ability to stand perfectly still.[1] (*Courtesy of the Imperial War Museum, Q 6902*)

1   Grayson, R. S., *Belfast Boys: How Unionists and Nationalists Fought and Died Together in the First World War* (London, 2009), p. 126.

Soldiers who were wounded or injured were often sent home to recuperate. Families were understandably filled with a sense of dread when that leave came to an end. Michael O'Donnell, or Mícheál an Táilliúra Shéamuis Mhóir as he would have been known to his neighbours, from Lettermore, Co. Galway, was killed soon after returning to the war from leave. He had been wounded and had the option of staying at home, but decided to return to his unit. (*Courtesy of Bertie Ó Domhnaill*)

In Loughgall, Co. Armagh, Mary Halligan's local paper informed its readers that her husband, Robert, had been killed in action. That was June 1916, but in September he wrote to her with word that he would be home on leave. He came home, but was noticeably suffering from the effects of being gassed. However, his family failed to persuade him to stay and he returned to his unit, where he contracted pneumonia and died. Robert and Mary are pictured here with their daughter Daisy. Before dying, Robert wrote to his wife: 'Try and do the best you can; I am sure you always have. God keep and comfort you my dear wife.'[1] (*Courtesy of John Henderson*)

1   Cousins, C., *Armagh and the Great War* (Dublin, 2011), pp. 167–68.

Over the course of the war many Irishmen were taken prisoner by the Germans. Amongst the men pictured above at Sennelager POW camp in Germany is Dr Bill Egan (*front left*) from Dungarvan, Co. Waterford. He was later released, a reasonably regular practice as both sides off-loaded medical personnel and wounded prisoners. The day after arriving back in London Egan married Norah Wall. The photograph on the right was probably taken at their wedding. (*Courtesy of Noel Harty*)

Internment also gave people time for thought. Archdeacon Thomas Duggan was a Catholic chaplain from Cork. Captured by Germans he was presented for registration in a camp. When he described himself as Irish rather than English one of the Germans spoke Irish to him. When Duggan was unable to engage him in conversation the disbelieving German recorded him as an Englishman.[1] On his release Duggan took up Irish and learned to speak it fluently. (*Courtesy of the Diocese of Cork and Ross*)

1   Ó Maoileoin, S., *B'fhiú an Braon Fola* (Baile Átha Cliath, 1958), pp. 117–18.

BELOW

Not all of those who spent time in a camp were captured by the enemy, however. The neutral Dutch interned belligerents who crossed their frontier, including this group of British officers. (*Courtesy of Collins Barracks, Cork, Clarke collection*)

Ireland accommodated German prisoners at Templemore, Co. Tipperary. Historian John Reynolds notes that the prisoners were generally positive about their experience in Ireland, certainly compared with the experience of the same group of prisoners when sent to Britain. While two prisoners died in Templemore (both of medical complaints), a number of them were shot while trying to escape in England. Pictured is the funeral of one of the prisoners who died in Templemore. (*Courtesy of the Garda Training College Museum, Templemore*)

BELOW

German prisoners in Templemore. (*Courtesy of the Garda Training College Museum, Templemore*)

The official reason that the prisoners were moved from Templemore to England was that the barracks was needed for training and that there was a problem with sanitation. It may also have been feared that Pierce McCan (*pictured*) and other local Republicans intended to liberate German prisoners to help in an uprising against the British. It seems that McCan did indeed intend to do so.[1] (*Courtesy of Mercier Archive*)

1   Dennehy, J., *In a Time of War: Tipperary 1914–1918* (Kildare, 2013), p. 154.

This cup was carved by a prisoner who left it behind him during the removal of the prisoners from Templemore. (*Courtesy of the Garda Training College Museum, Templemore*)

127

4. THE IMPACT OF THE WAR DOMESTICALLY

'Nach glórmhar an cogadh é ... ná raibh deireadh choíche leis'[1]
(Isn't it a glorious war ... may it never end)

A Galway woman commenting on the separation allowances paid to the dependants of servicemen

1 Bairéad, T., *Gan Baisteadh* (Baile Átha Cliath, 1972), p. 66.

Harbour, Queenstown

Despite the efforts of the British government to censor certain events of the war, newspaper readers can have been in little doubt about the appalling casualties that were being suffered. Before they joined the war effort in 1917, the neutral Americans were also keenly interested in the course of the war, although sympathies tended to be coloured by ethnic factors. Irish-America tended to be anti-British for example. Pictured is James Brendan Connolly from Boston. The son of emigrants from the Aran Islands, Co. Galway, Connolly was one of the most prominent war journalists during the First World War. (*Courtesy of Colby College, Maine*)

As a major naval base Queenstown (Cobh), Co. Cork, played an important role in the war at sea, particularly after the Americans entered the war. From May 1917 a large force of American destroyers operated out of the port. During this year Connolly spent time with a US U-boat hunting ship that worked out of Queenstown. (*Courtesy of Collins Barracks, Cork, Clarke collection*)

The British Grand Fleet in Lough Swilly, Co. Donegal. One of the Royal Navy's tactics during the war was to blockade Germany's ports. In 1919 the Germans claimed that the blockade had caused malnutrition contributing to the deaths of three-quarters of a million people and increased the mortality rates of women and children by 50 per cent, an overestimation which was later revised.[1] (*Courtesy of Donegal County Museum collection*)

1   Nolan, L. and Nolan, J. E., *Secret Victory: Ireland and the War at Sea 1914–1918* (Cork, 2009), p. 38.

Mines were a constant fear for those at sea. One of the victims was the British warship HMS *Audacious,* shown here sinking after striking a German mine off the coast of Donegal on 27 October 1914. There were 200 mines in the minefield that the *Audacious* had entered. It was July 1915 before the mines were successfully swept.[1] For months the government refused to admit to its loss, even though hundreds of Americans on a nearby ship had witnessed it and German schoolchildren had been given a school holiday in honour of the achievement.[2] (*Courtesy of Bundesarchiv, Bild 102-03320A*)

1   Nolan, L. and Nolan, J. E., *Secret Victory: Ireland and the War at Sea 1914–1918* (Cork, 2009), p. 40.
2   Hastings, M., *Catastrophe: Europe Goes to War 1914* (London, 2013), p. 377.

Queenstown, 7. Mai 1915.

Germany began to use unrestricted submarine warfare on any ship sighted in British waters. The first passenger ship sunk was the SS *Falaba*, which was torpedoed off the south-east coast of Ireland in March 1915. (*Courtesy of Bundesarchiv, Bild 183-R25475*)

In May 1915 the *Lusitania*, carrying a substantial number of American citizens, was torpedoed and sunk off the south coast of Ireland, without warning, by the Germans. Pictured is a German postcard depicting the sinking and Admiral von Tirpitz, Secretary of State of the German Imperial Naval Office. The sinking of the ship led to a wave of anger in both Britain and Ireland. The scenes in Queenstown and on the Cork coast were harrowing, as the dead and survivors were brought ashore. *The Times* reported that 'Men broke down when they looked upon a young mother, lying there with her baby folded in her protective arms ... of a sailor who was found with a body of a little child strapped to his shoulders ... Two children who went down together with their arms wrapped around each other.'[1] (*Courtesy of Mercier Archive*)

1   Nolan, L. and Nolan, J. E., *Secret Victory: Ireland and the War at Sea 1914–1918* (Cork, 2009), p. 73.

Pictured are four of Germany's submarines, one of which (*second from left*) sank the *Lusitania*. (*Courtesy of Mercier Archive*)

Pictured are some of the survivors of the *Lusitania*, including the Gardeners (*opposite*), brothers from New Zealand whose parents died during the attack. One survivor later wrote about the reaction of the people of Queenstown (Cobh) to the survivors, saying that they had never seen: 'anything more spontaneous or genuine or more freely given'.[1] (*Courtesy of the Library of Congress, LC-USZ62-118927, LC-USZ62-76930 and LC-DIG-ggbain-19173*)

1   Nolan, L. and Nolan, J. E., *Secret Victory: Ireland and the War at Sea 1914–1918* (Cork, 2009), p. 74.

Among the casualties on the *Lusitania* was Irish art collector Hugh Lane, Director of the National Gallery. He bequeathed a collection of priceless paintings to Dublin city, changing an original will. However, the codicil was not witnessed and led to a dispute for decades regarding where the paintings would be displayed.[1] (*Courtesy of the Hugh Lane Gallery*)

1   Yeates, P., *A City in Wartime: Dublin 1914–18* (Dublin, 2011), pp. 135–36.

With the passing of the Defence of the Realm Act (DORA) just four days after the outbreak of war in 1914, which severely curtailed personal freedom, Ireland's domestic peacekeepers, the RIC and Dublin Metropolitan Police, were given significant new duties. They now fulfilled an additional intelligence function, maintaining a close eye on visitors to their areas as well as resources that might prove of interest to spies or invaders. It was not always easy to fulfil centralised orders. Constable Jeremiah Mee (*right*), then stationed at Sligo, recalled the difficulties of applying the complex and ever-changing strictures of supervision outlined in DORA to an isolated Sligo village.[1] (*Courtesy of J. Anthony Gaughan*)

1   Gaughan, J. A., *Memoirs of Constable Jeremiah Mee* (Cork, 2012).

Alongside the additional roles outlined in DORA, normal police work continued. John Morahan (*middle row, fourth from left*) from Leitrim, a policeman in Galway, saved a child from drowning in Barna and was decorated for his actions. (*Courtesy of Séamus Coll*)

Farmers of Ireland
JOIN UP & DEFEND
your possessions.

In Ireland recruitment was uneven, with farmers being particularly unresponsive to the call. In an attempt to reverse this trend, scaremongering tactics were used. Newspapers and politicians reported that the Germans and the Turks planned to relocate excess populations to Ireland. John Redmond told listeners in Galway that: 'If this war ends in the defeat of the allies there is imminent danger that every tenant-farmer in Ireland will be robbed of his ownership of the soil.'[1] What created further resentment of farmers was the high prices that they were getting for their produce as a result of wartime conditions. (*Courtesy of the National Library of Ireland, EPH F97*)

1   O'Connor Lysaght, D. R., 'The Rhetoric of Redmondism 1914–6', in *History Ireland,* Spring 2003.

Many suspected that conscription would follow a series of unsuccessful recruiting campaigns. In the cartoon by Ernest Kavanagh shown here, while the officer attempts to recruit his target, behind his back he hides the threat of conscription. John Redmond is also mocked for his continuing support of the British cause. (*Courtesy of the Military Archives, P27-12*)

THE COMING OF THE HUN.

Redmond's March on Wexford.

LEFT

There was concern about the impact of alcohol on the war effort. Lieutenant Colonel Stewart Blacker (*left*) of the 9th Royal Irish Fusiliers issued an appeal to people to stop purchasing drinks for his soldiers who were in training, because it was undermining the training that was being done. (*Courtesy of the Deputy Keeper of the Records, Public Records Office Northern Ireland, D1498/8*)

Members of the Irish gentry went to great lengths to assist the British war effort. Aside from joining the colours, they became recruiters, served as nurses, involved themselves with the Red Cross and entertained the troops home on leave. This photograph was taken at the home of the O'Callaghan-Westropp family in Co. Clare. Note the Scottish soldier seated second from the left having a ribbon tied in his hair by a young girl. (*Courtesy of Clare County Library*)

RIGHT

Efforts to make life a little more comfortable at the front line involved large numbers of people. Professor Alexander Anderson, President of University College Galway, issued an appeal in 1916 for books for men at the Front.[1] (*Courtesy of NUI Galway*)

1   Henry, W., *Galway and the Great War* (Cork, 2006), p. 125.

LEFT

Certain groups did well out of the war. One of these groups were the 'madams' of cities like Dublin and Cork, women like Becky Cooper. Prostitution wasn't a creation of the war, however. In the early years of the twentieth century it was estimated that 2 per cent of the female population in Dublin were working as prostitutes.[1] (© *Terry Fagan and the Inner City Folklore Project*)

1   Yeates, P., *A City in Wartime: Dublin 1914–18* (Dublin, 2011), p. 278.

ABOVE

There was concern right across the political spectrum about the impact of military service on the moral compass of young Irishmen and of the potential corruption of young women through contact with the military. Church of Ireland Archbishop of Dublin John H. Bernard wrote about the difficulty of supervising the behaviour of young women when so many of them in Dublin were living in one-bedroom flats.[1] (*Courtesy of the Representative Church Body*)

1   Yeates, P., *A City in Wartime: Dublin 1914–18* (Dublin, 2011), p. 279.

145

The political landscape was also being changed by the war. By 1915 John Redmond's bedrock of support was being eroded, one of the reasons being the heavy casualties suffered in the fighting. This anti-war poster parodies a previous recruitment poster. (*Courtesy of the National Library of Ireland, EPH A173*)

However, it was in 1916 that the most radical political change would occur in Ireland, as a result of the most significant wartime event in Ireland, the Easter Rising. With increasing discontent among the general public over the war and the growing realisation that this conflict would not end any time soon, more radical members of the IRB decided the time was now right to stage their planned rebellion against British rule. The plans for the rebellion were withheld from the more moderate IRB members such as Bulmer Hobson, including the idea of using the Irish Volunteers to carry out the insurrection. (*Courtesy of Mercier Archive*)

The conspirators believed that they would have a better chance of staging a successful rebellion with German assistance. Joseph Mary Plunkett, one of the chief conspirators, travelled to Germany as part of an IRB plan to import German arms for a rebellion. Note the scar of an operation on his neck in his passport photo. Plunkett had tuberculosis. (*Courtesy of the Military Archives, P24*)

Ultimately however it was Sir Roger Casement who was the most prominent Republican contact with the Germans. He arranged for a shipment of German guns to be sent to Ireland aboard the *Aud* (*above*). Previously known as the *Castro*, this had been a British ship, but was captured by the Germans at the start of the war.[1] It was on this boat that the Germans attempted to land arms for the Easter Rising. The ship reached Ireland safely but there it was engaged by British naval ships and rather than let it fall into their enemy's hands, the crew abandoned ship after laying charges to scuttle the ship. It sank near the entrance to Queenstown harbour. One of the *Aud*'s crew members was Kriegsmarine Heizer Jans Dunker (*left*). (*Courtesy of Mercier Archive*)

1   Nolan, L. and Nolan, J. E., *Secret Victory: Ireland and the War at Sea 1914–1918* (Cork, 2009), pp. 134–35.

ABOVE

Left to right: Lieutenant Johannes Speiss, Robert Monteith, Daniel Julien Bailey, Lieutenant Otto Walter, Roger Casement, Captain Raimund Weisbach and, just out of shot, Lieutenant Hans Kukat on the deck of U-19, April 1916. Bailey was one of a handful of Irish members of the British Army who defected to the German side while prisoners of war. The Germans and Casement planned to create an Irish Brigade, and Casement was heavily involved in recruiting for the brigade. (*Courtesy of Mercier Archive*)

OPPOSITE

Monteith and Bailey saluting a German officer, Lieutenant Rudolf Zenter, on the deck of the U-boat. Casement was landed from U-19 along with Bailey and Monteith at Banna Strand, Tralee, Co. Kerry, on Good Friday 1916. However, he was recognised and quickly arrested by the RIC. With this arrest, both his and any German involvement in the rebellion ended. (*Courtesy of Mercier Archive*)

ABOVE

The rebellion was originally planned for Easter Sunday 1916. Despite the setback of the loss of arms on board the *Aud* and the actions of Eoin MacNeill, the president of the Volunteers, who attempted to stop the Rising through a coded message in the press cancelling all Volunteer gatherings on that Sunday, the IRB decided to continue with the rebellion regardless. On Easter Monday, 24 April, the IRB, some of the Dublin Volunteers, the Hibernian Rifles and the Irish Citizen Army seized strategic buildings in Dublin and declared a Republic. Their headquarters was Dublin's General Post Office (GPO). Pictured is the clock outside the GPO that stopped during the Rising. (*Courtesy of Mercier Archive*)

OPPOSITE

The start of the Easter Rising was not the only action of note by Irishmen on Easter Monday 1916. Thousands of miles away a small group of men were starting out on a journey that sensible opinion would have judged to be impossible. Having lost his ship *Endurance* to the ice, Kildare-born Ernest Shackleton (*pictured*) had managed to cross the Antarctic with his men dragging lifeboats. He then brought them across 250 miles of sea to Elephant Island. Knowing that there was no hope of rescue there, Shackleton took five others and set off for South Georgia on 24 April, a journey of 800 nautical miles. Amongst the men he took were Kerryman Tom Crean and Corkman Tim McCarthy. Showing incredible skill and courage they sighted land on 8 May. The men on Elephant Island were rescued at the fourth attempt, on 30 August. Tim McCarthy was dead by March 1917, torpedoed while on an oil tanker. Crean resumed his work with the navy and Shackleton also became involved in the war effort. (*Courtesy of the Library of Congress, LC-DIG-ggbain-04779*)

SIR EARNEST SHACKLETON & WIFE.

1020-

OPPOSITE

A number of British-born or British-based Irish Volunteers travelled from Britain to take part in the Rising. Pictured (*left to right*) are Joe Good, John 'Blimey' O'Connor and Seán Noonan, three London-Irishmen. (*Courtesy of Kilmainham Gaol Museum, KMGLM 2012.0107*)

ABOVE AND RIGHT

The first casualties of Easter Week: on the British side Constable James O'Brien (*above in uniform*) of the Dublin Metropolitan Police was killed in Dublin Castle. He was a Limerick man. Seán Connolly (*right*) of the Irish Citizen Army was the first fatality on the rebel side. O'Brien was killed at Dublin Castle by Connolly's men, Connolly at City Hall by British forces. (*Courtesy of Kilmainham Gaol Museum, 17PO-1A24-13 and 17PD-1A18-08*)

The first attempts by British forces to engage the rebels ended badly, so they switched tactics. Their new plan included creating a cordon around the city centre and cutting off the rebel positions from each other. Pictured is a British machine-gun post at Clontarf. (*Courtesy of Kilmainham Gaol Museum, 17PC-1A53-29*)

Significant numbers of the troops that the rebels faced were Irish. There were even cases of brothers finding themselves on opposing sides during the week. Pictured are arrested Republicans from Wexford, one of the few places outside Dublin where the Volunteers were active during the Rising, with members of the Connaught Rangers. (*Courtesy of Kilmainham Gaol Museum, 17PC-1B14-20*)

The Rising led to widespread looting in Dublin. While these girls are carrying future firewood, the looting was often of non-essential goods. (*Courtesy of Mercier Archive*)

LEFT

There was major destruction in the centre of Dublin as a result of shelling. (*Courtesy of Mercier Archive*)

Much of the damage done to Dublin's centre was carried out by the British gunship *Helga*, which started shelling targets on 25 April. (*Courtesy of Mercier Archive*)

A group of Irish Volunteers who took part in the Easter Rising. Seated in the centre is Tim Finn. He later joined the Irish Guards and was killed in France on 27 August 1918. (*Courtesy of Bernard Bermingham*)

ABOVE

The Rising caused much disruption to everyday life and was greeted with resentment by Dubliners, many of whom were already struggling to cope with the rise of food prices and wartime scarcity without the additional shortages created by the Rising. Pictured is the mail gathering in Kingstown (Dun Laoghaire), Co. Dublin, during the Rising, when distributing it was an impossibility. (*Courtesy of Mercier Archive*)

OVERLEAF

British troops gathered in the grounds of Trinity College Dublin during the Rising. Although the rebels had planned to take the college as part of their strategy, they failed to do so and it became a staging post for their opponents instead. (*Courtesy of Mercier Archive*)

ABOVE

There were a small number of incidents outside Dublin. In Cork, when the RIC was sent to arrest members of a well-known Republican family, the Kents barricaded themselves into their house and a gun battle followed. One member of the RIC, Head Constable William Rowe, was killed before the Kents surrendered. Thomas Kent (*centre*) was subsequently executed. He is barefoot in this photograph, having been refused permission to put on his boots.[1] (*Courtesy of Mercier Archive*)

1   Ó Ruairc, P. Óg, *Revolution: A Photographic History 1913–1923* (Cork, 2011), p. 71.

LEFT

Pádraig Ó Fathaigh was in a position to view the impact of the Rising on RIC men, isolated in vulnerable, rural barracks: 'Suddenly a constable rushed in to the Barracks saying that the rebels had a machine gun outside every barrack in the county, that the smaller barracks were being evacuated, that Ardrahan were preparing to evacuate and when they reached Kinvara, Kinvara were to evacuate and all were to hasten to Gort. Ardrahan peelers soon arrived and the panic spread: Constable McBirney ... flung his rifle against the ground saying he was finished with the RIC. The RIC fled helter-skelter to Gort, expecting to be attacked on the way.'[1] (*Courtesy of Finian Ó Fathaigh*)

1   McMahon, T., *Pádraig Ó Fathaigh's War of Independence* (Cork, 2000), p. 36.

RIGHT

British troops on the quays in Dublin. The superior artillery and numbers of the British forces soon told against the rebels, who surrendered on Saturday 29 August. (*Courtesy of Mercier Archive*)

BELOW

The tall man at the back of this photograph is Detective Daniel Hoey from Rhode, Co. Offaly, who picked out the rebel leader Seán Mac Diarmada among the surrendered rebels. Mac Diarmada was then court-martialled and executed. Hoey was shot close to Trinity College Dublin in September 1919, during the War of Independence. (*Courtesy of Mercier Archive*)

LEFT

Pictured is Paddy Paul from Waterford city, a member of the Royal Irish Regiment who was in Salonika in Greece when news of the Rising broke. Years later he recalled information about events at home being posted up, with one bulletin reading: 'Rebels still holding out', and the news of this 'brought about a spontaneous cheer throughout the camp'.[1] (*Courtesy of Waterford County Museum, UK 264*)

1   Paddy Paul, BMH WS 877, p. 3.

BELOW

Nationalist Tom Kettle (*left*) was killed in action in 1916. Robert Lynd (*right*), a journalist and supporter of Sinn Féin, described Kettle 'as the most brilliant Irishman of his generation'. Lynd described the inner conflict that Kettle and many other soldiers felt because of Easter Week: 'His attitude with regard to the Dublin insurrection in Easter Week was typical of the conflict of his sympathies, as of the sympathies of many Irish soldiers during the last few months. He was aghast at the insurrection: he fought in the streets of Dublin to suppress it. But he was equally aghast at the manner of its suppression and the execution of the leaders of the revolt.'[1] (*Courtesy of Mercier Archive*)

1   Lynd, R., *If the Germans Conquered England and Other Essays* (Dublin and London, 1917), pp. 137–39.

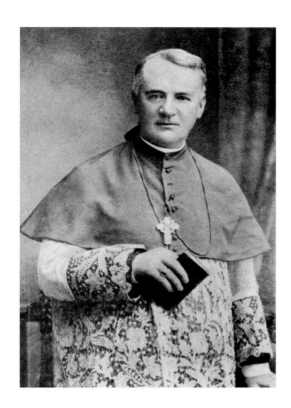

The executions of the leaders of the Rising and the secretive manner in which they were carried out, as well as wholescale arrests of anyone suspected of Republican sympathies, angered nationalists. One of the first prominent critics was Bishop Edward O'Dwyer of Limerick (*pictured*), who clashed with Sir John Maxwell about his policies. (*Courtesy of Mercier Archive*)

The executions also angered and depressed many serving soldiers. Francis Ledwidge of the Royal Inniskilling Fusiliers (*pictured*) had known and respected the executed rebel leader Thomas MacDonagh and wrote the following poem upon hearing of his death:

> He shall not hear the bittern cry
> in the wild sky, where he is lain,
> Nor voices of the sweeter birds
> Above the wailing of the rain.

Increasingly disillusioned with the war, Ledwidge, who was from Slane, Co. Meath, was killed by a shell in 1917. (*Courtesy of the Ledwidge Museum*)

Initial anger amongst the Irish general public at the rebels began to shift towards the British as a result of stories that emerged about their conduct during, and the executions carried out following, the Rising. One target of this anger was Captain J. C. Bowen-Colthurst. He killed several prisoners in cold blood, including Francis Sheehy-Skeffington and two journalists, one of whom was Thomas Dickson (*top*). Another of Bowen-Colthurst's victims was J. J. Coade (*bottom, on the right*), who was completely innocent of any involvement in the Rising. Bowen-Colthurst was tried and found guilty but insane; he spent two years in a mental institution.[1] (*Courtesy of Kilmainham Gaol Museum, 17PD-1A18-17 and 17PO-1A24-09*)

1 Ó Ruairc, P. Óg, *Revolution: A Photographic History 1913–1923* (Cork, 2011), p. 57.

The manner in which raids and arrests by the police and the military were carried out also alienated public opinion. A good example of how this shifting opinion could affect later events can be found in the figure of Liam Lynch (*pictured in July 1914 with Volunteers in Clogheen, Cork; marked with an X*), who later became a senior IRA leader. He originally 'hated the Irish Volunteers' after the split of 1914, but the Rising changed him. His godmother recalled how 'he saw Thomas Kent being brought bleeding through the town of Fermoy and his poor mother dragging along after them ... He said that when he saw the Kents ... it was like a sword going through his heart.'[1] (*Courtesy of Mercier Archive*)

1 Hart, P., *The IRA and Its Enemies* (Oxford, 1998), pp. 204–5.

ABOVE

Republican prisoners were housed in jails at first, before most of them were sent to Frongoch Internment Camp in Wales. This picture was taken in Stafford Gaol. Michael Collins is fifth from the right. (*Courtesy of Mercier Archive*)

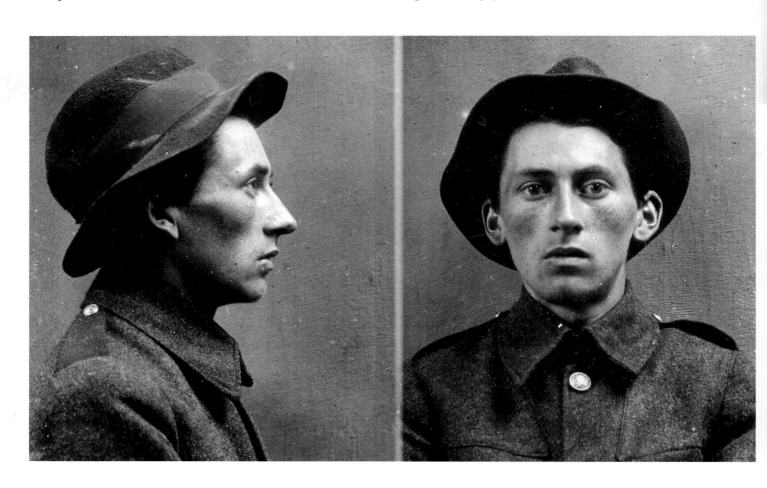

Some rebel prisoners began to plan for the future. One British officer who stood out for his poor behaviour in the aftermath of the Rising was Percival Lea-Wilson, an RIC District Inspector who had joined the Royal Irish Regiment. Later Liam Tobin (*pictured*), one of Michael Collins' key officers, was to recall: 'Lea-Wilson was responsible ... for whatever ill-treatment was received there [amongst the captured rebels at the Rotunda]. I know that when he refused to allow me to stand up I looked at him and I registered a vow to myself that I would deal with him at some time in the future'.[1] On 15 June 1920 Lea-Wilson was shot dead in Gorey, Co. Wexford, on Michael Collins' orders. (*Courtesy of Kilmainham Gaol Museum, 17PO-1A22-19*)

1   Liam Tobin, BMH WS 1753, p. 7.

Efforts were made to identify Irishmen from, or living in, England among the interned men, who were liable for conscription. One of them was Hugh Thornton, who is in this photograph taken inside the GPO during Easter Week (*probably third from right*). Despite efforts to shield Thornton from the authorities in Frongoch, he was found. They 'gave him a khaki uniform to put on. Instead of putting it on, he danced on it. Then he was court-martialled and sentenced to a term of imprisonment.'[1] (*Courtesy of the Military Archives*)

1   Mícheál Ó Droighneáin, BMH WS 374, p. 10.

ABOVE

As soon as the Easter Rising was over all sides began to attempt to explain and to represent it. Pictured is a postcard sent by a Cork soldier to his mother. The photograph was probably staged by the British for press photographs: note the soldiers standing totally relaxed to the right of the picture, one of whom is identified with an x by the writer of the postcard as a Major Farmer. (*Courtesy of Collins Barracks, Cork, Clarke collection*)

LEFT

The Germans used news of the Easter Rising to attempt to sow discord among Irish troops, and also for anti-British propaganda. The pictured sign was posted in no man's land, telling its Irish readers that 'English guns are firing at your wifes and children!' Francis (Frank) Biggane from Sunday's Well in Cork city, a member of the Royal Munster Fusiliers, was one of two men who entered no man's land at night-time to claim the sign, which was later presented to the king. The following year Biggane was killed by a shell at Passchendaele.[1] (© *Illustrated London News Ltd/Mary Evans*)

1 Borgonovo, J., *The Dynamics of War and Revolution: Cork City 1916–1918* (Cork, 2013), p. 188.

Immer wieder fühlen sich die englischen Zeitungen bemüßigt, über die Behandlung der Polen durch Deutschland sich aufzuhalten und durch unwahre Berichte über Unterdrückungsmaßnahmen die Gemüter aufzuwiegeln. Das edle, selbstlose England! Betrachten wir

Englands Wirken — England hat: — in den Kolonien!

In Irland durch Bluturteile gegen das ausgehungerte, zur Empörung getriebene Volk gewütet. Wir bringen hier die letzten Märtyrer der englischen Blutherrschaft in Irland: links den Führer der Aufständischen, Major Bride, rechts (in Uniform) die Brüder Plunkett — sämtlich inzwischen hingerichtet!

Zur Revolution — in Irland.

Lord Kitchener, der englische Kriegsminister.

Die Ruinen der Dubliner Freiheitshalle. (An den Wänden sind die Einschlaglöcher der Geschosse deutlich sichtbar.)

Der Würger von Irland: General Sir John Maxwell.

Images of the Easter Rising of 1916 from a German newspaper, the *Schweinfurter Volksblatt*. Having been roundly condemned because of their conquest of Belgium, the German media was happy to point out the willingness of the British to use artillery against an Irish city. Incredibly the German media had access to photographs of most of Dublin's main buildings as well as key characters in Irish and British politics and the military, such as John Redmond, Jim Larkin, Lord Kitchener and General Sir John Maxwell, who was responsible for the suppression of the Rising. (*Courtesy of Aribert Elpelt and the Main-Post GmbH & Co. KG*)

The witnesses who testified during Roger Casement's trial for treason. (*Courtesy of Mercier Archive*)

Casement at his trial in London. He was found guilty and, despite pleas for clemency from such well-known figures as W. B. Yeats and Sir Arthur Conan Doyle, was hanged at Pentonville Prison on 3 August 1916, the last man to be executed for his involvement with the Rising. (*Courtesy of Mercier Archive*)

175

ABOVE

As a result of the Rising, Brigadier-General Sir Joseph Byrne (*above left*), a Catholic, was appointed inspector-general of the RIC. He held this post until 1920, at which time he was pushed aside because it was felt that he was not prosecuting the campaign against the IRA with sufficient vigour. Also pictured (*right*) is Captain Walter Edgeworth-Johnstone, chief commissioner of the Dublin Metropolitan Police during the First World War. (*Courtesy of Military Archives CD 227-35*)

LEFT

British recruitment had been in decline for some time before the Rising, but despite the changing political atmosphere following it, there was still a trickle of Irish recruits to the British Army. Gunner Malachy Goode from Aughrim, Co. Galway, joined the Royal Artillery in November 1916. (*Courtesy of Paul McLoughlin*)

5. TOWARDS VICTORY

'In '16 beidh Éire dearg le fuil,
In '17 beidh daoine á gcrochadh gan coir,
In '18 déarfaidh na mná, 'Cá ndeachaigh na fir?'

(In '16 Ireland will be red with blood,
In '17 people will be hung without a crime,
In '18 the women will say, 'Where did the men go?')[1]

Irish regiments were not solely based along the Western Front. From early in the war British commanders had debated whether they should open up other fronts to try to stretch the forces of Germany and its allies. Those who wanted to damage Germany by diverting resources away from the Western Front and launching major campaigns against Germany's allies became known as Easterners. Many Irishmen saw service in the Balkans fighting against Germany's ally Bulgaria in a campaign that began in 1915 and lasted for much of the rest of the war. Pictured are members of the Connaught Rangers on a route march at Salonika, Greece. Note the stretcher-bearers standing behind the men. (*Courtesy of the Imperial War Museum, Q 55117*)

Fr Dominic O'Connor is pictured here in his British military uniform. Fr Dominic volunteered for chaplaincy work with the British forces during the First World War. After spending two months with a Scottish brigade in England, he transferred to a hospital unit bound for Salonika, Greece. After approximately two years of service, Fr Dominic resigned his post in 1917, returned to Ireland and became chaplain to the Cork No. 1 Brigade of the IRA. (*Courtesy of the Irish Capuchin Provincial Archives*)

A sustained and unsuccessful attempt to break Turkey was made at Gallipoli in 1915, but the Allies failed to make any headway, partly due to poor leadership. British forces, including a significant number of Irishmen, were landed on beaches, but under extremely difficult conditions failed to take the high ground occupied by Turkish forces who were backed up by German expertise. Irish units suffered terrible losses. Pictured are members of the Royal Dublin Fusiliers looking for shelter on the beach, while in the foreground casualties of the Royal Munster Fusiliers can be seen on the deck of the landing craft. (*Courtesy of the Imperial War Museum, Q 50473*)

INSET

A photograph of a British landing taken by Waterford man Bill Egan. (*Courtesy of Noel Harty*)

OPPOSITE

General Sir Bryan Thomas Mahon, commander of the 10th (Irish) Division at Gallipoli. (*Courtesy of the Library of Congress, LC-DIG-ggbain-20492*)

RIGHT

Pictured (*second from left, middle row*) is Corkman Vincent McNamara. McNamara, a member of the Royal Engineers, was an Irish rugby international. He was killed in action at Gallipoli. (*Courtesy of University Archives, University College Cork*)

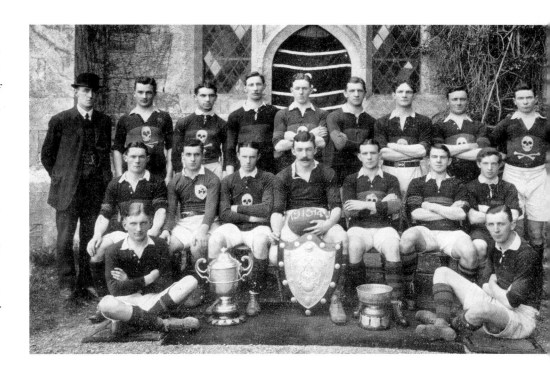

BELOW

Other ways of breaking the stalemate on the Western Front were also being considered, including the development of new technologies. With this in mind, great efforts were made by the British to develop a functioning tank. This image shows one of the early tanks used at the Front. (*Courtesy of Noel Harty*)

LEFT

Lieutenant Walter Wilson from Blackrock, Co. Dublin was one of those chiefly responsible for the development of the British tank. (*Courtesy of the Tank Museum*)

RIGHT

The new tanks were intimidating, but weren't as effective as the British had hoped. They broke down and the heat inside them made them almost unbearable for the crews. It was also difficult to determine where you were going. Captain Clement Robertson, VC, born in South Africa, was raised in Delgany, Co. Wicklow. He was killed while leading his tanks on foot during an attack on German lines in October 1917. (*Courtesy of the Tank Museum*)

Another major technological development of the war was in the sky. Flying aces provided an impersonal war with individual heroes who harked back to an age that was thought to have been more heroic and gentlemanly. David Lloyd George referred to them as 'the cavalry of the clouds'.[1] The most famous pilot on the Allied side may well have been Major Robert Gregory (*pictured*), 40 Squadron. Gregory was the son of Lady Augusta Gregory and inherited Coole Estate, Gort, Co. Galway, in 1902. He became famous not so much because of his own impressive character, but because his death in mysterious circumstances in 1918 inspired W. B. Yeats to compose the poem 'An Irish Airman Foresees His Death':

I know that I shall meet my fate,
Somewhere among the clouds above;
Those that I fight I do not hate,
Those that I guard I do not love;
My country is Kiltartan Cross,
My countrymen Kiltartan's poor,
No likely end could bring them loss
Or leave them happier than before.
Nor law, nor duty bade me fight,
Nor public men, nor cheering crowds,
A lonely impulse of delight
Drove to this tumult in the clouds;
I balanced all, brought all to mind,
The years to come seemed waste of breath,
A waste of breath the years behind
In balance with this life, this death.

(© *Colin Smythe*)

1   Morrow, J. M., 'Knights of the Sky: The Rise of Military Aviation', in Coetzee, F. and Shevin-Coetzee, M. (eds), *Authority, Identity and the Social History of the Great War* (Providence, Oxford, 1995), p. 317.

There were many other Irish flying aces, including Edward Mannock, VC, born of an English father and a mother from Ballincollig, Co. Cork. Although raised in England, he had spent at least some time in Cork and apparently spoke with a Cork accent. Called Pat at home, he acquired the nickname 'Mick' in France. As a Catholic member of the working class, Mannock initially suffered some prejudice at the hands of other pilots, but this dissipated because of his incredible talent. He was killed in action in July 1918.[1] (*Courtesy of the Imperial War Museum, Q 60800*)

1   Smith, A., 'Major Robert Gregory, & the Irish Air Aces of 1917–18', *History Ireland*, Winter 2001, pp. 29–33.

Many pilots suffered horrific deaths. Laurence Maguire (*centre standing*) from Ballycanew, Wexford, died from burns and wounds after being shot down by Turkish forces in Mesopotamia. (*Courtesy of Mary Kenny and Colin Stone*)

Technological advances increased casualties without being enough to deliver a knockout blow. The Somme was, for those from Britain and Ireland, the most famous battle of the war. Some 20,000 members of the British Army were killed on its first day. After a week's bombardment of the German lines with artillery, a major assault by British forces on German lines began on 1 July. However, the bombardment had not destroyed the German lines, barbed wire or morale. The casualties suffered by the British were horrendous. A sergeant of the Tyneside Irish described what happened to his unit: 'I heard the "patter patter" of machine guns in the distance. By the time I'd gone another ten yards there seemed to be only a few men left around me. By the time I'd gone another twenty yards I seemed to be on my own. Then I was hit myself.'[1] Pictured are the Tyneside Irish advancing towards German lines. (*Courtesy of the Imperial War Museum, Q 53*)

1   Keegan, J., *The First World War* (London, 1999), p. 317.

ABOVE

The Ulster Division, many of them former members of the UVF, suffered terrible losses. Pictured is Captain J. C. Proctor, taken at a UVF demonstration at Limavady, Co. Derry. Captain Proctor helped form the UVF battalion in Limavady in 1912. He was killed at the Somme in July 1916. (*Courtesy of the Deputy Keeper of the Records, Public Records Office Northern Ireland, D1784/2/6*)

LEFT

Lurgan man Billy McFadzean of the Royal Irish Rifles won his VC for an incredible act of selflessness, throwing himself on a box of hand grenades that had fallen in a trench. Despite occurring amidst the slaughter of the Somme, his heroism was recognised.[1] (*Courtesy of Colin Cousins*)

1   *Irish Independent*, 11 September 1916.

A letter from Belfast man William Lynas, a lance corporal in the Royal Irish Rifles, to his wife expresses how one Ulsterman felt about events at the Somme. Doing their duty was ingrained in Lynas and his comrades, not just to king, country and empire but to each other. Lynas wrote: '… a shell paid us a visit and buried us in our dugout … we were choking the gas from the shell near suffocating us … I lit a candle to find Charlie just lying nearby, we got him up and off he went to hospital. I was a little bit shaken … whatever little bit of good work I done I consider I only done my duty the only thing I can say is that I hope that I will be spared to do many a little turn for our boys in the trenches.' (*Courtesy of Stiofán Ó Direáin*)

ABOVE

While the carnage continued on the continent, the repercussions of the Rising and its aftermath were still being felt in Ireland. In the summer of 1917 the last of the Republican prisoners were released. Éamon de Valera, pictured here with other returning prisoners in 1917, became the new posterboy for the Republican movement. (*Courtesy of Mercier Archive*)

LEFT

The Republican revolution had begun, but it was disorganised. The Roscommon North by-election gave it back its focus. An agreed radical candidate, George Noble Count Plunkett (*seated*), was nominated and easily saw off two nationalist rivals. He was the father of Joseph Mary (*standing*), one of the Rising leaders who had been executed. (*Courtesy of Kilmainham Gaol Museum, 13PC-1K43-11*)

OPPOSITE

The second opportunity to demonstrate the growing support for the Republicans presented itself in another by-election, in Longford South. Republicans ran prisoner Joe McGuinness against an IPP candidate using what was to become a famous slogan: 'Put him in to get him out'. (*Courtesy of the Irish Capuchin Provincial Archives*)

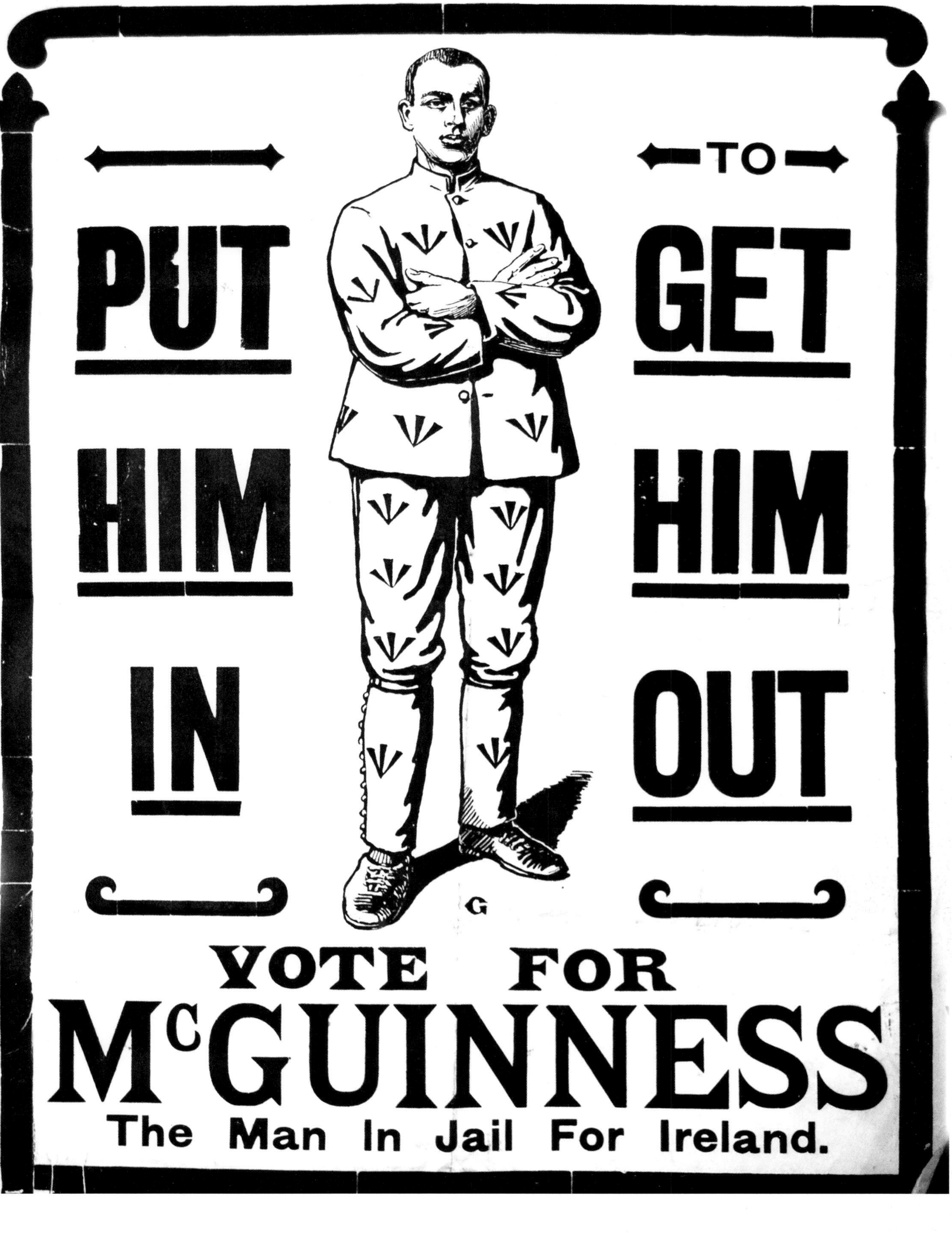
TO
PUT
HIM
IN
GET
HIM
OUT
G
VOTE FOR
McGUINNESS
The Man In Jail For Ireland.

ABOVE

McGuinness' opponent, Paddy McKenna, also had his supporters mobilised. These included members of a small but very visible minority in Ireland which came to be nicknamed 'Separation Women' because of the allowances paid by the government to them as dependants of men at the Front. They were considered urban, violent, unrespectable drinkers who neglected their children. Violently hostile to Republicans, their support for the IPP damaged the party's standing among nationalists who were wavering between moderate and radical parties. McKenna lost the by-election. (*Courtesy of Mercier Archive*)

OPPOSITE TOP

Republicans also clashed with soldiers home on leave and sought confrontations with the RIC. Pictured is a scene from the East Clare by-election that clearly shows early signs of trouble brewing – the RIC man has drawn his baton. (*Courtesy of Mercier Archive*)

OPPOSITE BOTTOM

The East Clare by-election was caused by the death in action of Willie Redmond (*centre*). Willie was one of a number of Irish MPs who had joined the British Army. This was a major blow to the IPP. Éamon de Valera, the most senior Republican officer to survive the Rising, was the Sinn Féin candidate and he took the seat. The IPP's power was dwindling rapidly. (*Courtesy of the Library of Congress, LC-DIG-hec-01513*)

RIGHT

Supporters of the IPP grew increasingly alienated from a southern public that was turning against the war. Cork Crown Prosecutor Jasper Wolfe, a supporter of Home Rule, complained about a man who was arrested after hissing at a cinema reel showing the king and queen visiting wounded soldiers, saying that in another country the defendant would be 'taken out and shot'.[1] (*Courtesy of Jasper Ungoed Thomas*)

1   Borgonovo, J., *The Dynamics of War and Revolution: Cork City 1916–1918* (Cork, 2013), p. 53.

LEFT

Maurice Dockrell, a prominent unionist businessman in Dublin, was critical of the general public's refusal to invest in war bonds. He warned that if the Empire collapsed, Ireland would soon follow. (*Courtesy of Morgan Dockrell*)

In America Woodrow Wilson (*foreground, left*) won the 1916 presidential election partly because he had kept the United States out of the war, which was an extremely popular policy at the time. This was a period where America sought isolation from the rest of the world, a period that saw Wilson rail against 'hyphenated Americanism' and also saw the Ku Klux Klan resurrected. Fear of Catholic immigrants, including the Irish, was a major factor in the rise of the Klan.[1] (*Courtesy of the Library of Congress, LC-DIG-hec-13265*)

1   Franklin, D. B., 'Bigotry in 'Bama: De Valera's Visit to Birmingham, Alabama, April 1920', *History Ireland*, Winter 2004.

One of the reasons why the United States ultimately entered the war was the German attempt to encourage the Mexicans to recapture territory in the southern United States, which they had lost in the nineteenth century. One of the most effective and prominent leaders in Mexico at the time was Alvaro Obregon (*pictured receiving a medal*), a Mexican of Irish extraction. (*Courtesy of the Library of Congress, LC-DIG-ppmsca-35150*)

America's entry into the war was a massive boost for the Allies, who were struggling against increased German naval aggression. 'Germany at last inaugurates war for the Liberty of Humanity! Unrestricted Submarine Warfare Commenced Feb. 1: Freedom of Ireland and India is desired' was a headline in the Irish-American newspaper *The Butte Independent* in 1917.[1] This renewal of unrestricted submarine warfare led to a major American naval presence in Queenstown (Cobh), Co. Cork. The USS *Melville* (*pictured*) was the flagship of the American force. The presence of American sailors and their relations with the local Irish women proved extremely contentious and led to some outbreaks of mob violence in Cork city against sailors and the women in their company. When angry American sailors aboard the *Melville* were caught manufacturing knuckle-dusters, it was decided by their officers to ban sailors from the city. The Americans apparently breached social norms of behaviour, with the British military referring to 'the disrespectful attitude' they showed local women. The most serious confrontation occurred when a sailor from the *Melville* struck and inadvertently killed a local man in a row caused by the sailor making inappropriate comments to the local's girlfriend. A charge of manslaughter was dropped after the attorney-general intervened. The sailor was transferred and efforts to obtain compensation for the local's family were refused by the US government.[2]
(*Courtesy of the US Naval History and Heritage Command, Washington, NH 43616*)

1   *The Butte Independent*, 3 February 1917.
2   Borgonovo, J., *The Dynamics of War and Revolution: Cork City 1916–1918* (Cork, 2013), pp. 122–33.

ABOVE

In an attempt to stifle the growth of the Republican movement in Ireland, the British arrested a number of Republican activists and sent them to live in England. Treating it as a holiday at the king's expense, Republicans merely left when they wanted. Photographed is a group of Republicans at Fairford in England. (*Courtesy of the Irish Capuchin Provincial Archives*)

LEFT

Pictured is leading Republican Tom Ashe (*at the back*) at a commemoration for Roger Casement at Banna Strand, Co. Kerry. Ashe died in October 1917 after being force-fed while on hunger strike in Mountjoy Prison. He had been arrested for making a seditious speech and was seeking prisoner-of-war status. A huge crowd attended his funeral, with Republicans using it as an opportunity to show their strength. Michael Collins delivered the oration, speaking briefly in Irish before adding thirty telling words in English: 'Nothing additional remains to be said. That volley which we have just heard is the only speech which it is proper to make above the grave of a dead Fenian.'[1] (*Courtesy of Mercier Archive*)

1   Yeates, P., *A City in Wartime: Dublin 1914–18* (Dublin, 2011), p. 208.

198

Distracted by the war, and hoping that a more conciliatory attitude would quell nationalist anger over the death of Ashe, as well as being determined to avoid creating any more martyrs, the government released the other hunger strikers. Pictured are hunger strikers from Co. Clare after their release. Celebrated as heroes, released men often became key Republican leaders in their home areas. Some, such as Michael Brennan of Meelick, Co. Clare (*second from right, middle row*), became national figures. (*Courtesy of Mercier Archive*)

Physical confrontations with the police led to violence being used to enforce the law or to prevent it being enforced. Pictured are Cathal Brugha and Count Plunkett being arrested after a public rally in Dublin. The affair turned ugly and a police inspector who was struck on the head with a hurley died as a result of the blow. (*Courtesy of Kilmainham Gaol Museum, 18PC-1A25-20*)

In an effort to shelve the Irish question until the war could be resolved, future British Prime Minister David Lloyd George (*pictured*) met with both John Redmond and Sir Edward Carson in July 1916 to discuss the possible partition of Ireland on the introduction of Home Rule. He met them separately and kept the nature of the discussions secret. When it was announced that partition was to be permanent, Redmond was furious, having gained the impression that it was to be temporary. This undermined Redmond and the IPP both for their acceptance of some measure of partition and the fact that Lloyd George was judged to have played Redmond for a fool. (*Courtesy of Mercier Archive*)

Another factor in the decline of the IPP was the association of the party with corruption at local government level and the inability of the party to maintain levels of patronage because of massive reductions in government expenditure as a result of the war. In a speech in the House of Commons in the aftermath of the Easter Rising, maverick nationalist MP from Cork Tim Healy (*left*) launched a stinging attack on the party, warning them that they were losing the support of the youth and the most idealistic men of the country.[1] (*Courtesy of the National Library of Ireland, HOG 192*)

1 Yeates, P., *A City in Wartime: Dublin 1914–18* (Dublin, 2011), p. 132.

Bribery, nepotism and cronyism were felt to be rampant in the securing of local appointments. Brian Cusack, a Republican who applied for a local government job in Galway, recalled: 'We travelled around interviewing members of the Council and everywhere we went the members of the public whom we mentioned the matter to all said "That will cost you a bit of money doctor".'[1] (*Courtesy of NUI Galway*)

1 Brian Cusack, BMH WS 736, p. 9.

In rural Ireland the IPP lost support because of a decision they had taken to halt land agitation during the war. The government also suspended land division except on land that was already being processed, which only exacerbated the problem. On one occasion Connemara MP William O'Malley criticised cattle driving, but the reaction of his local organisation was so negative that he had to withdraw his criticism. O'Malley was an active recruiter whose son was killed in the war. Note the message on his horse blanket: 'We are not Sinn Féiners.'[1] (*Courtesy of the Hulton Archive/Getty Images 2668685*)

1 Varley, T., 'A Region of Sturdy Smallholders? Western Nationalists and Agrarian Politics during the First World War', *Journal of the Galway Archaeological and Historical Society*, 2003, pp. 130–31.

As well as physical confrontations, the government used other methods to try and blunt the Republican threat. The Defence of the Realm Act legislation could be used to restrict any aspect of regular life. Head Constable Peter Folan (*pictured*), a native Irish speaker from Spiddal, Co. Galway, who worked in Dublin Castle, wrote about his unenthusiastic attitude towards being a censor: 'When the Press Censorship was established in Ireland, there was very little printed matter given to us for examination. After the Rising every scrap that was printed in Irish in any paper in Ireland had to be submitted to Dublin Castle, and I read every document and I allowed them all to pass. I used to draw a blue pencil under an occasional sentence (to show that I was doing the job) and bring it in to the Chief Censor, Lord Dunsany, and when he left, to Major Cooper (I should mention that the latter had his daughters taught Irish).'[1] (*Courtesy of Enda Folan*)

1   Peter Folan, BMH WS 316, pp. 5–6.

Similar legislation was used in Australia to prevent anti-war agitation. Pictured are suspected Irish Republicans in Darlinghurst Gaol, Sydney (1918–19), who were interned during the war for the perceived danger they presented to the Allied cause. A more controversial case was that of a group of International Workers of the World activists, who came to be known as the Sydney Twelve, including Thomas Glynn from Monivea, Galway. They were charged with sedition and arson in 1916 but there was widespread suspicion that they were framed because of their involvement in anti-war agitation. They were released in 1920 by a judge who re-examined the case. (*Courtesy of the National Library of Australia, nla.pic-vn3313979*)

While the political unrest in Ireland was growing, the majority of the people faced more basic problems. Rising food prices were the cause of great hardship amongst the country's poorest families. In an attempt to help alleviate the suffering, Bishop Daniel Cohalan of Cork and Ross (*left*) organised for wealthy citizens to subsidise the price of milk for poor people.[1] (*Courtesy of Mercier Archive*)

1   Borgonovo, J., *The Dynamics of War and Revolution: Cork City 1916–1918* (Cork, 2013), p. 172.

Daily  Mail

MONDAY, AUGUST 28, 1916.

LABOUR PROTEST AGAINST HIGH

YESTERDAY'S GREAT FOOD DEMONSTRATION.—The increasingly serious question of Food Prices, to which "The Daily Mail" has given daily attention for some weeks, came to a head in London yesterday, when a great procession, organised by the National Union of Railwaymen, marched to Hyde Park to be addressed from five platforms. The picture shows one division of the procession leaving the Embankment. One of the banners carried is super-imposed on the picture. ["Daily Mail" Photograph.

Die Lebensmittelteuerung in England. Titelbild der englischen Zeitung „Daily Mail", das englische Arbeiter bei einem Protestumzug gegen die Teuerung zeigt.

OPPOSITE

The Germans knew that unrest was being caused by the hardships of war in Britain. Pictured is a report in a German newspaper showing the front page of the *Daily Mail* of 28 August 1916. It shows a protest by workers against the rise in food prices. The German 1917–18 U-boat campaign was specifically geared to break Britain by preventing the importation of food. (*Courtesy of Aribert Elpelt and the Main-Post GmbH & Co. KG*)

RIGHT

The increased pressure on the British food supply led to fears in Ireland that famine would be caused through the exporting of food to the British market. Sinn Féin mobilised to prevent that occurring. In Cork Irish Volunteer leader Tomás MacCurtain was appointed director of food for the city in order to prevent the exporting of foodstuffs. In various parts of the country force as well as persuasion was used in order to maintain food supplies. For example, in Dublin pigs that were destined for the British market were seized and butchered. (*Courtesy of Mercier Archive*)

LEFT

There was also an explosion of land agitation, directed and encouraged by Republican leaders. This involved the driving (scattering) of cattle and ploughing unused or grazing land. Markets aimed at helping the poor and food collections were organised. The epicentre for this agitation was the west, where violent agrarian agitation and Republicanism had long been linked. Even during the Easter Rising in Galway, led by Irish Volunteer organiser Liam Mellows, efforts appear to have been made by some Volunteers to utilise the rebellion to advance a radical agrarian agenda. Although Mellows was to advance left-wing ideas during the Civil War, he refused to allow the Rising to be used in this manner. (*Courtesy of Kilmainham Gaol Museum, 13PC-3N26-10*)

LEFT

Not all Republicans were enthusiastic about the marriage of the agrarian and national struggles. Cathal Brugha (*pictured*), for one, was concerned about the influence of agrarian activists within the Republican movement. Brugha questioned their commitment to Republican ideals, telling a Republican cleric in Galway that agrarian activists had tried to use previous Republican and nationalist organisations for their own benefit. One thing he was happy about was the increasing involvement of the clergy in the movement, telling Fr Tom Bourke from Castlegar, Co. Galway: 'the closer the connection between the clergy of the right kind and the movement the better for both and for the country as a whole.'[1] (*Courtesy of Mercier Archive*)

1   Cathal Brugha to Father Tom Bourke, 21 October 1917 (CD 161/2 Bourke Papers, Military Archives).

RIGHT

Priests of the right kind would have included Fr Michael O'Flanagan, a radical cleric from Roscommon, an enthusiast of the Irish language, an agrarian radical and a Republican. There were significant numbers of clergymen of this type, particularly in the west of Ireland. (*Courtesy of Kilmainham Gaol Museum, 2012.0260*)

Despite the growing support for Sinn Féin, the Republicans did not have it all their own way in election contests. John Redmond (*centre*), the leader of Irish nationalism for almost two decades, died on 6 March 1918. In the subsequent by-election for his vacant Waterford seat, the Sinn Féin candidate was beaten by Redmond's son William Archer Redmond (*right*). Aside from personal sympathy for the Redmond family, Redmond's cause was strengthened by the fact that some potential conservative Sinn Féin supporters were concerned about land seizures and arms raids being carried out by members of the Volunteers. (*Courtesy of the National Library of Ireland, IND_H_0003*)

Local Republican courts began to spring up in the south and in the west to maintain the peace, and had to take sides in bitter local disputes, risking alienating potential or actual supporters. Fr John O'Meehan (*pictured*) presided over one such court in Kinvara, Co. Galway. John Diviney claimed that a particular farm 'was held by his father until grabbed by Peter Kelly's father about 38 years ago'. The court resolved that Kelly would keep the farm he currently occupied but provide Diviney with another farm that Kelly had been provided with after a grazing farm had been subdivided.[1] (*Courtesy of Siobhan Watson*)

1   County Inspector Report, Galway West Riding, November 1918 (TNA: PRO CO 904/107).

John Dillon (*centre*) succeeded Redmond as leader of the IPP and is pictured addressing a meeting in Enniskillen, Co. Fermanagh, in March 1918. Despite Redmond having agreed to partition, Ulster remained a staunch IPP stronghold. Republicans remained a minority among northern nationalists. (*Courtesy of Kilmainham Gaol Museum, 18PO-1A31-02*)

Partition remained a cause of intense anger among nationalists, moderate and radical, at home and abroad. At a rally of the Irish community which tens of thousands attended in Melbourne, Australia, motions were passed against partition, for the exhumation of the remains of the bodies of those executed after the Easter Rising, and that Irish delegates should be welcomed to post-war conferences. The most prominent speaker was Corkman Daniel Mannix, Archbishop of Melbourne and Bishop of the Armed Services.[1] Pictured are the rally committee and speakers. (*Courtesy of the National Library of Australia, nla.pic-vn4507070*)

1   *Bendigo Advertiser*, 6 November 1917.

To try to settle the Irish question, the Irish Convention was held in 1917–18 to reach agreement across the political spectrum. Leaders of all major political organisations in Ireland were invited to take part, but Sinn Féin refused to participate, knowing that complete independence would be refused regardless of the views of the delegates. The convention was a failure. Pictured is artist Walter Paget's impression of the event. (*Courtesy of the National Library of Ireland, PD HP (1917) 1(A)*)

Irish Republicans were not the only radicals to take advantage of wartime conditions to rebel against their political leaders. Two Russian revolutions saw the Tsarist regime overthrown and ultimately replaced by the Communist Bolsheviks. When news of this reached Ireland it spurred the growth of trade unionism. Even moderate Labour leader Tom Johnson, a reformist rather than a radical, briefly became caught up in the excitement.[1] (*Courtesy of Kilmainham Gaol Museum, 19PC-1B51-04*)

1   O'Connor Lysaght, D. R., 'Labour in Waiting: The After-Effects of the Dublin Lockout', *History Ireland,* July/August 2013, p. 46; Yeates, P., *A City in Wartime: Dublin 1914–18* (Dublin, 2011), p. 228.

The line between trade union and Republican activists was often very thin. Sligo Labour leader and trade unionist John Lynch was alleged to have told a meeting: 'I am a soldier of the Republic and I expect you are all the same. The time is coming when we will have our own soldiers, our own navy and our own police. This is not our war. We are at war with no one, the only enemy we have is England.'[1] He was sentenced to three months imprisonment. (*Courtesy of Betty McGowan*)

1   M. Farry, *Sligo 1914–1921: A Chronicle of Conflict* (Trim, 1992).

214

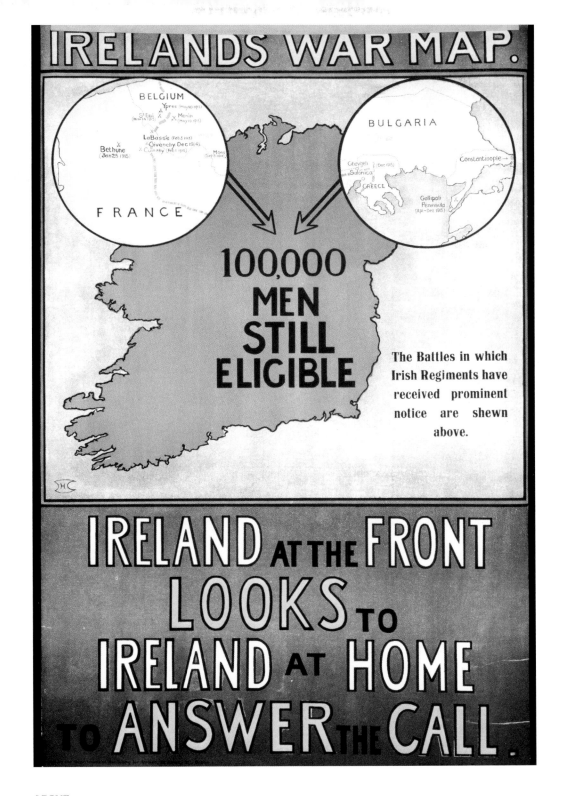

Despite the difficulties in Ireland, the government still needed substantial numbers of volunteers for its wartime forces. Targets were set outlining how many troops were needed. An increasingly significant theme in recruitment as the war dragged on was the need to enlist large numbers of men to avoid conscription and to meet the need that men at the Front had for reinforcements; issues that this poster hints at. However, the recruitment drive failed to have the necessary effect. (*Courtesy of the Library of Congress, LC-USZC4-10975*)

ABOVE

Due to increasing pressure on the Western Front the British government considered extending conscription, which had already been introduced in Britain in 1916, to Ireland. They were unprepared for the violent backlash this would cause in Ireland, even amongst their Irish supporters. All of nationalist Ireland mobilised in opposition to the plan. Irish Volunteer companies sprang up in areas where previously there were none. Nationalist rivals such as Éamon de Valera and John Dillon appeared together on platforms such as this one in Ballaghaderreen in Co. Roscommon. In Co. Antrim members of the Orange Order marched side by side with Republicans against the threat. A local Republican later commented: 'These men were never very bitter in their attitude towards Republicanism afterwards.'[1]
(*Courtesy of Mercier Archive*)

1   Liam McMullen, BMH WS 762, p. 5.

Though previously moderate, Primate of All Ireland Michael Logue strongly and publicly opposed conscription, with priests denouncing the plan from the altar. (*Courtesy of the Archdiocese of Armagh*)

The threat of conscription was viewed in almost apocalyptic terms. Note the banners pictured at Ballaghaderreen referring to a blood tax. (*Courtesy of UIG/Getty Images, 152236405*)

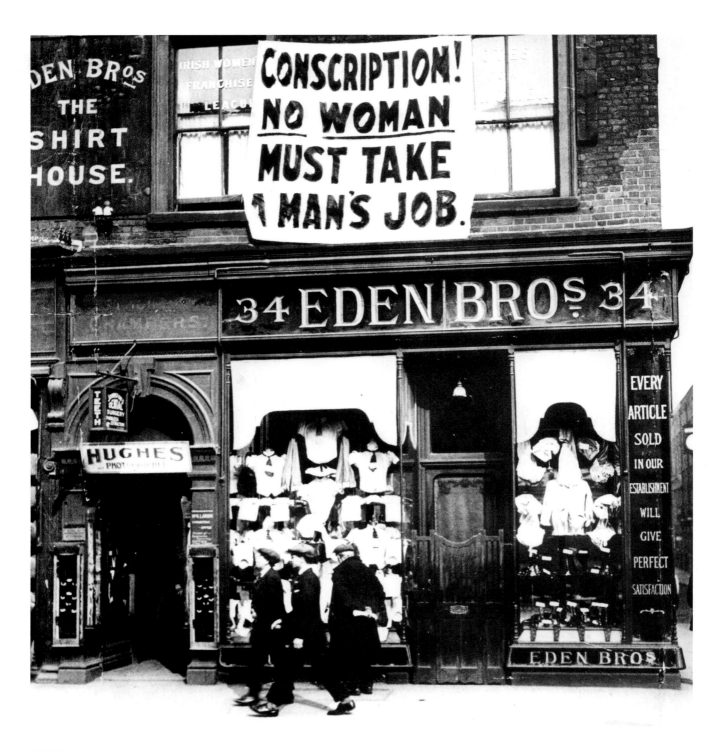

ABOVE

The most obvious way of defeating conscription was to make its implementation too costly. Republicans talked openly in terms of killing more soldiers than the British would gain. Another tactic involved the women of Ireland. In the event of conscription being enforced women would be expected to fill the void created in transport systems, factories, etc. The banner (*pictured*) hung from the offices of the Irish Womens' Franchise League in Dublin outlined what was expected in those circumstances. Facing such strident opposition from all sides, the British government eventually shelved the idea of conscription for Ireland. (*Courtesy of Popperfoto/Getty Images, 78950889*)

ABOVE

In an attempt to ensure that a new rebellion could not take place with German support, prominent Republicans became the target of arrests in May 1918. One of those who was a target was Pádraic Ó Máille. His attempted arrest near Maam, Co. Galway, backfired, with Ó Máille firing on the police, who then fled.[1] (*Courtesy of Emer Joyce*)

1   Ó Máille, T., *An t-Iomaire Rua* (Baile Átha Cliath, 2007 edition), pp. 21–23.

ABOVE

While all this was going on back home, Irish casualties continued to mount on the battlefields as the war ground on. Pictured is a doctor dressing the wounds of Lieutenant Guy Morgan of the Irish Guards at the start of what came to be known as the Third Battle of Ypres or the Battle of Passchendaele, a campaign that took place over the second half of 1917. One interviewer of First World War veterans concluded that soldiers considered it worse than the Somme.[1] (*Courtesy of the Imperial War Museum, Q 5732*)

1   Grayson, R. S., *Belfast Boys: How Unionists and Nationalists Fought and Died Together in the First World War* (London, 2009), p. 120.

Pictured is Robert O'Connor (1880–1917), a sergeant with the 2nd Battalion, Leinster Regiment and brother-in-law of Captain D. D. Sheehan MP. Born in Tralee, Co. Kerry, he had also served in the Boer War. When on home leave in Youghal, Co. Cork, in April 1916, he married, but met his death on 31 July 1917, during Passchendaele. His only son, Robert (Bob), was born in August 1917 and later joined the Irish Army. (*Courtesy of Niall Ó Síocháin*)

Even in the midst of all the carnage the ordinary mundanities of everyday life were carried on, such as getting a hair cut. Here the barbers of the 2nd Leinsters are hard at work in their camp. (*Courtesy of the Imperial War Museum, Q 5850*)

Members of the 2nd Leinsters at rest in camp during the Battle of Passchendaele. Officers often wrote letters to the relatives of soldiers who were killed, praising the soldier regardless of the reality of his service or his death. One proud woman published a letter written to her by an officer of the 9th Royal Irish Rifles. The officer later wrote to his father: 'My blood ran cold when I saw the balls I wrote Mrs Hill in print.'[1] (*Courtesy of the Imperial War Museum, Q 6186*)

1 Grayson, R. S., *Belfast Boys: How Unionists and Nationalists Fought and Died Together in the First World War* (London, 2009), p. 89.

Pictured at the right of this photo is Private Paddy Flynn, Glendalligan, Co. Waterford, who emigrated to New Zealand and was conscripted into the New Zealand Expeditionary Force. He died near Tyne Cot, Belgium, on 23 December 1917, aged thirty-five. The other two soldiers were probably from the Kilmacthomas area of Waterford. (*Courtesy of the Waterford County Museum, UK 3754*)

The war in the air was also continuing apace. Lieutenant Daniel J. Sheehan, Royal Flying Corps, son of D. D. Sheehan MP, was killed on 10 May 1917, reportedly by the German flying ace Lothar von Richthofen (brother of the Red Baron) near Arras. (*Courtesy of Niall Ó Síocháin*)

In the fight for naval supremacy the Allies had adopted new tactics in order to destroy the German U-boats: nets, ramming them and mining areas around U-boat bases. The 1917 U-boat campaign came close to defeating the British, but ultimately the adoption of a convoy system, protected by destroyers, put a halt to the danger it posed. Pictured is U-63, a German submarine that was sunk off the coast of Ireland in 1918 by depth charges, massive explosive devices dropped into the water by Allied ships. (*Courtesy of the Bundesarchiv, Bild 134-B0511*)

German submarines were still capable of inflicting casualties. Bartley Keane of Furbo, Co. Galway, a member of the Royal Navy, died in 1918 after his ship was torpedoed. (*Courtesy of Vera Cahill*)

RIGHT

Pictured is John 'Jack' Lundy (*seated right*) from Carrickfergus, Co. Antrim, during naval training. Lundy served on several ships, including the HMS *Hindustan* which was used as a depot ship during the Zeebrugge raid of 1918. During that raid the Royal Navy attempted to block the port of Zeebrugge, which was used by the German navy as a base for U-boats. The mission was a propaganda, rather than a military, victory. (*Courtesy of Stiofán Ó Direáin*)

LEFT

The massive resources that the United States possessed made a huge difference to the Allied war effort from their entry to the war in April 1917. Significant numbers of the American forces were Irish or, like General Frank McIntyre, of Irish extraction. (*Courtesy of the Library of Congress, LC-DIG-hec-16938*)

OPPOSITE

The most famous American-Irish regiment was the 69th Infantry Regiment, a regiment that even today retains a keen sense of Irishness. Its proud history is a theme of this recruiting poster. (*Courtesy of the Library of Congress, LC-DIG-ppmsca-08405*)

ENLIST TO-DAY

— IN —

THE 69TH INFANTRY

JOIN THE FAMOUS IRISH REGIMENT

THAT FOUGHT IN ALL THE GREAT BATTLES OF THE **CIVIL WAR.** FROM BULL RUN TO APPOMATOX

GO TO THE FRONT WITH YOUR FRIENDS

DON'T BE DRAFTED INTO SOME REGIMENT WHERE YOU DON'T KNOW ANYONE

MEN WANTED FROM 18 TO 40

APPLY AT THE ARMORY

LEXINGTON AVENUE and 25th STREET

Major Bill Donovan (*left*), whose parents were the children of emigrants from Cork and Ulster, was a prominent Irish-American soldier in the 69th Regiment. Fr Francis Duffy (*right*) was the legendary chaplain of the Fighting 69th and was decorated several times for his bravery. Donovan went on to found the OSS (forerunner of the CIA) during the Second World War. (*Courtesy of the 69th Regiment*)

Captain John T. Prout (*right*) was a Tipperary man who also served in the 69th Regiment. Towards the end of the war he was transferred to the 370th Infantry Regiment, the ranks of which were made up of African-American soldiers. Their experience of the war was more pleasant than that of many of their ethnicity. They were brigaded with French troops and so avoided their own white countrymen. Their positive treatment may have had an impact on their martial spirit. It was noted that 'Prout's Battalion distinguished itself at the Sal [*sic*] St. Pierre where it captured a German battery'. Prout was presented with the Croix de Guerre by the French government.[1] (*Courtesy of Chicago History Museum, Chicago Daily News negatives collection, DN-0070768*)

1   Scott, E. J., 'The Participation of Negroes in World War One: An Introductory Statement', *The Journal of Negro Education*, Summer 1943, p. 291; Mason, M., *The American Negro Soldier with the Red Hand of France* (Boston, 1920), p. 177.

Irish-Americans were not the only ones being awarded for their bravery. Lieutenant Donald Moodie of the 2nd Battalion of the Irish Guards was awarded the Military Cross: 'For conspicuous gallantry and devotion to duty. On the company commander becoming a casualty, he took command and successfully checked several enemy attempts to get round the flank of his company, which was for some hours critically situated. Later, when the trenches held by his company were attacked and entered by the enemy, he directed his men with great skill and judgment, and himself fought with splendid courage and determination.'[1] (*Courtesy of Dave Donatelli*)

1   Kipling, R., *The Irish Guards in the Great War: The First Battalion* (Staplehurst, 1997).

Private Martin Moffat from Sligo was a member of the Leinster Regiment. Moffat rushed a house at Ledgehem, Belgium, from which he and some other men were being fired on. For his action he was awarded the VC. (*Courtesy of Mellows Barracks*)

RIGHT

By autumn 1918 Germany and her allies were losing the war, a spring offensive having failed. However, the fighting dragged on and men continued to die. John Folan (*left*), from Derrygimla, Clifden, Co. Galway, served in the 5th Battalion of the Connaught Rangers and was killed in action in France on 9 October 1918, aged twenty-six. His two brothers also served in the army. Thomas O'Toole (*right*), from Cloghaunard, Clifden, Co. Galway, was luckier than his friend. He enlisted on 6 October 1915, was promoted to sergeant in the 3rd Battalion of the Connaught Rangers, and survived the war to be demobbed on 24 June 1919. Of the seated man nothing is known except his surname, O'Hara. (*Courtesy of Kathleen Villiers-Tuthill*)

Martin Joseph Sheehan (1896–1918) was a second lieutenant with the Royal Munster Fusiliers. This photograph shows him on home leave in Cork in 1917. He was serving with the Royal Air Force when he was killed on the Western Front. The second of three sons of Captain D. D. Sheehan, MP for mid-Cork, he went out on observation duty over the enemy lines on the morning of 1 October 1918 and met his death near Cambrai, France, but in what circumstances has never been known. (*Courtesy of Niall Ó Síocháin*)

ABOVE

Sergeant William Bartley (*pictured*) was a member of the Canadian Army. Wounded for the fourth time, he was in hospital in England in October 1918 when his father, Rev. J. R. Bartley, a Presbyterian minister in Tralee, Co. Kerry, but originally from Bailieborough in Co. Cavan, decided to visit him. Rev. Bartley was drowned when the ship he was travelling on, the RMS *Leinster*, was torpedoed in the Irish Sea. William died soon afterwards. (*Courtesy of Dave Donatelli*)

ABOVE

Many of those who had sacrificed greatly for the British war effort wanted either vengeance against Germany or at least its weakening as a global power. Events like sinking of the *Leinster* fed the hatred. Church of Ireland Bishop of Ossory, Ferns and Leighlin, Dr John Gregg (*above centre*), told a crowd at Stephen's Green, Dublin, that 'the deed showed the absolute necessity of carrying the war to the end so that Germany may be deprived of the power of making the earth a hell.'[1] (*Courtesy of Mercier Archive*)

1   *Irish Independent*, 15 October 1918.

Then, suddenly, it was all over. Germany sued for peace and an Armistice was declared for 11 November 1918. In this photograph Irish Guardsmen remain at their post near Maubeuge, France, still on the alert, five minutes before the Armistice.

Not surprisingly, one of them seems to be watching the time. The ceasefire was due to come into effect at 11 a.m. The last soldier to be killed in the war was shot at 10.58 a.m. (*Courtesy of Hulton/Getty Images, 3425869*)

Patrick Murray from Doocastle, at the junction of the Sligo, Mayo and Roscommon borders, was among the last soldiers to die in the war. He was a member of the United States Army. He was killed by shellfire at 9 a.m., just two hours before the Armistice. (*Courtesy of Diarmuid Murray*)

There was little sense of euphoria at the announcement of the cessation of hostilities. Pictured are a Royal Field Artillery crew on 11 November, having just received their rations. Note the muted expressions on their faces. Malachy Goode from Aughrim, Co. Galway, is standing on the extreme right. (*Courtesy of Paul McLoughlin*)

ABOVE

In Dublin a mob, allegedly involving soldiers, their wives and students from Trinity College, attacked the Sinn Féin headquarters on Harcourt Street on Armistice Day and tried to set it on fire.[1] Pictured in October 1918 are a number of Sinn Féin members at the Dublin headquarters, including Michael Collins (*standing fourth from left*). (*Courtesy of Mercier Archive*)

1   Joseph O'Connor, BMH WS 487, p. 10

RIGHT

A parade was organised in Dublin to celebrate the Armistice. Joe McGrath (*pictured*), an IRA officer, sent his unit out to prevent the taking of photographs. One Volunteer later recorded: 'the idea being that this British military parade was not to be given any publicity in the local papers … As the Artillery were passing I saw a camera-man with a tripod camera on the south side of Capel Street Bridge endeavouring to take photographs of the parade. As we were making our way towards him to prevent him from doing so I observed two more Volunteers approaching him from the Quay side. I recognised these as Paddy Holohan and Pat Doyle – the latter was afterwards executed. They reached the camera-man first and I heard an altercation going on between them. The next thing I saw was the camera and the man (the operator) being thrown into the Liffey. We resumed our patrol.'[1] (*Courtesy of Kilmainham Gaol Museum, 20PO-1A58-10*)

1   James Harpur, BMH WS 536, pp. 1–2.

For some, tragedy was yet to come. Pictured is the USS *Dixie*, which docked at Queenstown (Cobh), Co. Cork, in May 1918. It was aboard this ship that the first verifiable cases in Ireland of what came to be known as the Spanish flu were recorded. A global pandemic, the flu claimed at least 20,000 Irish lives during 1918–19, with at least 800,000 people affected. Those who worked in the medical service, or who had most contact with people, such as transport workers, teachers and clergymen, were most vulnerable to contracting the disease. Most terrifying of all, the disease seemed to target the young and healthy. Fear of catching the disease led to hostility towards returning soldiers, who were identified as being one of the causes of the disease spreading.[1] (*Courtesy of the Library of Congress, LC-DIG-npcc-32727*)

1   Foley, C., *The Last Irish Plague: The Great Flu Epidemic in Ireland 1918–19* (Dublin, 2011).

It is difficult to quantify how many Irish served and died in the First World War. Estimates of the Irish dead in the British Army have ranged from 27,000 to 49,000.[1] A precise total figure of Irish casualties is uncertain because of the deaths of Irishmen who enlisted in other countries, as well as the fact that others, whose place of birth was not Ireland, regarded themselves, with justification, as Irish. Why they volunteered is even harder to quantify, but one set of figures suggests that many, perhaps a majority of, recruits joined for reasons other than patriotism, whether Irish or British. 51,141 soldiers were recruited in Ireland in 1915. 10,794 were members of the National Volunteers, 8,203 were members of the UVF, 32,144 recruits were unconnected with either body.[2] Pictured is the grave of one soldier who was never identified. (*Courtesy of Patrick Lynch*)

1 Fitzpatrick, D., 'The Logic of Collective Sacrifice: Ireland and the British Army, 1914–1918', *The Historical Journal*, 1995, p. 1017; Fitzpatrick, D., 'Militarism in Ireland 1900–1922', in Bartlett, T. and Jeffery, K. (eds), *A Military History of Ireland* (Cambridge, 1996), p. 392.

2 Ó Ruairc, P. Óg, *Revolution: A Photographic History 1913–1923* (Cork, 2011), p. 40.

6. AFTERMATH

'Like everyone else I was at a loss to know what to do.'[1]

Captain David Campbell writing about life after the war

1 Campbell, D., *Forward the Rifles: The War Diary of an Irish Soldier* (Dublin, 2009), p. 144.

LEFT

In December 1918 a general election was held that led to the obliteration of the IPP. Violence was pronounced in urban areas where the party was strong, in villages like Inniskeen, Co. Monaghan, and in the cities of Waterford and Belfast, where West Belfast was dominated by Joe Devlin.[1] (*Courtesy of the Deputy Keeper of the Records, Public Records Office Northern Ireland, D1919/2*)

1   Dooley, T., *Inniskeen 1912–1918: The Political Conversion of Bernard O'Rourke* (Dublin, 2004), p. 55; *Irish Independent*, 2 December 1918; Kevin O'Shiel, BMH WS 1770, pp. 801–3.

Galway provides a good example of the manner in which the IPP was swept aside. Pictured is the South Galway Sinn Féin election committee. It was a relatively easy campaign in an area with a long tradition of agrarian agitation and Republicanism. There were really only two problems for Sinn Féin canvassers: the violent opposition of Loughrea's ex-soldiers and censorship of their election material which was regarded as seditious. The police reported: 'The S.F. manifesto was put up in a few places but the police tore it down'.[1] In Loughrea even Republican priests were attacked. Shortly afterwards one of those who had been most strident in his hostility to the Republican priests died suddenly: 'his fellow companions are very nervy over it ... He was one of the many that insulted the priests.'[2] (*Courtesy of Kilmainham Gaol Museum, 18PO-1A31-07*)

---

1   County Inspector Report, Galway East Riding, November 1918 (TNA: PRO CO 904/107).
2   Letter to Bernard Fallon from Kathleen Fallon, 9 February 1919 (Internees Letter Censorship TNA: PRO CO 904/164).

LEFT

The local IPP MP for South Galway, William Duffy, was highly regarded, but Sinn Féin's Frank Fahy (*pictured*) easily won the seat with over 85 per cent of the vote. Sinn Féin exercised a policy of abstention from the British parliament and formed their own Irish parliament, the first Dáil Éireann, the inaugural meeting of which was held in January 1919. (*Courtesy of Kilmainham Gaol Museum, 17PO-1A24-14*)

RIGHT

Fr Michael Griffin, a curate in Galway city and an active Republican, spoke about why he supported Sinn Féin. He wanted to 'fight against England's tyranny, corruption and wealth'. Referring to returning British soldiers, he told his audience that some also supported Sinn Féin and were 'determined to be on the right side in the election'.[1] (*Courtesy of Clare County Library*)

1   *Connacht Tribune*, 14 December 1918.

RIGHT

Older clergymen, such as Monsignor Patrick McAlpine in Clifden, Co. Galway, were often reluctant to change and remained hostile to Republicanism during both the War of Independence and the Civil War. (*Courtesy of Mercy Archives*)

BELOW

The replacement of politicians who had supported the British war effort did not end with the general election. Sinn Féin and its allies in the Labour Party largely dominated the local government elections of 1920 as well. One IPP man who kept his seat, barely, in Galway city was Thomas Christopher McDonogh (*seated*) who secured only nine votes on the first count in the East Ward and relied on his brother's massive surplus to retain his seat. His brother, also an IPP candidate, topped the poll. However, Michael Crowley, 'a staunch recruiter', was defeated.[1] (*Courtesy of an t-Ionad Oidhreachta, Leitir Mealláin*)

1   *Galway Express*, 10 January 1920.

ABOVE

It took some time to demobilise the British Army on the continent after the end of the war. This photograph of British troops in Calais, France, in September 1919 was taken by Belfast man Captain Tommy Byers. The slow pace of demobilisation and the living conditions of the soldiers led to much dissatisfaction. The worst manifestation of this discontent came in January 1919 at Calais, where 5,000 soldiers went on strike. Field Marshal Haig sought permission to execute the ringleaders. When one British general pointed out that while German prisoners were accommodated in huts, British soldiers slept in tents, he was confidently told by Haig that tents were 'not really colder than huts'.[1] (*Courtesy of Dave Donatelli*)

1   James, L., *Warrior Race: A History of the British at War* (London, 2002), pp. 534–35.

FAR LEFT

Tommy Byers inspecting a British Army company on the Rhine, 1919. (*Courtesy of Dave Donatelli*)

LEFT

Tommy Byers (*centre*) at Queenstown, Cork, waiting to be demobilised. (*Courtesy of Dave Donatelli*)

Soldiers waiting to be demobilised were not the only ones disappointed after the war ended. Expecting support for nationalist political aspirations because of Woodrow Wilson's rhetoric about creating a new and just world order, and expecting too much from Irish-America's legendary lobbying ability, the Dáil's representative at the post-war peace conferences, Seán T. O'Kelly (*pictured*), was ignored. (*Courtesy of Mercier Archive*)

RIGHT

Soldiers struggled to settle back into civilian life for various reasons. Kathleen Lynn, one of Sinn Féin's co-directors of health, estimated that at least 15,000 returning ex-servicemen were infected with venereal diseases.[1] While many people comforted themselves that such diseases were unknown outside the British military centres, a 1926 Free State report shattered their illusions. The problem was so extensive that it was briefly suggested that the state would begin to regulate prostitutes. An even more disconcerting conclusion was that 90 per cent of the infections in the Free State Army originated with women who 'could not be classed as a prostitute'.[2] (*Courtesy of Kilmainham Gaol Museum, 17PO-IB52-13*)

1 Matthews, A., *Renegades: Irish Republican Women 1900–1922* (Cork, 2010), p. 205.
2 Howell, P., 'Venereal Disease and the Politics of Prostitution in the Irish Free State', *Irish Historical Studies*, May 2003, pp. 321–26.

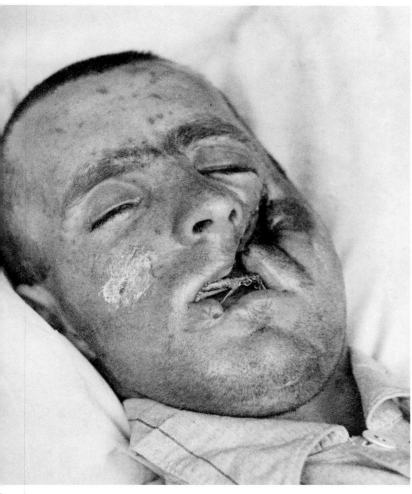

The end of the war did not mean the end of suffering for many of the wounded. Captain Herbert Crowther Foxton of the Australian Army, born in Kilkenny in 1890, was a watchmaker before enlisting in January 1915. He served at Gallipoli, then at the Western Front, where he reached the rank of captain. In October 1917 he was gassed, and following treatment in England returned to his unit in France. On 17 July 1918 a shell explosion rendered him blind, unable to speak and with major wounds to his face; initially he was not expected to survive. He was transferred to the 3rd London General Hospital, Wandsworth, where he underwent twenty-five operations. His face was rebuilt to a natural shape and the sight in one eye was partially restored. He went to Australia in early 1925 and in the same year married Ruth Love. He had met Ruth in Dublin whilst doing his apprenticeship in watchmaking, then again in 1921 in Belfast whilst recuperating from his wounds. They had four children. During the Second World War Foxton worked for a time in an engineering factory and this was his only paid employment after the First World War. In the 1950s his eyesight failed and he returned to using braille to read. Herbert Foxton died in 1984, aged ninety-four. The pictures show Foxton before, during and after reconstruction. (*Courtesy of the Australian War Memorial Museum, P06131.013, P06131.002 and P06131.010*)

For those who made it back to Ireland, life was often difficult. Despite the vast crowds that gathered to celebrate Victory Day in Dublin in 1919 (*pictured*), the marching men found it difficult to gain sympathy or work. Unemployment was a common problem. In January 1921 39 per cent of ex-servicemen in Munster, 23 per cent in Connacht, 17 per cent in Leinster and 12 per cent in Ulster were unemployed. Cork was highest with 54 per cent, Carlow lowest with 6 per cent.[1] Part of the reason was the changed political situation, part of it was economic. Efforts to provide ex-servicemen with employment at the expense of those who hadn't enlisted further alienated people from them. (*Courtesy of Mercier Archive*)

1 Fitzpatrick, D., 'Militarism in Ireland, 1900–1922', in Bartlett, T. and Jeffery, K. (eds), *A Military History of Ireland* (Cambridge, 1996), p. 502.

ABOVE

While not on the scale of France or even Britain, there were thousands of war widows in Ireland. Some, like Ellen Rush, pictured (*above left*) with her husband James who was killed in action, later married ex-soldiers. In Ellen's case she married William Diver, pictured (*above right, seated*) with his brother John James (*standing*), from Derry. John James was killed at the Battle of Loos. (*Courtesy of Gerald Diver*)

RIGHT

D. D. Sheehan, nationalist MP, campaigned for the provision of land for ex-soldiers in both Britain and Ireland. However, in the charged atmosphere in Ireland at the time, anybody, regardless of politics, who was provided with land at the expense of the locals who coveted it was in real danger, and this rendered any effort at such a scheme pointless in vast areas of the country. Some ex-soldiers were provided with houses. (*Courtesy of Niall Ó Síocháin*)

ABOVE

The war had a massive impact on the Irish gentry. Pictured before the end of the war is Henrietta O'Callaghan-Westropp, in Co. Clare with an unidentified British soldier. One member of the gentry wrote after the war ended about their devastated social network: 'The world we had known had vanished. We hunted again but ghosts rode with us.'[1] (*Courtesy of Clare County Library*)

1   Hart, P., *The IRA at War 1916–1923* (Oxford, 2005), p. 227.

Those who had been heavily associated with the British war effort and who weren't Republicans had to maintain a delicate balancing act during an increasingly bitter campaign between the IRA and the crown forces. Tact and shrewdness were essential. When British forces burned the home of Galway Republican Thomas 'Baby' Duggan (*pictured*) near Castlegar, the first visitor who came to the house and offered financial assistance was a local unionist who had been a prominent recruiter. (*Courtesy of John Commins*)

Captain Alan Lendrum, a resident magistrate in west Clare, was a veteran of the First World War, having served with the Royal Inniskilling Fusiliers, and was fatally shot by members of the IRA. A sensationalised fictional account of his death, published in 1922, implausibly claimed that the local IRA buried him in sand hoping to drown him, succeeding at the second attempt, despite the fact that there were large numbers of British forces combing the area. This account was ridiculed by the local RIC District Inspector, a friend of Lendrum's, but was reported as fact by *The Irish Times* as late as the 1980s and in a history of the RIC a decade later. (*Courtesy of the Deputy Keeper of the Records, Public Records Office Northern Ireland, D1163/8*)

Despite fighting as part of the British Army during the war, many Irish ex-soldiers joined or supported the Republican cause when they returned home. The IRA mostly attempted to recruit contacts from within the crown forces rather than infiltrate them. Many of those recruited would have seemed to be beyond suspicion. In Grangegorman Cemetery in Dublin lie two men who took opposing sides in the intelligence struggle during the War of Independence. Pictured is the grave of Martin Doyle from New Ross, Co. Wexford, a company sergeant major who won a VC. Returning home he gained employment working at a military barracks in Ennis, Co. Clare, where he gathered intelligence for the IRA.[1] (*Courtesy of Patrick Lynch*)

1   Fitzpatrick, D., 'Militarism in Ireland, 1900–1922', in Bartlett, T. and Jeffery, K. (eds), *A Military History of Ireland* (Cambridge, 1996), p. 401.

Close to Doyle's grave is the final resting place of Brian Fergus Molloy, a shadowy figure of whom relatively little is known with certainty. A member of the British Army, he was one of several agents who attempted to infiltrate Michael Collins' inner circle and who paid for it with their lives. (*Courtesy of Pádraig O'Reilly*)

A prominent example of an ex-soldier working for the IRA is David Robinson (*middle row, second from left*). A Dubliner and son of a Church of Ireland clergyman, he served in the Canadian Army and in the Royal Marine Artillery during the war. He went on to join the IRA and achieved legendary status. Frank O'Connor wrote: 'Robinson was supposed to have planned one attack on the village of Inchigeela (Cork), in which, disguised as a tinker and carrying a baby he would drive on an ass-cart to the barrack door, shoot the sentry, and hold the way open for his men ... before the engagement he addressed his troops, warning them that this would probably be the last time some of them would meet, and put such terror into them that they made at once for the hills, while Robinson, going from door to door trying to borrow a baby, complained of the lack of patriotism in Irish mothers. I find that difficult to believe, unless Robinson, with his dotty English sense of humour, was doing it as a joke, but there is certainly some truth in another story ... (in) Kenmare ... his troops took to the hills. Someone told me that the last he saw of Robinson was as he knelt in the middle of the Main Street firing at the advancing [Free State] troops, and shouting over his shoulder in his English public-school drawl: "Come back, you Irish cowards!"'[1] Robinson was part of the Irish delegation to the negotiations for a treaty between Britain and Ireland in 1921, some of whom are captured in this photograph. (*Courtesy of Mercier Archive*)

1   O'Connor, F., *An Only Child* (London, 1961), p. 186.

ABOVE

Ex-soldiers were highly prized as training officers in the IRA because of their experience and skill. Pictured is Emmet Dalton (*left*), IRA director of training in 1921. Beside him is Michael Collins. Dalton was a member of the 7th Battalion, Leinster Regiment, and served in France and in Palestine. As IRA director of training he was responsible for efforts to improve the standard of IRA units by training men in leadership as well as how to handle weapons. These men were then sent to rural units. (*Courtesy of Mercier Archive*)

Some were suspicious about the motivation of key Republicans who had been involved with the British, such as Erskine Childers (*front*) and John Chartres (*back*). Childers, who worked in naval intelligence during the war, became a prominent Republican and was a particular target of loathing for the British establishment that he had once been part of. He took the Republican side in the Civil War and was executed in November 1922. Chartres had been involved in gathering intelligence on Labour activists in Britain for the Ministry of Munitions during the war.[1] (*Courtesy of Mercier Archive*)

1 Murphy, B., *John Chartres: Mystery Man of the Treaty* (Dublin, 1995).

At a local level many IRA units recruited individual ex-soldiers. Pictured is Jimmy Flaherty, a member of the West Mayo Brigade, IRA flying column. Flaherty had spent nine years in the Connaught Rangers. (© *J. J. Leonard, courtesy of Anthony Leonard*)

Ignatius O'Neill from Co. Clare, who served with the Irish Guards, is pictured here (*front row, extreme right*) in a photograph taken just before the Civil War. He was one of the driving forces of the Rineen ambush, 22 September 1920, which saw six policemen killed and O'Neill himself seriously wounded. (*Courtesy of Clare County Museum*)

LEFT

Ex-soldiers were often more ruthless than other IRA members. The two IRA ambushes that inflicted most fatalities were at Dromkeen in Limerick and Kilmichael in Cork. Both IRA units involved were effectively dominated by an ex-serviceman, and both saw men shot after they attempted to surrender, though in Kilmichael men were shot after what was perceived to be a deliberate false surrender. In Dromkeen the ex-soldier who shot several men who had surrendered told his comrades that he had seen British soldiers racing into trenches to kill surrendering Germans.[1] Pictured is Tom Barry, leader of the Kilmichael ambush. In his own words he gives us an idea of why it was easy for some who had served in the British Army to support the Republicans: 'I had decided to see what this Great War was like. I cannot plead I went on the advice of John Redmond or any other politician, that if we fought for the British we would secure Home Rule for Ireland, nor can I say I understood what Home Rule meant. I was not influenced by the lurid appeal to fight to save Belgium or small nations. I knew nothing about nations, large or small. I went to the war for no other reason than that I wanted to see what war was like, to get a gun, to see new countries and to feel a grown man.'[2] (*Courtesy of Mercier Archive*)

1   Ó Maoileoin, S., *B'fhiú an Braon Fola* (Baile Átha Cliath, 1958), p. 160.
2   Barry, T., *Guerilla Days in Ireland* (Cork, 2013), p. 18.

LEFT

Ex-soldier Con Healy (*pictured*) shot Major McKinnon, a company commander in the Auxiliary Division, RIC, on Tralee golf course, Co. Kerry. (*Courtesy of Mercier Archive*)

Other Irish ex-soldiers chose to remain on the British side. District Inspector Thomas O'Brien Gore-Hickman from Co. Clare was a lieutenant in the Royal Dublin Fusiliers during the First World War. He later joined the RIC and served in Co. Leitrim during the War of Independence. He left the country having guided the military to an IRA flying column, an attack which led to the deaths of six IRA men. (*Courtesy of Military Archives CD 227-35*)

Michael Fitzgerald from Ahascragh in Co. Galway also joined the RIC after leaving the army, but, unhappy with British policy in Ireland, resigned and joined the IRA. During the Civil War he joined the National Army. (*Courtesy of J. Anthony Gaughan*)

ABOVE

This photograph shows a group of Auxiliaries, a crack unit composed of ex-British Army officers who were sent to areas where the RIC were struggling to cope with the Republicans, in Galway city. One of them, Burke, was a Scot of Irish extraction. Burke was implicated in the torture and murder of the Republican Loughnane brothers, Pat and Harry, near Gort, Co. Galway, part of which involved them being dragged behind a lorry. It was Burke who commandeered the rope. Another was a local man, Carr, who acted as a guide for the Auxiliaries. (*Courtesy of Military Archives CD 227-35*)

RIGHT

Ex-soldier T. Redmond, born in Wicklow but living in Dublin, was a member of the Auxiliaries based in Beggars Bush, Dublin. He was shot in May 1921, having been captured by two members of the IRA. Their frank report gives a chilling insight into the last few moments of Redmond's life as they openly admitted in their report that they used a belt to choke information out of him.[1] (*Courtesy of Military Archives CD 227-35*)

1   Augusteijn, J., *From Public Defiance to Guerrilla Warfare: The Experience of Ordinary Volunteers in the Irish War of Independence 1916–1921* (Dublin, 1996), p. 171.

Captain Campbell Joseph O'Connor Kelly from Ballyhaunis in Co. Mayo was a British Intelligence Officer based in Victoria Barracks, Cork. Kelly served in the Royal Garrison Artillery during the First World War. He was a hate figure for Republicans because of his torture of two IRA officers which led to one of them going insane. He was highly regarded by the British state and by the French. He was, at various times, awarded the Military Cross, Croix de Guerre, an OBE and, during the Second World War, the George Medal.[1] (*Courtesy of Military Archives CD227-35*)

1 http://www.cairogang.com/other-people/british/castle-intelligence/kelly/kelly.html.

Some ex-soldiers proved completely unable to settle back into regular life and sought easy money, getting involved in crime or adventure. Harry Timothy Quinlisk (*pictured extreme right*), motivated more by reasons of money and adventure than loyalty to the crown, attempted to infiltrate Michael Collins' intelligence network and paid the ultimate price. (*Courtesy of Mercier Archive*)

A lot of the evidence advanced by Republicans against executed informers, including a large number of ex-soldiers, was circumstantial. Police reports regularly referred to those who were shot as being friendly with the crown forces, even if they disputed IRA claims that they were informing. In 1921 Thomas Morris, a tramp, an ex-soldier and an ex-policeman, was executed by the IRA in Kinvara, Co. Galway. He was suspected locally of picking out houses to be burned by the crown forces. Morris was part of a working group which included Seamus Davenport (*standing, right*), who was on the run. Davenport allowed Morris to overhear where he was supposedly going to stay that night and the IRA waited to see what would happen. Morris was ordered to leave the area when crown forces raided only the house Davenport had mentioned. Morris did so, but not long afterwards returned to Kinvara and was seen spending money freely. Within hours he had been picked up by the local IRA. He was hurriedly shot.[1]

Many ex-servicemen suffered at state hands as well. In Limerick more ex-soldiers were shot by members of the crown forces than were shot by the IRA.[2] (*Courtesy of Finian Ó Fathaigh*)

1 *Connacht Tribune*, 9 April 1921; Joseph Stanford, BMH WS 1334, pp. 61–62; Thomas McInerney, BMH WS 1150, p. 8; Michael Hynes, BMH WS 1173, p. 9.
2 O'Callaghan, J., *Revolutionary Limerick* (Dublin, Portland, 2010), p. 183.

ABOVE

It might be tempting to speculate about a missed opportunity of bonding unionists and nationalists arising out of the First World War, but whatever collective sense of unity people had in the trenches was temporary. Upon returning home veterans segregated themselves into different organisations based on political attitudes. In the words of Niall Ferguson: 'The World was not weary of war ... just weary of the First World War.'[1] Many loyalist ex-soldiers joined the Ulster Special Constabulary, hoping to use their military experience to prevent IRA attacks. This force was heavily criticised by nationalists and by the military, with allegations of sectarianism, murder and reprisals dogging them throughout their fifty-year history. Sir Basil Brooke (*pictured, standing*), an ex-officer of the British Army, was involved in the organisation. Later Lord Brookeborough, he went on to be prime minister of Northern Ireland for twenty years. (*Courtesy of the Deputy Keeper of the Records, Public Records Office Northern Ireland, INF/7/A/5/57*)

1   Ferguson, N., *The Pity of War 1914–1918* (London, 2009).

In 1920 Belfast exploded in an orgy of violence. Previous service in the British Army was no protection against loyalist violence, which targeted 'Rotten Prods' (Protestants with nationalist or socialist beliefs) as well as Catholics. Catholic veterans were expelled from the shipyards and were even moved out of the UVF hospital as a result of threats made in 1922. Pictured are Catholic workers being chased by a mob. (*Courtesy of Kilmainham Gaol Museum, 19PO-1A-32-17*)

ABOVE

On 22 June 1922 Field Marshal Sir Henry Wilson was assassinated close to his home in London by Reggie Dunne and Joe O'Sullivan, one of whom can be seen in this photograph with his head bandaged. They were both Londoners, both British Army veterans (O'Sullivan lost a leg in France in 1918) angered by partition and anti-Catholic violence. Crucially, in terms of the Civil War that followed, both men were executed without ever identifying who, if anybody, ordered the shooting. (*Courtesy of Mercier Archive*)

ABOVE

1922 also saw the withdrawal of British forces from the twenty-six counties that made up the new Free State. Pictured above are British troops driving out of Athlone. This was a massive blow to the economy in garrison towns. Terry Judge (*inset*), an Athlone ex-soldier, had opened a shoemaking business on his return to the town, but in 1928 he turned the key in the lock and emigrated to America. His business plan had been based on being able to use his own past service to gain contacts in the military.[1] (*Courtesy of Athlone County Library and Tadhg Carey*)

1   Carey, T., *When We Were Kings: The Story of Athlone Town's 1924 FAI Cup Triumph* (Athlone, 2009), p. 183.

RIGHT

Ireland wasn't the only country which saw ex-soldiers suffer in the years after the First World War. Mickey O'Rourke from Limerick had emigrated to Canada before the war. A former member of the Royal Munster Fusiliers, after the war began he joined the Canadian Army in February 1915. An unruly but brave soldier, he was decorated for leading a spontaneous counter-attack at the Somme. As a stretcher-bearer he won the VC for his bravery in rescuing wounded comrades over the course of three days and nights despite coming under fire and being partially buried by exploding shells several times. Years later O'Rourke commented: 'sure I don't know what all the fuss is about, it was me job'. Severe sciatica and being gassed rendered him unfit for active service and he returned to Canada. The war stayed with him and he suffered physically, struggled to cope with drinking, was nervous in crowds and was unable to settle into regular employment. Despite the fame he had achieved, O'Rourke found the state ungenerous. Granted a limited pension, he lived in poverty in some of the poorest parts of Vancouver. One business gave him work to keep him from 'starving to death', but found him a liability. O'Rourke was far from the only one disenchanted with post-war life. Wearing his VC he led a dockers' strike march which was then batoned by the police. A further controversy followed when he refused to meet members of the royal family, citing his health and the crowds at such an event. His mental and physical health continued to deteriorate. Beaten, robbed, short of friends who were in a position to give him the help he needed, he was sectioned when a family member who spent some time looking after him became unable to cope. He died in 1957 and received a large funeral attended by many dignitaries. (*Courtesy of the Canadian Department of National Defence (DND)*)

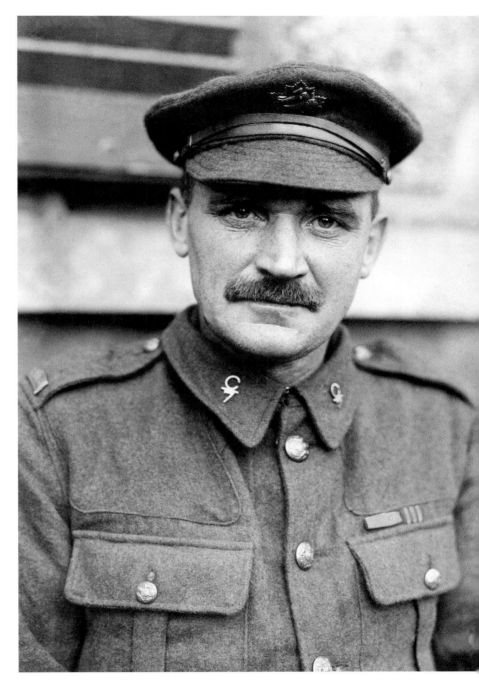

Mike Curran, a conscript to the United States Army is pictured here (*far left*). A native of Cornamona, Co. Galway, Curran's family was informed that he was missing in action. When no additional information was received, the worst was assumed. Year after year Masses were offered up in his memory. Then, out of the blue, in the 1960s a nurse in an institution for war veterans in the United States contacted Mike's family. He had just told her who he was. (*Courtesy of Seán Ó Tuairisg*)

A minority of returning veterans failed to settle into their families. The vast majority of ex-servicemen, however, settled down and lived normal lives. A typical case was Jeaic Ó Cluanáin from Baile na Cille, Lettermullen, Co. Galway. A naval veteran, he raised six children and intrigued neighbours with stories about the places he had seen. (*Courtesy of John Bhaba Jeaic Ó Conghaile and Ionad Oidhreachta Leitir Mealláin*)

Tommy Muldoon, born in Granard, Co. Longford, was a member of the Leinster Regiment. In the years after the war he played professional football with Aston Villa, Tottenham Hotspur and Walsall as well as Athlone Town. (*Courtesy of Tadhg Carey*)

Henry Hew Gordon Stoker from Dublin caught the acting bug while taking part in a play in a Turkish prison camp. He went on to become a very prominent actor, with thirty TV and film credits to his name. He is pictured here not in his own uniform but in costume. (*Courtesy of Dacre Stoker*)

Connemara man Lieutenant Jack King of the Connaught Rangers (*left*), graduated in law on his return and joined the civil service. He later contracted tuberculosis and, having taken medical advice, moved to South Africa where he spent the remainder of his life. His brother, Captain Leo King (*above*), also graduated in law and after the war he worked for the Electricity Supply Board in Dublin. He was killed in a motorcycle accident on 28 July 1935. (*Courtesy of Kathleen Villiers-Tuthill*)

ABOVE

In Ireland commemorations of the Armistice continued for years after the foundation of the Free State. These commemorations were controversial, particularly in the 1920s and early 1930s. There were a number of reasons for this: Republicanism, anti-imperialism, class resentments, hostility to the behaviour of certain groups associated with the day and hostility to a small number of uniformed British fascists who attached themselves to the occasion. The IRA, which was responsible for much of the violence associated with the occasion, organised an alternative commemoration not associated with the British Legion, a group that Republican leader Frank Ryan accused of 'ignoring the poverty of ex-servicemen and using them as pawns every 11 November', an allegation the Legion bitterly resented.[1] The Fianna Fáil government took the sting out of the occasion by giving the commemoration organisers a list of conditions which helped keep the peace. The conditions essentially involved removing British national symbols, banning uniformed fascists and restricting the sale of the poppy. Pictured is a crowd at College Green, Dublin, who were there for the unveiling of a cross to the memory of the 16th Irish Division. (*Courtesy of the National Library of Ireland, HOG 131*)

1   Hanley, B., *The IRA 1926–1936* (Dublin, 2002), pp. 72–74; Burke, T., 'Poppy Day in the Irish Free State', *Studies*, Winter 2003, pp. 349–58.

ABOVE

Pictured is Remembrance Day in Ballybricken, Waterford city, 1937. As time passed those who commemorated the First World War and its dead became fewer and fewer. As a result the issue became less contentious. In 2013 Waterford again saw commemoration of its First World War dead with the erection of a monument that remembers the names of those who fell in the war. John Deasy, a Fine Gael TD and one of those involved in the project, explained the new monument: 'Its intention is to recognise those who served and died rather than being a commentary on the political rights and wrongs of what was a catastrophic conflict.'[1] It is a fine sentiment. The challenge for historians will be to go beyond the names and the stereotypes of both supporters and detractors, and find the individuals, whether their motivation was financial, political, selfish or noble. The results of this investigation will be mixed. Some of their thoughts and beliefs may be offensive to twenty-first-century readers. Some of their deeds will cause us to question our own bravery and integrity. But above all else a forensic investigation of the war years will breathe life once more into those who lie in rest both at home and abroad. (*Courtesy of Waterford County Museum, UK 3665*)

1   *The Munster Express*, 27 September 2013.

BIBLIOGRAPHY

PRIMARY SOURCES

MILITARY ARCHIVES, DUBLIN

Bureau of Military History Papers

PUBLIC RECORDS OFFICE, THE NATIONAL ARCHIVES, KEW, LONDON

Admiralty: Royal Navy Registers of Seamen's Services
Colonial Office Papers
Irish Grants Committee (CO 762)
War Office Papers

NEWSPAPERS

Anglo-Celt, The
Bendigo Advertiser
Butte Independent, The
Connacht Tribune
Freeman's Journal, The
Galway Express
Irish Independent
Irish Press, The
Irish Times, The
Kerryman, The
Kildare Observer
Munster Express, The
Southern Star, The
Ulster Herald, The

WEBSITES

http//www.cairogang.com
http://www.census.nationalarchives.ie
http://www.europeana1914-1918.eu
http://www.irishnewsarchive.com
http://www.soldierswills.nationalarchives.ie
http://www.warofindependence.info

ANECDOTAL INFORMATION

Families of the people pictured provided photographs and anecdotal information on their relatives.

PUBLISHED SOURCES

Andrews, C. S., *Dublin Made Me* (Dublin, 1979)

Augusteijn, J., *From Public Defiance to Guerrilla Warfare: The Experience of Ordinary Volunteers in the Irish War of Independence 1916–1921* (Dublin, 1996)

Augusteijn, J., *The Memoirs of John M. Regan: A Catholic Officer in the RIC and RUC 1909–1948* (Dublin, 2007)

Bairéad, T., *Gan Baisteadh* (Baile Átha Cliath, 1972)

Barry, T., *Guerilla Days in Ireland* (Cork, 2013)

Bartlett, T. and Jeffery, K. (eds), *A Military History of Ireland* (Cambridge, 1996)

Beiner, G., *Remembering the Year of the French: Irish Folk History and Social Memory* (Madison, 2007)

Beiner, G., Marsh, P. and Milne, I., 'Greatest Killer of the Twentieth Century: The Great Flu of 1918–19', *History Ireland*, March/April 2009, pp. 40–43

Borgonovo, J., *Spies, Informers and the 'Anti-Sinn Féin Society': The Intelligence War in Cork City 1920–1921* (Dublin, 2007)

Borgonovo, J., *The Dynamics of War and Revolution: Cork City 1916–1918* (Cork, 2013)

Bourke, J. (ed.), *The Misfit Soldier: Edward Casey's War Story 1914–1918* (Cork, 1999)

Bowman, T., 'The Ulster Volunteer Force and the Formation of the 36th (Ulster) Division', *Irish Historical Studies*, November 2001, pp. 498–518

Braddan, W. S., *Under Fire with the 370th Infantry (8th I.N.G.) A.E.F: Memoirs of the World War* (Chicago?, n.d.)

Burke, T., 'Poppy Day in the Irish Free State', *Studies*, Winter 2003, pp. 349–58

Burnell, T., *The Waterford War Dead: A History of the Casualties of the Great War* (Dublin, 2010)

Campbell, D., *Forward the Rifles: The War Diary of an Irish Soldier* (Dublin, 2009)

Campbell, F., *Land and Revolution: Nationalist Politics in the West of Ireland 1891–1921* (Oxford, 2005)

Carey, T., *When We Were Kings: The Story of Athlone Town's 1924 FAI Cup Triumph* (Athlone, 2009)

Cooper, B., *The Tenth (Irish) Division in Gallipoli* (Dublin, 1993)

Corns, C. and Hughes-Wilson, J., *Blindfold and Alone: British Military Executions in the Great War* (London, 2002)

Cousins, C., *Armagh and the Great War* (Dublin, 2011)

Denman, T., 'The Catholic Irish Soldier in the First World War: The "Racial Environment"', *Irish Historical Studies*, November 1991, pp. 350–65

Denman, T., 'The Red Livery of Shame: The Campaign against Army Recruitment in Ireland 1899–1914', *Irish Historical Studies,* 1994–95, pp. 208–33

Denman, T., *A Lonely Grave: The Life and Death of William Redmond* (Dublin, 1995)

Denman, T., *Ireland's Unknown Soldiers* (Kildare, 2014)

Dennehy, J., *In a Time of War: Tipperary 1914–1918* (Kildare, 2013)

Dolan, A., *Commemorating the Irish Civil War: History and Memory, 1923–2000* (Cambridge, 2003)

Dooley, M. K., 'Our Mickey: The Life of Private James O'Rourke, VC MM (CEF) 1879–1957', *Labour/Le Travail*, Spring 2001, pp. 171–84

Dooley, T., *Inniskeen 1912–1918: The Political Conversion of Bernard O'Rourke* (Dublin, 2004)

Dungan, M., *Irish Voices from the Great War* (Kildare, 2014)

Fanning, R., *Fatal Path: British Government and Irish Revolution 1910–1922* (London, 2013)

Farry, M., *Sligo 1914–1921: A Chronicle of Conflict* (Trim, 1992)

Farry, M., *Sligo: The Irish Revolution, 1912–23* (Dublin, 2012)

Feeney, M., *Remembering Mayo's Fallen Heroes* (2008)

Ferguson, N., *The Pity of War 1914–1918* (London, 2009)

Fischer, L., *The Life of Mahatma Gandhi* (London, 1997)

Fitzpatrick, D., 'The Logic of Collective Sacrifice: Ireland and the British Army, 1914–1918', *The Historical Journal*, 1995, pp. 1017–30

Fitzpatrick, D., 'Militarism in Ireland, 1920–1922', in Bartlett, T. and Jeffery, K. (eds), *A Military History of Ireland* (Cambridge, 1996), pp. 379–406

Foley, C., *The Last Irish Plague: The Great Flu Epidemic in Ireland 1918–19* (Dublin, 2011)

Franklin, D. B., 'Bigotry in 'Bama: De Valera's Visit to Birmingham, Alabama, April 1920', *History Ireland*, Winter 2004, pp. 30–34

Gaughan, J. A., *Memoirs of Constable Jeremiah Mee* (Cork, 2012)

Gillis, E., *Revolution in Dublin: A Photographic History 1913–23* (Cork, 2013)

Goldberg, D., 'Unmasking the Ku Klux Klan: The Northern Movement against the KKK, 1920–1925', *Journal of American Ethnic History,* Summer 1996, pp. 32–48

Good, J., *Enchanted by Dreams: The Journal of a Revolutionary* (Kerry, 1996)

Grayson, R. S., *Belfast Boys: How Unionists and Nationalists Fought and Died Together in the First World War* (London, 2009)

Greenald, J., 'In the Forefront of Duty: Orangeism in World War One', in D. Hume (ed.), *Battles beyond the Boyne: Orangemen in the Ranks 1798–2000* (Belfast, 2005), pp. 26–44

Hanley, B., *The IRA 1926–1936* (Dublin, 2002)

Hart, P., *The IRA and Its Enemies* (Oxford, 1998)

Hart, P., *The IRA at War 1916–1923* (Oxford, 2005)

Hastings, M., *Catastrophe: Europe Goes to War 1914* (London, 2013)

Henry, W., *Galway and the Great War* (Cork, 2006)

Henry, W., *Forgotten Heroes: Galway Soldiers of the Great War 1914–1918* (Cork, 2007)

Herlihy, J., *The Royal Irish Constabulary* (Dublin, Portland 1997)

Hochschild, A., *To End All Wars: A Story of Protest and Patriotism in the First World War* (London, 2012)

Hogan, D. (Frank Gallagher), *The Four Glorious Years* (Dublin, 1953)

Horne, J. and Kramer, A., *German Atrocities 1914: A History of Denial* (New Haven and London, 2001)

Howell, P., 'Venereal Disease and the Politics of Prostitution in the Irish Free State', *Irish Historical Studies*, May 2003, pp. 320–41

James, L., *Warrior Race: A History of the British at War* (London, 2002)

Jeffery, K., *Ireland and the Great War* (Cambridge, 2000)

Johnston, K., *Home or Away: The Great War and the Irish Revolution* (Dublin, 2011)

Jourdain, H. F., *The Connaught Rangers, Formerly 88th Foot* (3 volumes, London, 1926)

Keegan, J., *The First World War* (London, 1999)

Kipling, R., *The Irish Guards in the Great War: The First Battalion* (Staplehurst, 1997)

Leeson, D., *The Black and Tans: British Police and Auxiliaries in the Irish War of Independence, 1920–1921* (Oxford, 2012)

Leonard, J., 'Survivors', in Horne, J. (ed.), *Our War: Ireland and the Great War* (Dublin, 2008), pp. 211–23

Lynd, R., *If the Germans Conquered England and Other Essays* (Dublin and London, 1917)

Martin, T. F., *The Kingdom in the Empire: a portrait of Kerry during World War One* (Dublin, 2006)

Mason, M., *The American Negro Soldier with the Red Hand of France* (Boston, 1920)

Matthews, A., *Renegades: Irish Republican Women 1900–1922* (Cork, 2010)

McDowell, R. B., *Crisis and Decline: The Fate of the Southern Unionists* (London, 1997)

McMahon, T., *Pádraig Ó Fathaigh's War of Independence* (Cork, 2000)

Metters, R. and Kilbeggan Heritage Group, *Who Answered the Bugle Call? Kilbeggan and Neighbourhood during World War One* (Kilbeggan, 2011)

Morrow, J. M., 'Knights of the Sky: The Rise of Military Aviation', in Coetzee, F. and Shevin-Coetzee, M. (eds), *Authority, Identity and the Social History of the Great War* (Providence, Oxford, 1995), pp. 305–24

Mortimer, G., *Fields of Glory: The Extraordinary Lives of 16 Warrior Sportsmen* (London, 2001)

Murphy, B., *John Chartres: Mystery Man of the Treaty* (Dublin, 1995)

Nolan, L. and Nolan, J. E., *Secret Victory: Ireland and the War at Sea 1914–1918* (Cork, 2009)

O'Callaghan, J., *Revolutionary Limerick* (Dublin, 2010)

Ó Comhraí, C., *Gaillimh 1913–23* (forthcoming)

Ó Comhraí, C., *Revolution in Connacht: A Photographic History 1913–23* (Cork, 2013)

O'Connor, F., *An Only Child* (London, 1961)

O'Connor Lysaght, D. R., 'Labour in Waiting: The After-Effects of the Dublin Lockout', *History Ireland*, July/August 2013, pp. 44–47

O'Connor Lysaght, D. R., 'The Rhetoric of Redmondism 1914–6', *History Ireland*, Spring 2003

O'Donoghue, F., 'Rescue of Donnchadha MacNeilus from Cork Jail', in *IRA Jailbreaks 1918–1921* (Cork, 2010), pp. 18–27

Ó Máille, T., *An t-Iomaire Rua* (Baile Átha Cliath, 2007 edition)

Ó Máille, T. S., *Seanfhocla Chonnacht* (Baile Átha Cliath, 2010)

O'Malley, C. and Horgan, T., *The Men Will Talk to Me: Kerry Interviews by Ernie O'Malley* (Cork, 2012)

O'Malley, C. and Ó Comhraí, C., *The Men Will Talk to Me: Galway Interviews by Ernie O'Malley* (Cork, 2013)

O'Malley, E., *On Another Man's Wound* (Dublin, 1979)

Ó Maoileoin, S., *B'fhiú an Braon Fola* (Baile Átha Cliath, 1958)

Orr, P., *The Road to the Somme: Men of the Ulster Division Tell Their Story* (Belfast, 2008 edition)

Ó Ruairc, P. Óg, *Revolution: A Photographic History 1913–1923* (Cork, 2011)

Ó Ruairc, P. Óg, 'The Worst Atrocity in the History of Irish Sadistic violence? The Killing of Alan Lendrum in fact & fiction' at www.warofindependence.info

Plowman, M. E., 'Irish Republicans and the Indo-German Conspiracy of World War I', *New Hibernia Review* 7.3, 2000, pp. 80–105

Reynolds, J., '"It's a Long Way to Tipperary": German POWs in Templemore', *History Ireland*, May/June 2008, pp. 23–25

Richardson, N., *A Coward if I Return, a Hero if I Fall* (Dublin, 2010)

Scott, E. J., 'The Participation of Negroes in World War One: An Introductory Statement', *The Journal of Negro Education*, Summer 1943, pp. 288–97

Shanahan, E., 'Telling Tales: The Story of the Burial Alive and Drowning of a Clare RM in 1920', *History Ireland*, January/February 2010, pp. 36–37

Shankman, A., 'Black on Green: Afro-American Editors on Irish Independence, 1840–1921', *Phlyon*, Third Quarter 1980, pp. 284–99

Sheehan, W., *The Western Front: Irish Voices from the Great War* (Dublin, 2011)

Shephard, B., *A War of Nerves: Soldiers and Psychiatrists 1914–1994* (London, 2002)

Simkins, P., 'The Four Armies 1914–1918', in Chandler, D. G. and Beckett, I. (eds), *The Oxford History of the British Army* (Oxford, 2003), pp. 235–55

Smith, A., 'Major Robert Gregory, & the Irish Air Aces of 1917–18', *History Ireland*, Winter 2001, pp. 29–33

Snape, M., *God and the British Soldier: Religion and the British Army in the First and the Second World War* (London and New York, 2005)

Sweeney, W. A., *History of the American Negro in the Great World War* (New York, 1919)

Switzer, C., *Unionists and Great War Commemoration in the North of Ireland 1914–39: People, Places and Politics* (Dublin, 2007)

Tomkins, P., *Twice a Hero: From the Trenches of the Great War to the Ditches of the Irish Midlands 1915–1922* (Gloucestershire, 2012)

Travers, T., 'The Army and the Challenge of War 1914–1918', in Chandler, D. G. and Beckett, I. (eds), *The Oxford History of the British Army* (Oxford, 2003), pp. 222–34

Ungoed-Thomas, J., *Jasper Wolfe of Skibbereen* (Cork, 2008)

Varley, T., 'A Region of Sturdy Smallholders? Western Nationalists and Agrarian Politics during the First World War', *Journal of the Galway Archaeological and Historical Society*, 2003, pp. 127–50

Villiers-Tuthill, K., *Beyond the Twelve Bens* (Galway, 1986)

Walker, S., *Forgotten Soldiers: The Irishmen Shot at Dawn* (Dublin, 2008)

White, G. and O'Shea, B., *A Great Sacrifice: Cork Servicemen Who Died in the Great War* (Cork, 2011)

Yeates, P., *A City in Wartime: Dublin 1914–18* (Dublin, 2011)

ACKNOWLEDGEMENTS

Research and writing are impossible without the help, facilities and tolerance of others. Míle buíochas mar sin leis na daoine seo a leanas: Jim Tierney of the 69th Regiment; The Archdiocese of Armagh; The Army Medical Museum; Gearóid O'Brien and Athlone County Library; The Australian War Museum; Bundesarchiv, Deutschland; The Canadian Department of National Defence; Brian Kirby and the Irish Capuchin Provincial Archives; Maureen Comber and the Clare County Museum as well as the families who allowed their photographs to be used; Patricia Burdick at Colby College, Maine; Jim Horgan and Margaret Daly in Collins Barracks, Cork; Collins Press; Cork and Ross Diocesan Archive; Daniel Breen and the Cork Public Museum; Department of the Defence, Ireland; Caroline Carr and the Donegal County Museum; Rosemary Yore and the Francis Ledwidge Museum; John Reynolds and the Garda Training College Museum, Templemore, Co. Tipperary; Jarlath Cloonan and the Galway GAA County Board; Galway County Library; Getty Images; Ronan Colgan and The History Press Ireland; Elizabeth Forster and the Hugh Lane Gallery; Imperial War Museum; Terry Fagan and the Inner City Folklore Project; *Irish Examiner* Archives; www.irishnewsarchives.com; Sarah O'Farrell and the Kerry County Museum; Niall Bergin and the Kilmainham Gaol Museum; Pat Delaney and the Laois GAA County Board; John Bhaba Jeaic Ó Conghaile agus Kathleen Nic Dhonnacha as Ionad Oidhreachta Leitir Meallán (Leitir Meallán Heritage Centre); Library of Congress; Lilliput Press; Susanne Weidemann and Main-Post GMBH; P. J. Maloney of Mellows Barracks, Galway; Mercy Archives; Military Archives; National Library of Australia; National Library of Ireland; Kieran Hoare and the James Hardiman Library, NUI Galway; Office of Public Works; Hugh Forrester of the Police Museum, Belfast; Perth Diocesan Archives; Presentation Archives; Sandra Ronayne and Emily Gushue of the Provincial Archive of Newfoundland and Labrador; The Deputy Keeper of the Records, Public Records Office Northern Ireland, as well as Neil Watt; the Representative Church Body; Peter Finnegan and the Royal Dublin Golf Club; Scott Polar Research Institute, Cambridge; The Tank Museum; Kieran Waldron and Tuam Diocesan Archives; Catríona Mulcahy and University College Cork; Mark Weber, Frank Arre, Robert Smith and the US Naval History and Heritage Command, Washington; Laura Bang and the Villanova University for the use of images from the Joseph McGarrity collection (licensed under a Creative Commons Attribution-ShareAlike 3.0 Unported License); John Callanan and Wanderers Rugby Football Club; Waterford County Museum and its donors; The London School of Economics; The Kiltartan Gregory Museum, particularly Rena McAllen who came out on a wet Sunday to let me into the museum; David Hume of the Orange Order; the Irish Jesuit Archive; Rachel Searcy at New York University Library; and The Ward Irish Music Archives.

Kerry Andrews; Aribert Elpelt; Bernard Bermingham; Seamus Breslin; Paul Browne; Dillon Bryden; Jason Burke; Tom Burke; Vera Cahill; Tadhg Carey; Martin Cleary; Rosie Coffey; Séamus Coll; John Commins; John Corry; Peter Cottrell; Dominic Cronin; John Cunningham; Richard de Stacpoole; Donal Fallon; Rónán de

Bhaldraithe; Gerard Diver; Maurice and Morgan Dockrell; Dave and Maureen Donatelli; Simon Draper; T. Ryle Dwyer; Linda Ervine; Warren Fahey; Dawn Ferguson; Seán Gannon; J. Anthony Gaughan; Liz Gillis; David Grant; Michael Guilfoyle; Senator Jimmy Harte; Noel Harty; Patricia Haselbeck Flynn; John Henderson; William Henry; Martin Higgins; Seán Hogan; Declan agus Tim Horgan; Mary Kenny; Tom Kenny; Anthony Leonard; Joe Loughnane; Patrick Lynch; James MacCarthy; Alex Maskey; Ann Matthews; David McCallion from www. waryearsremembered.co.uk; Patrick McCarthy; Fergal McCluskey; Betty McGowan; Paul McLoughlin; Darren McMahon; Norman McNarry; Nick Metcalfe; Ray Metters; Redmond Morris, Thelma Mansfield and the Morris family; Hazel Morrison; Éamon Murphy; Diarmuid Murray; Willow Murray (IRFU Honorary Archivist); Máirtín Ó Catháin; Seán and John O'Connell; Louise O'Connor; Seosamh Ó Cuaig; Stiofán Ó Direáin; Bertie Ó Domhnaill agus a mhuintir; Cóilín Ó Domhnaill; Darach Ó Dúbháin; Finian Ó Fathaigh; Gus O'Halloran; Kathleen O'Kelly; Páraic Ó Labhradha; Lillis Ó Laoire; Cormac O'Malley; Karen O'Rawe; Rory O'Shaughnessy; Niall Ó Síocháin; Seán Ó Tuairisg; Aimee Olcese; David Parlsow; Sandy Perceval; Jean Prendegast; Eoin Shanahan; Thomas Simmons; Colin Smythe; Dacre Stoker; Henry Stuart; Jackie Uí Chionna; Jasper Ungoed-Thomas; Kathleen Villiers-Tuthill; Siobhán Watson and the family of Father John O'Meehan; Karen Willows; Pádraig Yeates. Special thanks to Seán MacDonncha; Martin Ridge; Pádraig O'Reilly; Colin Stone; Colin Cousins and Richard Grayson.

Buíochas le mo chara dílis Pádraig Óg Ó Ruairc.

To all the staff at Mercier for their professionalism, support and patience: Patrick, Sarah, Dominic, Wendy and Mary, of course, who took a punt on this book.

Albert Muckley; Cal and Theresia Muckley; Albert; Lynn, Cian and Conor; my sisters Laoise, Orla and Caoimhe; Ann Muckley; mo thuismitheoirí Laoise agus Stiofán Ó Comhraí; mo bhean Sarah-Ann Muckley agus ar deireadh thiar thall mo mhac Ben-Eoghan.

INDEX